AMY FINE COLLINS

THE GOD OF DRIVING

How I Overcame Fear and Put Myself

in the Driver's Seat with the Help

of a Good and Mysterious Man

SIMON & SCHUSTER

New York   London   Toronto   Sydney

SIMON & SCHUSTER
Rockefeller Center
1230 Avenue of the Americas
New York, NY 10020

For information about special discounts for bulk purchases,
please contact Simon & Schuster Special Sales:
1-800-456-6798 or business@simonandschuster.com.

Designed by Jeanette Olender
Manufactured in the United States of America

1   3   5   7   9   10   8   6   4   2

Library of Congress Cataloging-in-Publication Data
Collins, Amy Fine.
The god of driving : how I overcame fear and put myself in the driver's seat
with the help of a good and mysterious man / Amy Fine Collins.
p. cm.
1. Collins, Amy Fine—Friends and associates. 2. Women automobile
drivers—United States. 3. Automobile driver education—Psychological aspects.
4. Automobile driver education teachers—United States. 5. Phobias. I. Title.
TL140.C68A3 2004
629.28'3'07107471—dc22   2004045362

ISBN 0-7432-4421-4

Acknowledgments

First, I thank Larry Ashmead, who got me started and keeps me going. Suzanne Gluck, who understood the idea and made sure others did too. David Rosenthal, who took a chance. Chuck Adams, who presciently and soothingly presided over the book, and expertly made sure I didn't go astray. The dynamic Rob Weisbach, the right man who arrived at the right moment. Aimée Bell, who has intelligence, belief, courage, and strength. Graydon Carter, who has loyally provided an ideal and inspiring home base. Chris Garrett, who has been a steadfast supporter, and David Harris and Ann Schneider, both of whom have made me look good. John Marciano, who has persistently guided, encouraged, and challenged me with astonishing skill. I also thank early readers Martine Singer and Stephen Rubin, both selfless and wise. Nancy Novogrod gave me many needed boosts, as did Sheila Glaser. Elizabeth Hayes, Victoria Meyer, and Sandi Mendelson made a gifted and powerful team. Jeffrey Shaw, David Kornblau, and Grace Pollack straightened me out. Generous, sympathetic, and essential help came from Joe Richardson, Andrew Torres, Annette Koch of Bentley Motors, Seema Mehta, Jim Kloiber, Miranda de Kay, Marion Rosenfeld, and the three Varnas.

And to my friends who listened: Eleanor Lambert, Babs Simpson, Geoffrey Beene, Robert Rufino, Gene Meyer, Robert Couturier, Cathryn Collins, Andrew Solomon, Ken Silver, David Kuhn, Lars Nilsson, Dana Cowin, Mish Tworkowski, Myriam and Vivien Lesnick, Ward Landrigan, Leila Hadley Luce, and my mother.

Names of places, people, and things have been changed and identities and events combined or condensed.

To Brad, who let me go
To Daddy, who didn't
and
Flora, who came along for the ride

CONTENTS

THE GOD OF DRIVING

It Shouldn't Happen to Us

This is the recurrent nightmare:

I am inside my father's Morris Minor convertible, scarcely filling the driver's seat, and the oyster gray automobile is hurtling, helter-skelter, down a steep hill.

My hands can neither hold the steering wheel nor grasp the stick shift, and my feet dangle uselessly, high above the pedals. The car is going so fast I am unable to see anything through the windows except a rushing, murky blur, a whizzing smudge of motion.

The dream has no beginning or end, just movement and terror.

THE NOCTURNAL scenario is now unreeling in broad daylight, in actual time and real space—with a few crucial changes of location. This time I'm seated inside a different vehicle, a '92 Acura Integra. My legs are more than long enough to reach the pedals, but for all the control my right foot possesses, it could be kicking right through the windshield. There is no high hill here, but the car might as well be rocketing skyward, upside down, so disoriented is my sense of vertical and horizontal, right and left, earth and atmosphere. And this time I can see, with too much clarity, what's outside the window: a throbbing digital traffic sign, skipping white and yellow lines, a curving cement retaining wall, and a looming suspension bridge, maybe a thousand feet ahead. And all of them are angled fiercely, about to collide and converge on me like the falling planes of a Cubist painting.

The driving instructor in the passenger seat beside me grabs the wheel and guides the car away from a hulking SUV in the adjacent lane.

Saved. The dream begins to ebb away.

FOR MY entire adult life I had no use for automobiles, and no ability to drive them. Unlike most Americans, I never drove to work—in my case, the *Vanity Fair* offices on the twenty-second floor of 4 Times Square in New York City. Every morning I commuted, instead, from my silver-and-pink bedroom, on upper Park Avenue, to a large black-and-gold desk in my adjacent dressing room. The clothes in the closets opposite this ornate desk (formerly the property of Hugh Hefner) were part of my working life too. All were custom-made by Geoffrey Beene—he was my fashion mentor, I was his muse. Fifteen years before, I had donated my previous wardrobe of Giglis and Alaïas to one of my charities, the Metropolitan Museum's Costume Institute, and never looked back. This drastic divestiture also was performed in the line of duty. As a special correspondent to *Vanity Fair*, I wrote features about style, fashion, society, old Hollywood, and other glamorous subjects. I was obsessed not just with flawless design but also with painstaking research and writing about vanished people, places, and things.

Arranged on the walls of my lacquered fuchsia work cell were souvenirs from the stories I had published during my fourteen-year association with the magazine—studio shots of Claudette Colbert and Hedda Hopper, red luggage tags stamped "Diana Vreeland," whimsical sketches of me by Karl Lagerfeld and Hilary Knight, handwritten notes from Geoffrey Beene, and a triple portrait of me by Horst. Images of my daughter, now nine, were displayed on this trophy wall too, taken by the photographers with whom I had collaborated over the years.

I never drove my daughter to school either, of course—she rode the yellow school bus. And whenever I needed to go to the office at 4 Times Square, to a lunch appointment (I had one almost daily), a dinner party, or a fund-raising event (this could happen almost nightly—it's where my job blended into my social life), I traveled by taxi, car service, or, on rare occasions, bus or train. In New York I had at my disposal a round-the-clock, on-tap abundance of transportation alternatives.

If a *Vanity Fair* story—such as the ones I wrote on Chanel and Valentino—took me to L.A., London, Paris, or Rome, I got around there by car service or taxi too. And if I needed to travel out of New York on a family holiday—to Thanksgiving dinner at my aunt's house in Pennsylvania, for instance, or to my beach rental in August—then my husband, a subway-loving city man, drove me in an Avis auto. It was a lopsided arrangement that went unquestioned.

My dependency on my husband, friends, colleagues, and strangers evolved almost into an affectation, in keeping with the impractical, cerebral, hothouse tone of my life. I didn't own sneakers (at the gym I wore ballet slippers), not even jeans (Beene jumpsuits worked fine in the country). I wore high Manolo heels (which I have collected since 1985, the year they arrived in America) even throughout my pregnancy, and blood red lipstick at all times. And I accumulated rarefied useless objects with impressively quirky provenances at auctions and at flea markets, such as 1930s *Vogue* fashion illustrations and Lucite furniture from the same period, examples of which I had lent to museum shows. Though not comfortable to most people (comfort, I argued, was a state of mind), my apartment was highly photogenic, and was showcased repeatedly in magazines and decorating books.

Before I became a journalist, I spent nine years at Swarthmore College and Columbia University earning three degrees in art history, a precious, scholarly field that deals in ideas more than things and that encouraged my inclination for reflection over action. In all my endeavors I was a perfectionist, setting such impossibly high standards for myself that eventually I eliminated pursuits—painting, cooking, ballet, French—in which I couldn't measure up. I could not tolerate mediocrity in anything. Among the many reasons I had resisted driving—something 190 million Americans did 2.6 times daily—was that I knew I had no natural aptitude for it.

MY PHOBIA about driving was a legacy passed down from my father. On a frigid late-November day when I was four, his 1960

Morris Minor, the oyster gray convertible of the nightmare, skidded on an icy road in Bucks County, Pennsylvania. It smashed into a red delivery van, also spiraling out of control. My father's car was demolished. His head was gashed open, his leg pierced by the steering column, his neck thrown permanently out of alignment, and some of his teeth were knocked out. A psychoanalyst, he was on his way to a hospital for consultation on a case. He reached his intended destination, but as a patient.

This was the second of three accidents that my father miraculously survived—a fate that eluded both of his parents. My paternal grandfather, scrambling to catch a ferry when my father was three, was mowed down by a hit-and-run trucker. Twenty-seven years later, my paternal grandmother was killed under similar circumstances, while crossing a shopping center's parking lot on foot.

On the road with my family—traveling in one of our Ford station wagons or, later, our garnet Volvo sedan—my father would utter a Yiddish incantation, *"Nisht fur dich gedacht,"* whenever we passed the scene of an accident. I thought this was one old Jewish word for "accident," but later I learned that the phrase translated more or less as "It shouldn't happen to us."

But the fact of the matter is that over two million Americans are injured every year in car accidents. That comes down to around forty-three thousand deaths annually—a figure exceeding the total U.S. casualties in the Vietnam War, and ten times greater than the number of fatalities caused by all other forms of transportation combined.

The father of this book's first editor, Chuck, died in a car wreck; the father of Simon & Schuster's publisher, David, killed a man in an accident; my literary agent, Suzanne, crushed her face when an Amtrak Metroliner ran into her family's car at a railroad crossing (every ninety minutes someone is hit on a train track); my upstairs neighbor's child perished in a collision when she was a college freshman; my *Vanity Fair* editor's best friend was immolated in an automobile soon after her marriage. Even First Lady Laura Bush killed a high school classmate, track star Michael Douglas, in 1963 when she ran a stop sign on Farm Road 868 and smashed into the seventeen-year-old's Corvair.

Both my sister and I obtained our learner's permits and driver's licenses in Tennessee, where our road tests consisted of driving out of one parking lot and into its counterpart across the street. Though we were rarely given car privileges, we learned to negotiate our way to school, to our favorite shops, to our father's offices, but not onto a highway, and certainly not out of town. My sister and I were both academic stars and able athletes, but as drivers we were failures.

Though he repeatedly disparaged me for having no "depth perception," my father once tried teaching me to drive standard shift, in a 1974 Ford Capri. But like many fathers, husbands, and boyfriends who try to instruct their children, spouses, and girlfriends, he exploded in anger each time I made a mistake— a vicious cycle in a pedagogical setting.

Whatever particles of confidence remained to me as a driver were wiped out for good after my sister and I were stopped by a Florida policeman during my sophomore-year spring break for making a perilous, illegal turn. In fact, the only pleasurable driving I knew before giving it up entirely in my late teens was a few bumpy seconds bouncing a battered truck over an empty pasture at my college boyfriend's tobacco and horse farm in Versailles, Kentucky.

FROM SWARTHMORE, Pennsylvania, where I attended college, and New York City, where I moved afterward, I renewed my Tennessee license—a false but legal document—on schedule every four years, via U.S. mail. And then one year I let it expire.

A decade passed—a pivotal one, during which I abandoned academia for magazine journalism and became a mother. Then, in late January 2000, acting on a millennial New Year's resolution, I signed up for a ten-hour package with a Manhattan driving school. I'd had the company's number filed in my Rolodex for two years, slipped to me by a friend who apparently felt she had given me one lift too many. Initially, I was motivated less by a desire to drive than by exasperation with the new FAA rules requiring airline passengers to show government-issued photo identification. It seemed like an imposition to carry my U.S. passport, the only such document I possessed, aboard domestic flights; I felt discriminated against as a nondriver.

The school assigned to me an earnest Asian instructor named Fred, adept at teaching for the road test. (His pass rate: 94 percent.) The essential skills to master for the New York City exam, reputedly the toughest in the nation, are parallel parking, the broken U-turn, right and left turns, attentiveness to signs, and good hand-eye-and-foot coordination. Every action must be accompanied by the correct head checks, mirror checks, and turn signals. For each maneuver, Fred had in his repertoire a fail-safe technique that, properly understood and executed, worked like a charm. Still, the lessons—totaling thirty hours in the end—were a trial. Over the course of three brutal winter months, I assimilated these fundamentals with painful slowness, considerable difficulty, and enormous self-consternation.

Fred's sound teaching and my perseverance paid off. I passed the test on my first try, at Havemeyer Avenue in the Bronx, on April 4, 2000. Along with the license (with its penitentiary-like portrait photo) I had acquired some good rudimentary motorist's habits and—thanks to the state-mandated five-hour class, taught by a Filipino named Carl—a heightened sense of safety. (His computer-simulation video of Princess Di's car wreck effectively closed the case on the subject of safety belts.) Still I could not drive, not well. For around a year and a half, in fact, I drove only on the stringy byways of the thumbprint-sized island where I spend every August—because there are no highways, no traffic signals, no traffic, and a maximum speed limit of 30 miles per hour.

Fred proposed I advance with him to the next stage, highway driving. I wanted to oblige him, but I had hit a psychological wall. Facing down the phobia had tapped out my psychic reserves; another year and a half had to pass before they would replenish.

The Driving Instructor

Five weeks after the attack on the World Trade Center, I made myself dial the school again and book an introductory one-hour-and-a-half session of its advanced highway driving program—for Friday, October 19, at two o'clock. Given the timing, a reflex to escape the city or at least diminish my dependency on airplane travel must have motivated me. Consciously, however, what prompted my return to driving school was a wish to lose myself in a challenge so absorbing, compelling, and demanding that it nullified all my other anxieties, personal and professional. Maybe it was a precocious manifestation of a midlife crisis, or a mild case of post-9/11 trauma, but I had, during that autumn, begun to feel disenchanted with the life I'd been leading. I had just met *Vanity Fair*'s deadline for a story on director Luchino Visconti, and had only an introduction for a book on jeweler Fulco di Verdura to write. My daughter was at school. Making time, for once, was not a problem.

I requested Fred again, but Marilyn, a school receptionist, said he was on leave until summertime. (Later I learned his teaching certificate had been revoked as a result of two speeding tickets—a typical case of instructor burnout.) I then asked for Carl, the safety enthusiast who had conducted the five-hour class. Any familiar face would have been welcome at the onset of a journey that I had been postponing for twenty-five years.

On the 18th, the day before the lesson, I called the school and canceled my appointment. A haircut took priority over driving. I did force myself to reschedule for the next available opening, Monday, the 21st of October, at two. Marilyn advised me that Carl would not be on duty at this time. Would I mind if she sent someone else "very good"? Having already been placed on hold three times, I wanted to cut the conversation there, before I canceled again. So I told Marilyn no, I didn't mind, send anyone as long as he was an older and experienced teacher.

Just before my first advanced highway-driving session I had lunch near home with Tina, a *New York Times* columnist. She told me that her two regrets in life were that she had never learned to drive or to play bridge. "One would have given me freedom, the other would have kept my mind sharp." We split the check and I hurried out, in nervous anticipation of the lesson. I race-walked around the corner, to the spot by the fire hydrant where overworked, wizened Fred used to await me in his dented gray Nissan. Replacing this familiar sight was an immaculate pale-brown Acura Integra from whose roof jutted a prism-shaped driving-school signboard, as brassily yellow as a wedge of Wisconsin cheese. A dark-haired, broad-shouldered man with a tiny silver hoop through his left ear leaned propri-etarily against the car. His arms were crossed confidently against his chest, and though he was chewing on a tiny piece of gum, he was also smiling—just a shade too cockily, I thought. He had been anticipating that I would enter the street from my apartment building, directly in front of him, but I had ambushed him from the left.

"You're not whom I expected," I said frostily. Perhaps it was the unabashed way he seemed to be sizing me up that made me want to greet him with an arctic blast.

"Who were you expecting?" he replied evenly.

"A Filipino man, Carl. Or Fred." That wasn't even true.

I raked my eyes over his black T-shirt, his tough-guy black boots, and his camouflage cargo pants—two last-year's trends in one. By inspecting his outfit, I was trying to avoid meeting his unnerving gaze, and he knew it.

"Well, I'm Andrew," he said, extending his right hand to me. "If you decide you don't like me, it's all right to ask for someone else afterward."

I gave him a prickly glance. At that moment he reminded me, smoky voice and all, of Mickey Rourke playing Boogie in *Diner*.

"Excuse me, I'll be right back down." I tore into my apartment building and hastened up the elevator. I shook off my green suede heels and switched to olive ballet flats. Agitated, trying to compose myself, I unclasped my tiger's-eye choker, hoping to get more comfortable.

This Andrew already had me pegged as an uptown ice queen, and I was fully living up to his expectations.

I returned to the Acura, where a little power play was speedily enacted.

"Have a seat," he said.

"Am I driving?" I asked, in a futile bid for the upper hand.

"Yes," he said, chivalrously opening the front left door.

I slid into the chair. The automatic Japanese shoulder harness snaked itself around my chest like one of Laocoön's attacking serpents. I reached for the ignition key. But Andrew wasn't about to let me make a move without his first having commanded it.

"No, not yet. First, check to see if your mirrors are adjusted correctly. Out of the left and right mirrors you should see just a sliver of the car's sides."

"Oh, right. Fred taught me that. I see now. Just a sliver of the car on each side, thin and long like a banana peel."

He liked that. He smiled.

"Now the rearview mirror. Do you see the whole back window? And just the little brake-light box beneath?"

"Yes," I said, fiddling with the looking glass anyway, to get a glimpse of my face. Lipstick check.

"The average car has twelve blind spots. Now the seat position."

"I feel too far away." He was just maybe an inch taller than I—five eleven, probably claiming six. So why had he placed the seat so far back?

"New drivers feel more comfortable if they're a little closer to the wheel. But you don't want to be too close because you tense up more and start controlling the pedals with your quadriceps instead of your ankle. When you become as relaxed with driving as I am," he said, "then you can recline more. What do you call this?" he asked, resting a silver-banded finger behind the nape of my neck.

"A headrest," I said impatiently.

"No," he contradicted. "It's a head *restraint*. If it's not in the right position, you can injure your neck if you're rear-ended. Make sure it's at ear level—neither too high nor too low. Next, look at the placement of your hands on the steering wheel— they should be at nine o'clock and three o'clock. In a car without air bags, ten and two is the best position. But at ten and two, if, God forbid, an air bag is deployed, it could send your knuckles flying into your face at over two hundred miles per hour. Turn the key, put on your left signal, and pull out."

We were off.

I signaled right and we went up Park Avenue and turned left at Ninety-seventh Street, where I failed to notice both a red light and a pedestrian. Andrew stopped us with his dual brakes.

"Who taught you to drive?" I asked, trying, in an uphill battle, to collect myself. We were heading through Central Park on the Ninety-sixth Street transverse.

"These two lanes become one—the sign is warning us. My father. He was a pilot with the Turkish air force and a former general."

That sounded serious enough for me. I liked the fact that Andrew wanted to inform me he was not a creature from the bottom of the food chain. That piqued my curiosity. He was the kind of man who normally was invisible to me. Had I been missing something? I stole a sideways glance at him, and was nearly sideswiped by a taxi.

"You didn't notice him because he was in your blind spot."

We had made it to Columbus Avenue. "Turkish? I thought maybe Italian."

It occurred to me that my right side, my second-best profile, was the one on view to him.

"Most people do," he said. "Keep going. You shouldn't have turned into the right lane—if you were looking far enough ahead you would have seen two double-parked cars."

His accent didn't sound Turkish either. It had the coarse cadences of Queens, mixed with a touch of Black English and, I noted, something else, vaguely Continental. He spoke slowly —as deliberately as I, but not as softly.

"I couldn't even imitate a Turkish accent if I tried," he said. "The first Americans I ever spent any time with were from the South—black guys, in Germany."

That was it—German. His *th*'s became *d*'s, and he interchanged his *v*'s with his *w*'s. "Army guys?"

"No."

He had talked me right onto the West Side Highway. And that's when panic struck, and when the recurrent childhood nightmare unspooled into the daylight.

The Swiss architect Le Corbusier, exhilarated by the soaring vision of the George Washington Bridge, exalted it as "the only seat of grace in the disordered city."

At that instant, my response was not quite so euphoric. "I felt like the bridge was collapsing on me," I tried desperately to explain to Andrew, after he grabbed the steering wheel and guided us away from the hulking SUV and into the adjacent lane. "The flashing sign was hypnotizing me, the cement wall was caving in on me."

"Do not focus on any object," Andrew replied. "Keep your eyes moving. If you stare at anything for more than a fraction of a second, you will head for it. When I grabbed the wheel, you were focusing on the broken white line, your left lane markings."

I had been. And I had barely been aware of it. How did he know?

"That's why you drifted out of your lane. With your central vision, scan fifteen to twenty seconds ahead, a distance of two city blocks at thirty miles per hour. Sweep your eyes into the curve, to the car's intended path of travel. Then bring your eyes back to where they started. And scan wide to every moving and stationary object in the unfolding panorama. If you don't look far enough ahead or high enough, you're not giving your brain enough information. Your eyes should make little jerky movements—fixating but never focusing. That will pull you right into your safe cushion in the middle of your lane."

"So your eyes move in and out, sort of like a zoom lens?"

"Sure, that's one way to think of it."

These words, variations of which I would come to hear often, didn't quite make sense to me on that first day out. Still, they started to take effect. It felt as if taut, invisible cords were now securing my eyes to the road ahead, keeping me correctly positioned, and connected to the rushing stream of events outside the car. The vertical and horizontal axes righted themselves. I found the center of the lane.

"What is a safe cushion?" I asked. I liked the term. The sound of it alone made me relax, a little. I imagined my safe cushion as a huge, buoyant satin damask pillow, bearing me gently along the highway.

"You're in your safe cushion—or your space cushion—when you're riding in the center of your lane and, at thirty miles per hour, you are preserving a distance of at least three car lengths between you and the vehicle in front of you. At sixty miles per hour it should be six car lengths. That's on dry pavement. To see if you are maintaining the proper distance, use the two-second rule. Choose a landmark on the road—that speed limit sign will do."

The white Dodge Intrepid in front of us flew by the sign.

"Start counting: *one thousand one, one thousand two*. And keep up with the traffic."

We arrived at the sign, just where the white car had been two seconds before.

"Anyone who invades your safe cushion is a potential danger to you. You have to drive defensive."

"Defensively?"

"Yeah. Defensively."

I had never understood the term "defensive driving"—it had always sounded combative.

"Defensive driving doesn't mean you're fighting back," Andrew said, reading my mind. "What you are defending—or protecting—is your safe cushion. Allow that car to pass you. All right. Now on wet pavement, the two-second rule becomes a four-second rule. Do you understand?"

"I'm not sure. Would you mind repeating it?" Now that the nightmare had receded, my first highway driving lesson was turning into that math class scourge—the word problem.

Andrew started over. Though I still didn't fully absorb what he was saying, the sound of his voice helped calm my leaping nerves.

"You know, I've had nightmares about this all my life."

"Yes, my students always have driving dreams. Pick up speed."

"I think maybe driving fears are about the fear of losing control."

I think maybe I wanted him to know that even though I drove like an idiot, I wasn't one.

I once more tried to rationalize my incompetence.

"My father almost died three times in car accidents, and both of his parents were killed by cars."

"Every twenty-three minutes someone in America will be killed in an alcohol-related car accident," the instructor replied impassively, hyperalert eyes fixating simultaneously on the road, highway signs, the movements of other vehicles, his extra set of mirrors, my erratic driving.

It seemed like a somewhat unfeeling response to a rather dramatic personal revelation.

"In five years I've taught thirteen hundred students," he recited. "None that I know of has ever been in an accident. In the thirty years that I've been driving, I've logged two million kilometers. I myself have not been in a car accident since 1986."

He had me there.

At three-thirty, the lesson's end point (Andrew, it seemed, was maddeningly punctual), we found that the little spot by the hydrant was occupied. He had me turn right, to double-park along the avenue. I remembered, from Fred's training, to flip on my hazard lights. But I couldn't locate the switch on the dashboard.

"Here," he said, reaching over. "Would you like to pay me by credit card, or by check?"

I looked at him, trying to guess his meaning.

"You mean, pay you directly, under the table?" I asked suspiciously.

Andrew looked at his wary student and laughed, little judgments forming behind his opaque eyes. "No, I don't do that."

"Last time, with Fred, I always paid the school over the phone, by credit card. I didn't even know you could pay the driver. So I really didn't understand what you meant." I didn't want him to think I had assumed he was corrupt.

"That's fine. So, Amy. Would you like to change instructors?"

"No, I'll stick with you." I smiled. It felt odd, maybe too familiar, to be called by my first name. Andrew opened the door for me and gave me his hand to help me out of the car. Another handshake and then he slipped back into the driver's seat. Like an Olympian arrow launched from Diana's bow, he shot onto Park Avenue with a precision, grace, and assurance that I had never before seen in a car or a driver.

I want to learn to do that, I thought as he disappeared—not realizing how far this wish would take me from the corner on which I stood.

Moving Chicane

Between the first and second lessons I had a minor fashion crisis. What should I wear for driving? My wardrobe seemed slightly out of context, for both the car and the instructor. I wandered into a neighborhood boutique and ended up with a pair of black corduroy hip-huggers, my first since adolescence, and a pair of black leather pants with toreador ruffles stitched down the sides, as well as a pair of gray stretch gabardine trousers, possibly too tight. Now that I knew what—and whom—to expect, I was rather looking forward to seeing Andrew, and I wanted to look good.

I SELECTED the corduroys with a Beene camel-hair jacket for lesson number two, which didn't take place until early November, because I had been away in Dallas.

"Two questions," I said to Andrew as he offered me his seat behind the Acura's wheel.

"Yes?"

"What is your opinion of sunglasses? And how do you feel about heels?"

"Sunglasses are good. I don't recommend high heels."

"For neither men nor women?"

"Well, some like these could be OK," he said carefully, indicating his motorcycle boots.

Andrew warmed me up with city driving—I was comfortable knowing his eyes and his reflexes (and his brake in his foot well) were in charge, not my own. From the West Side, Andrew nudged me to the Henry Hudson Parkway, and at its tollbooth he refused to let me pay. I could not understand why he would want to use cash from his own pocket. "All right, then, keep a running tab," I said. "You'll be able to collect a big bill later."

"I'll never ask you for one," he said.

Next we entered the Saw Mill River Parkway. "The Saw Mill has a lot of hairpin turns, many tight situations, but the same speed as an expressway," Andrew explained. "Like all parkways, it has no trucks. I noticed on Amsterdam they made you nervous."

Andrew was not euphemistic about the seriousness of our undertaking.

"More accidents occur on two-lane highways than on any other kind of road," Andrew warned. "Head-on collisions are the most common. When driving you have to make constant life-and-death decisions. The risk of injury and fatalities is much higher than in anything else you'll do in daily life. The point of our lessons is to beat the odds."

Hunched over the wheel, not knowing where to look or for how long, or what to think about, I felt my left shoulder grow tense and sore. I told him it seemed like I was using only the left side of my brain. In fact, I was drifting so much to the left, I was "giving up my safe cushion."

"Apply gas, apply gas," he repeated, flicking his left fingers forward. "Do you see how you've become an obstacle to the other cars? On a racetrack they'd call you 'moving chicane.'"

I flashed back to my father haranguing my maternal grandfather: "Sam, speed up! You're pausing at every intersection even when there's no stop sign!"

"Quiet," my grandfather had growled, sotto voce, glancing at me in the rearview mirror. "*Die Kinder.*" Both men went silent, puffing cigars.

"You're too tense to control the acceleration," Andrew said, intruding on my thoughts. "You're somewhere else right now. Concentrate on the task at hand. Do you see we're going uphill? You need more power—*now.*"

I felt like a speed demon, but the needle was only hovering at 40. And now I was hearing my mother scolding my father, on our way to the lake cottage, to slow down, and my big sister crying next to me in the backseat. Both she and my mother were white-knuckling their armrests with their right hands. I observed their noisy drama in silence.

"Relax," Andrew said finally, touching my right arm. I had not noticed until that instant that both were as rigid as petrified twigs. Under the gentle pressure of his fingertips—unusually well manicured, I noticed—they became supple.

"You were so tense, Amy, you were just looking into a little box, seeing nothing. You were gripping the wheel so tight you could have squeezed water out of it."

"My daughter has a parallel fear," I said, recovering. "She's afraid to ride a bicycle."

21

Andrew proposed that he teach her, free of charge. Moved by the kindness of this offer, I asked, "Have you ever taught a child to ride a bike before?"

"No, but I can do it. Let me think about it for a few days, and I'll come up with a strategy." This man probably could teach anybody anything, I decided—he had a gift. How had he managed to coax me onto the Saw Mill and now back again? I was wondering if it were possible really to know something unless you *could* teach it.

At the lesson's end, we pulled into our fire hydrant spot at the corner of my apartment building.

"I'll give you my cell phone number. Here, take one of the school's cards to write on."

I wrote on the card, "Andrew."

"Andrew's not my real name."

I looked at him.

"What is your real name?"

"Attila."

"*Attila?* Like Attila the Hun? Then why do you call yourself Andrew?"

"Andrew is the name I took when I became an American citizen. It's on my passport. I use it at work."

"So you're an American citizen."

"For ten years now."

There was still so much raw tension and lurking suspicion left over from the World Trade Center attacks that if he were Muslim—and as a Turk surely he was—the fact that he had adopted U.S. citizenship made me feel less skittish.

"What would you like me to call you?"

"Attila."

"OK. And when I call the school to make my next appointment, shall I refer to you as Andrew, or Attila?"

"Andrew."

I programmed his phone number into my cell. On my alphabetized directory, "Attila" landed immediately after the entry "Amy," for my own home number.

Breakthrough on Bear Mountain

I had booked a four-hour lesson for the next Saturday, which turned out to be a spectacularly beautiful autumnal day. Again, I dressed down for the occasion with care. Attila met my daughter, whom we were taking to a playdate, and charmed her right away by taking her hand, looking her in the eyes, and helping her into and out of the car as if she were a great lady instead of a little girl. He was evaluating me, I sensed, by studying her, just as I was assessing him by watching his manner with my child. During the ten-block trip to her playdate, I recounted for both of them the plot of Puccini's *Turandot*, which I had seen at Lincoln Center the night before.

"Look at your shoulder belt," Attila said as we prepared to take off again, now without my daughter. "You will not be protected in a crash!" The harness was slung under my arm, like a fashion accessory rather than a safety device. I obediently yanked the strap over my shoulder.

He directed me, via the Henry Hudson Parkway, onto the Saw Mill again, and over the long, arcing Tappan Zee Bridge, which spans the Hudson at its broadest point—a feat of locomotion that elated me. I felt as if the oval egg of the world were hatching open, spilling its infinite contents over a watery, newborn horizon. If I could do this, I imagined, anything was possible. I was awed—by him, by me, by the all-encompassing vista. And I knew I was on the verge of liberation from my fear. Trying to contain my exuberance (lest it revert to terror), I asked Attila if he knew the origin of the bridge's name. I explained that it was part American Indian (the Tappan tribe) and part Dutch ("Zee" referred to a wide body of water). I also told him that the French artist Marcel Duchamp, who sat out World War II in New York, believed that the only works of art that America had contributed to society were its plumbing and its bridges. I couldn't tell if he was paying any attention to my anxiety-induced pedantry.

His priority at that moment was not local history but teaching me to control the acceleration—to ease up on it as we cruised downhill and apply gas as we climbed uphill, in order to maintain consistency. He was also training me to "manage curves." I had been "pre-steering," he said, treating curves as turns.

"It's enough to apply pressure to the wheel—without gripping it or turning it, while sweeping your eyes into the curve far ahead. Physics will do the rest of the work for you."

"You mean centrifugal force?"

"Yep," he said.

We worked on lane positioning and merging, probably the scariest highway task.

"Start judging the length of the ramp six to seven seconds ahead by looking at the right edge of the road with your central vision," Attila said. I repeated his words to myself as he spoke, the better to steady myself and absorb their meaning. "If it's a short runway," he added, "do a head check. If it's a long runway, check the mirror first, and when you get parallel to the road, do the head check. Before you accelerate, make sure that the reflection of the car you see in the mirror is small.

"Don't hesitate! *Go!*"

I felt like a kid, nose pinched, sprinting to the edge of the high dive.

Splash! I had merged successfully.

WE TOOK exit 13N off the Palisades Parkway and spiraled up, at 25 miles per hour, to the highest lookout point of Bear Mountain. The view spread beneath us was intoxicating. A train far below, reflected upside down in the glassy water, puffed like a toy through gaudy autumn foliage, past a Victorian depot. It was a framable picture straight off the brush of a Hudson River School painter.

"I wish I had taken a camera, or a sketch pad," I said, removing my denim jacket. We had stepped out of the car. "But I'm a lousy photographer and I don't really draw anymore. My mother's the artist in the family. What about you?"

"My friend Russ is a good photographer. He took pictures up here with me a long time ago."

We followed Seven Lakes Drive down, and at a junction for West Point, Attila taught me how to negotiate a circle.

"Who has the right of way in a circle?"

I had read about traffic circles in my manual when I had crammed for my learner's permit. But I had long since forgotten the rules that governed them.

"Whoever's already in the circle has the right of way," Attila answered for me. "Whoever is about to enter the circle has to yield. There's the red-triangle Yield sign. Now, are you going to give up your right of way? You were trying to be polite with the other car, I know, but too polite, like too slow, can do you harm on the highway."

And off it too, I thought.

I asked him if he knew he was using the Socratic method—asking questions rather than lecturing—and then realized that Greek philosophers were unlikely to have figured in his Turkish school curriculum.

"Mathematics and science were important at my high school," he informed me. "Physics and psychology were my best subjects. Also sports. They all come together in this job. Afterward I studied sports medicine at the university, but I never finished. If I ever go back to school I'd like to get a degree in marine biology, or maybe computer science."

Another of Attila's thankless tasks on this day was to try to inculcate in me a sense of direction, first by reading a lot of signs. "You've got to learn—if you start from point A—how to return to point A. Do you know why you were drifting out of your lane again?" He had rotated the steering wheel toward himself, a marginal but deft correction.

"No, why?"

"Because your eyes were focusing on the sign too long. Read signs one line at a time, scanning into the distance in between."

"Everyone says driving will finally teach me a sense of direction," I said. "But I'm not convinced."

I gave him the background of this handicap, which long predated the driving phobia. In Manhattan, I told him, I had always resided uptown, where because the streets are laid out in ruler-and-pencil grids, it was impossible to lose my way. If I ventured downtown below Fourteenth Street, where the streets began to branch and divide as bewilderingly as the channels of the Minotaur's labyrinth, I was lost, without bearings. I chose to attend a small college because I worried about finding my way around a large campus. In foreign cities I had to be driven, or walked like a child. "I can't read a map," I admitted. "I can't even fold one."

"You waited too long to put on your blinker, Amy," he answered. "You should start signaling your intentions a hundred feet ahead." He observed me in silence for another mile or two, surreptitiously probing for something, I sensed, and then came back with a reply. "Attila will help you learn to find your way."

We rolled along quietly for a few more minutes on 87. He turned on the radio, which played only one station, a hard rock channel that seemed to suit him. It didn't take long for our conversational lull to make me jittery all over again—I was anxiously anticipating my next driving faux pas. I fidgeted with my hands, dropping them to the crossbar of the steering wheel.

"I've felt deficient for so long, because I didn't know how to drive. But I'm realizing for the first time that though most people drive, very few drive well."

"I'm going to make you one of those few," he promised. "Now put your hands back on the wheel. You're not driving a motorcycle."

THE NIGHT before, I had shared my new insight with Edward, a writer friend, at a dinner party at Daniel, the French restaurant on East Sixty-fifth Street. He had replied, "Well, then, it's just like my epiphany about marriage. For the longest time I wondered, What's wrong with me? Why is it that so many unlovable people are able to marry and mate, and I'm still single? And then it finally occurred to me that though most people do in fact wed, very few marriages are truly happy." I repeated this simile to Attila, who told me (without going into detail) that he had been married once, but was now divorced. "No children—I live alone with my dog, Ajan, half rottie and half German shepherd. I'll bring you a picture of him."

"Well, Edward will never marry," I continued, "because he decided he's gay."

We stopped at a gas station, where he bought me a Diet Coke from a vending machine (again he wouldn't let me pay). And he took a pack of Dunhill Blues out of a side pocket of his cargo pants (they were olive drab this time). He lit one in the parking lot.

"I didn't know you smoked," I said.

"I didn't want you to know."

"So that's why you chew Winterfresh gum." He kept a pack handy by his seat. "I love the smell of tobacco. I'm a second-hand smoker."

"I quit once for a long time," he said. "But I started again five years ago. In America, when you smoke too much they say you 'smoke like a chimney.' In Germany they say you 'smoke like a Turk.' "

"What made you start again?"

"Somebody died," he said, his eyes rising to the treetops behind the station, away from me. Densely fringed and dotted with a mole on the upper and lower left lids, they were his smallest features. His jaw was strong, his chin shallowly cleft, and his brow a bulky visor.

"Time to get back in the car," he said.

Attila opened the door for me and took the passenger seat. "I started it already," he said, pulling my hand away from the ignition key.

"When'd you do that?"

"I'm quick with my fingers—Mandrake the Magician. When I was a kid in Turkey that was my favorite comic book," he explained. Back on the road he opened the window and lit another cigarette. "You know, this isn't really my profession." His refutation of an obvious fact reminded me of my long-ago friend Alex, a beautiful boy who grew fat. He would introduce himself by saying, "Hello, I'm Alex. I used to be thin."

"What do you mean—you moonlight as a magician?"

"No, but I did learn a few tricks from a kid in Turkey who's now famous there."

Attila, it turned out, didn't have one other "real" profession—he had run though an epic series of them. In Turkey, Germany, Switzerland, and New York he had been (and, he cautioned, not in this order) a textile designer, a musician, a motorcycle racer, an inventor, a soccer player, a furniture importer-exporter, a folk dancer, a trucker, a snowboarder, part of an airline ground crew, a nightclub owner, a masseur, a gym trainer, an Internet entrepreneur, and a sculptor.

"But I only carved one sculpture—of a naked man and woman kneeling and holding each other. I called it *One on One*. My plan was to cast it and market it as an automobile air freshener."

"So which job did you like the best?" I asked, trying to picture this figurine and what circumstances in his life inspired him to carve it.

"Inventor. My partner, Claude, and I designed reusable, adjustable dress patterns. We patented special machinery to manufacture them, and made a lot of money. I'll show one to you sometime. But then Claude got sick, and he was never the same after that, and . . . I don't want to go into it." He had begun to sound angry or regretful, and had caught himself. He waved his thoughts away with his hand.

"This job I found in the newspaper," he continued. "Maybe now it's my favorite—definitely not the best money, though. I saw an ad that said, 'Wanted: Driving Instructors.' I had taught my two younger brothers and some of my friends how to drive, so I knew I could do it. And I've always liked cars. I've owned a lot of them."

"Can you remember them all?"

Over the next ten minutes, like a Don Juan paging through his little black book, he recited his list, watching the road and my eyes as he spoke, hitting his dual brake twice, and grabbing the steering wheel once. The roster ran the gamut from a VW Beetle, a 1985 Mercedes 190E AMG, and a Rolls-Royce Silver Wraith to a Mercury Cougar, a Series III 1978 Excalibur, and a Lincoln Town Car. He stopped at car number forty-three. "That averages out to one car for each year of my life," he said.

RESPECTFUL, Attila didn't ask me any personal questions, nor did I trouble him with any. Off the cuff, he remarked that he would like to write a collection of short stories based on his experiences with his students, "sort of like *Coffee, Tea or Me?*—a book I read in Germany."

"I read that book in ninth grade on a Christmas break in Florida," I said. "Years later I heard it was not written by stewardesses at all but by a couple of gay men." I told him that I was a writer. He had never seen, or even heard of, *Vanity Fair* before—very refreshing to me.

I asked him to tell me, one by one, some of the tales about his students that he would compile for a book. It was a pleasant way to pass the time as we drove cityward through thickening traffic —not unlike Scheherazade's narrations in *Arabian Nights*. He had an almost eidetic memory for details and events, and he lingered longest over the story of dyslexic twins, brother and sister.

"When I told them to turn right, they'd go left. They were the toughest cases I've had so far."

But by the time they had finished their lessons with him—
about thirty-five hours per twin—their dyslexia was unscram-
bled, not only on the road but in their other endeavors as well.
Attila, it seemed, had an uncanny ability to plumb his students'
psyches.

"If you could succeed with them, then there's hope for me," I
said. "I'd like to hear the story from the dyslexic twins' point of
view. Do you think it would be a good idea for me to meet
them?"

"Sure. Why not?"

"You really like working with problem students, don't you?"

"I like poking into the sorest places, and healing them."

"I've got plenty of sore spots for you."

"Maybe. But have you noticed they're not wounds anymore?"

He explained that he preferred zero-mileage students. "I like
to leave my imprint on smooth wax. Otherwise I waste time
grinding away bad habits." I told him he was like George Balan-
chine, who preferred directing an older starting ballerina to a
young girl trained by another choreographer.

"I've never been to a ballet," he said. "But I wouldn't mind trying out a ballet class because I've always been a good dancer."

This small boast brought to mind a conversation I'd had at a
neighborhood Italian restaurant, Centolire, a few nights before
with two friends—Kate, a decorator, and Joseph, a photographer. It was reaching the point where all I wanted to talk about
was my driving lessons.

"In my experience," Kate had said, pushing away her raw ar-
tichoke salad, "if a man is a great driver, he's also a great dancer.
And great in bed."

"What do you think those three skills have in common?" I
had asked her.

33

"Rhythm and flow," Kate had answered without hesitation. "And empathy—an ability to anticipate another person's responses, needs, and reactions."

Joseph, recalling an affair he had had as a teenager with an auto mechanic, noted, "I'm not so sure I agree, Kate. You've heard the saying about lumberjacks? 'They make love when they chop wood and chop wood when they make love.'"

I did not repeat this conversation to Attila. But I did guess his secret wish to open his own driving school.

"You're good," he said. "There isn't nobody else who I've mentioned that to."

I corrected his double negative. "Your English doesn't do justice to your intelligence," I told him. "Do you mind if I help you improve it?" He welcomed my linguistic instruction, and the Henry Higgins teacher-student role reversal helped make me feel less defenseless.

"With you I'm studying," he said. "I've been trying to learn not just better English, but a whole way of life."

At the end of the Henry Hudson Parkway he handed me a twenty-dollar bill to pay the toll—and I passed the cash on to the toll taker and kept going. I had to put the car into reverse to collect his $18 in change. This mistake did not embarrass me—not with him.

By the time we were back in Manhattan, my right hamstring was so sore from manipulating the accelerator that at a red light on Columbus Avenue, I got into a lotus position to relieve the ache.

And in the lesson's last few minutes he mentioned that his talking to me was a didactic technique, the "only way I could find to get you to relax, and pay attention to the road." I was a little let down—it felt as if we had been laying down the foundation for some kind of friendship.

But in front of the East Seventy-fifth Street building where my daughter awaited me, her playdate over, Attila said, "This is the hot seat, sweetheart. Everyone who sits in that seat ends up talking to me, telling me things that even their best friends, husbands, boyfriends, and parents don't know. This is the first time that I'm doing the talking. I never talk about myself to my students."

I felt better.

FIVE DAYS after the Bear Mountain run, I had lunch with Larry, a veteran book editor friend, at Michael's, the publishing industry fishbowl on West Fifty-fifth Street. For nearly three years, we had been meeting there monthly. Originally, our objective had been to find the right book project for me. On Larry's urging I had started a novel, based on a true experience, about an evil nanny, a reverse Mary Poppins who had disturbed the sanity of a series of Manhattan families. But in the process Larry and I had discovered what I had already suspected—that I didn't have the temperament for fiction—and so we had agreed to shelve the book, whose title was to have been *Nursery*. After that, our lunches had turned into a nonworking social ritual, pleasant and gossipy.

But on this particular day, I dispensed with the tittle-tattle and talked instead about Attila, my lessons, Bear Mountain, and how I had suddenly discovered that my accountant, my hair salon's manager, my daughter's friend's mother, my cousin, my favorite antique dealer, and my agent's assistant all had paralyzing driving phobias—and they had all opened their hearts to me on the subject. "I directed every one of them to Attila," I told Larry. "Attila's more than an instructor," I pressed on. "He's a healer, a guru, a sage, a road philosopher."

"Amy, you're obsessed with your lessons and with your instructor," Larry said, when I finally gave him a chance to speak. "Take notes. Keep a diary. Start now. There's a book in this—and I bet you're going to have more fun working on it than anything else you've ever written."

Real Life

I acted on Larry's advice—I usually do. All that follows (and everything that preceded) is a result of his lunchtime exhortation.

THE NEXT Friday, Attila picked me up on East Seventy-seventh Street after lunch. In spite of Attila's recommendation I was wearing slender heels—but just in case, I packed pink ballet slippers in my silk houndstooth bag. He looked at my hair-calf pumps and approved them for driving; they were low enough. The night before, I had been to dinner at the SoHo loft of Robert (himself a new driver at forty-two), where another guest, Hervé, exclaimed, "It's absolutely ridiculous for your instructor to tell you not to wear heels! All the women in France drive around in stilettos, they always have!"

"He's right," Attila said. "They do in Turkey too."

We took the FDR Drive from Ninety-sixth Street to the Bruckner Expressway and got off at the Orchard Beach–City Island exit. Our original plan had been to go to Connecticut on

37

I-95—I wanted to learn the way to my beach house—but the traffic, as Attila put it, "got too crazy." On the Bruckner, he told me I seemed more relaxed, probably because he was keeping highway driving to a minimum. Though Manhattan streets were the terror of out-of-town drivers, I was still much more at ease on them—they were the known evil.

Attila seldom told me my mistakes overtly—he let me discover them myself. But timing was everything because he never interfered until the last possible moment—when my error had reached the point of life-threatening danger. He let me pass, knowing full well that a U-Haul van was coming up fast, about to overtake the space that I had marked out for myself. He floored the dual brake just as I was about to catapult us into a collision.

Obviously, he thrived on risk.

ATTILA EXPLAINED that on the first day when I got in the car and started driving, he saw "a blue screen with a lot of flashing red dots. The dots are now shrinking into small points of light. One by one they'll disappear until we will end up with a clear, empty blue screen. I'm letting you know things I normally never tell a student. But it's different now—because we're working on a book." (He had loved Larry's idea and was eager to participate.) "Whatever it is I do to students behind the *veel* will affect their behavior outside of the car," he said.

"So you mean if you teach them to be nice and calm while driving, they'll become that way in real life?"

"Of course they will," he said, tapping the dashboard with his thick index finger (no silver ring today). "This *is* real life. As real as it gets."

THAT DAY, things were starting to settle, Attila said as we crossed the Triborough Bridge. He offered the metaphor of an aquarium: "You begin with the empty tank. Then you get the gravel, and wash it. The gravel needs to settle for a while. Next you add the water. After that, you have to wait to put in the fish."

"You have one of those?"

"I used to," he said, his eyes darkening. "It's an expensive hobby. My fish were happy. They bred a lot."

He praised my broken U-turn on one of City Island's dead ends, a cramped alleyway that serviced a row of Monopoly-marker houses, each set off from its neighbor by a chain-link fence.

"Watch out for the cat!"

"You can't just tell a student, 'Stop panicking,'" he continued, once we were sure of the yellow tabby's safety, "any more than an eye surgeon can tell his patient to cut his own retina. I have to study the panic from her point of view. I shouldn't reveal more secrets to you—but with you I knew the fear wasn't about speed, because you were still nervous when I slowed you down."

He stopped himself there, though I wished he would proceed with his diagnosis.

"Sometimes we should come back here to City Island," he said. We were cruising slowly down its eponymous main drag, City Island Avenue. "One of these fish restaurants is supposed to be excellent. Maybe it's that one, the Lobster Box."

"Sometime," I corrected him.

On the way home we took the Throgs Neck Bridge to the Cross Island Parkway, detouring through Queens. When we stopped for gas I gave him an old Bob Dylan tape, with a song about Bear Mountain.

"I used to sing a little Bob Dylan when I had my guitar. It was an Ovation," he said wistfully. He pronounced it *Owation*. "I taught myself to play, on a bet."

I could only imagine what Attila sounded like doing Dylan's Jewish-boy country twang in his German-Queens-Turkish-black-inflected English.

"I'll bring you a demo tape I made of some songs I wrote. You won't understand the lyrics, though, because they're in Turkish. The tape deck has been broken for five months," he said. "But I'll give it a try anyway." By some fluke Dylan's music played.

"I don't understand! This is not supposed to work."

"Maybe I'm you're lucky charm."

"That you are."

The lesson finished, the tape ended. The cassette player never functioned again.

ATTILA planned to return to Bear Mountain for our next lesson, but I missed the exit on the FDR Drive to the Willis Avenue Bridge, and we ended up looping back to the city. We crossed the Harlem River on the 207th Street Bridge and followed the FDR south. The silvery cityscape viewed from the driver's seat at sunset was an uplifting, magical vision. Because of all the downtown detours, we ended up, not by design, at Ground Zero at twilight. The melancholy stillness there made our skin crawl.

"Can you feel the low energy?" he asked solemnly.

We left quickly.

I told Attila that Robert Moses—the commissioner who built

the FDR Drive, the Long Island and Cross Bronx expressways, and the Triborough, Bronx-Whitestone, and Henry Hudson bridges—did not know how to drive. This bit of trivia had come to me from my tablemate Owen during a lunch party several days earlier at Sotheby's. Owen, a rare-book dealer and (I quickly discovered) a nondriver, had insisted throughout the salmon course that "some people are just too intelligent to drive." But by the time the chocolate soufflé arrived, he admitted that he had been traumatized as a child by tales told by his father, a country doctor, "called away too many times" to the emergency room of his hospital to administer to mangled car-crash victims.

As the hydrant spot was filled, Attila nosed the Acura into a space half a block away, beside a synagogue, which over the past two months had been a target of bomb threats. He lit a Dunhill Blue, and while the ashes on his cigarette's tip grew alarmingly long, he talked about his country. Instinctively, I cupped a hand beneath the immobile tube of cinders (as a former pack-a-day smoker, I knew all too well the hazardous effect of gravity on ashes).

"You don't need to do that," he said. "They won't fall." And they didn't, ever—not until the whole jettisoned smoked-out butt hit the pavement.

It was 10 Kasim, he was telling me, a day of reflection commemorating the 1938 death of Atatürk, the founding father of modern Turkey. Atatürk had warned his people, Attila said, never to mix religion with politics—that it could only lead to conflict. Attila was convinced that Turkey was the best strategic ally and bulwark for the U.S., our greatest hope for shoring up the Mideast, because it was the only westernized Islamic nation. Turkey was the one country on the planet, he said, where the military (of which his father had been a part) protected democracy and kept the religious right at bay. He himself was a pacifist and a vegetarian, but not a practicing Muslim. Still, he recited prayers in Arabic, a language he didn't understand any more than Roman Catholics used to understand the Latin liturgy. His conception of God was ecumenical, personal, and mystical.

"If the U.S. made Turkey the fifty-first state," he reasoned, "it would solve America's foreign policy problems and Turkey's domestic ones.

"You handled the car well," he concluded. "You were not afraid at all."

And he took off, leaving me with just enough time to change my clothes and meet Sebastian, a magazine colleague, at the Broadway revival of *The Women*. During intermission Sebastian teased me about my driving lessons, going so far as to refer to my instructor as "Attila the Hunk."

Throughout the rest of the week I had an intermittent, odd, and not unpleasant sensation that a tinkering hand had been thrust into my brain, and was making adjustments—tightening some parts, loosening others. Other times I felt as if I'd swallowed a pill that enabled me to see the world with more clarity. At lunch at the 4 Times Square cafeteria, Sebastian accused me of having submitted myself to a cosmetic surgery intervention. "I've never seen you look so relaxed and happy before," he said. He then asked for Attila's phone number for his sister and a friend, both of whom had driving phobias.

The Colossus of Roads

A week later Attila collected me outside my daughter's ballet studio, where she had begun *Nutcracker* rehearsals. Running his right palm over his cheekbone, he apologized for not having shaved. Though gray specks had begun to proliferate among the black, on him the stubble was becoming. "I used to have a full beard—black then—and long, curly hair, past my shoulders. Nobody could believe it when they saw this hairy man with two pierced ears and torn worker's overalls stepping out of a Rolls."

We headed toward Connecticut again. Traffic on I-95 was abominable, and even worse on the return. But Attila remained the soul of patience. "Imagine what is taking place inside those cars," he said, indicating the ribbon of southbound vehicles. "An endless wave [pronounced *vave*] of anger and frustration." He accompanied his words with a ripple of his right hand. But not in our car. The unanticipated congestion left us plenty of time to talk, and the trip was fun. He talked about our "friendship."

"So you've given this a name," I said. It had begun to confuse

43

me, this indefinite amalgamation of teacher, subject, student, and confederate.

"Yes, it is a seed which will continue to grow," he predicted. "But when it does, I am not going to pull it up by the roots to examine what kind of plant it is."

Homeward bound, I did my first night driving. And as if summoned by Attila, Prospero-like, to test my tolerance further, raindrops began to splotch across the Acura's windshield. I complained that the road reflectors, the highway lamps, and the lights of other cars were blinding me.

"Take your central vision away from the source of glare," he advised, "using only your peripheral vision." Like all his techniques, it worked.

At the lesson's end, Attila kissed my hand.

"What's the matter?" he asked, holding a compact black umbrella over my head. "Did I do something wrong?"

"No, no, not at all." I could not tell him how reluctant I was to leave, and how these driving lessons had begun to supercede everything else in my life.

The next day I phoned *Vanity Fair* to turn down a story that would have taken me away to Paris for ten days—it was an assignment that not long before I would have fought to keep. Still, I was relieved that the article, on Yves Saint Laurent, wasn't reassigned to someone else.

ON THE Sunday after that, we headed down Second Avenue, through the Queens-Midtown Tunnel, onto the Long Island Expressway, and past Oyster Bay, while overhead, military jets' crystal trails iced the sky. Five days later we ventured into New Jersey. While Attila refueled the Acura at a gas station, I stood outside in the cold, shivering in a silver Beene T-shirt, and watched the cars streaking by on the turnpike. I could not believe that moments before I was one of them, and that I would soon be rejoining them.

Blocks away from home, as I was circumventing a double-parked car in the East Seventies, I told Attila I envied his self-sufficiency. Lately, I had been regretting that there was so little of any practical value that I could do well. He could cook, clean, do laundry, renovate a house, train a dog, tend a garden, build a computer from discarded parts. If I had to, how well would I fare on my own, without doormen or a housekeeper, in a small apartment in Queens? As I was speaking to him I had an uncanny feeling that this conversation had already taken place.

"Are you having a déjà vu?" he asked softly.

"Yes," I replied.

"Are you surprised that I knew that?"

"I'm getting accustomed to your ability to pull thoughts out of my head."

"You didn't mean to turn right on Seventy-ninth Street," he answered, as if to offer up proof of what I had just said. "Go around again on Seventy-seventh, and then back to Park. You were thinking Seventy-ninth was Eighty-sixth Street."

He was right again.

I HAD made up a list of destinations for future lessons—Stuy-vesant and Bridgehampton, New York; Kent, Connecticut; Three Bridges, New Jersey; Bucks County, Pennsylvania—locations, of course, of friends' country houses. He politely ignored these suggestions. Attila had his own program of routes, a calibrated system based on the level of difficulty and the type of challenges I was likely to encounter. So even though each successive trip required more complex and demanding driving skills, I didn't notice the increasing difficulty because of the corresponding rate at which he had me progress. Attila made the decisions, and gave the orders—partly why the routine had become so relaxing for me. "A student has to become a robot," he said—with him at the remote control. I did need to abandon myself to an egoless, empty, Zen-like state of mind to let the learning take place. Most of his students fought his control at first, but almost all, like me, ended up surrendering to him.

On upper Broadway, near the gates of Columbia University (scene of five years of art history graduate school), I ran another red light.

"Did I scare you?" I asked, heart pounding.

"You never scare me," he answered. "I only scare myself. Now turn right. We can get some good coffee near here on Broadway."

I put on my left blinker.

"You made that mistake because you were still thinking of your last error."

When he returned to the car from the Green Corner Deli on 122nd Street and Broadway, two scalding cups in one hand, he sniffed the sleeve of his black ribbed turtleneck and said, "Two minutes in there and now I've got the scent of the deli all over me. Poor ventilation." I couldn't smell anything except the Acura's pink Morning Fresh car deodorizer, and the faintest, cleanest whiff of Attila's Bulgari cologne.

ON ANOTHER day, back on the Saw Mill, he told me he would book me now only as his last student of the afternoon. "That way I won't have to rush off at the end of our lessons. We can spend a little time together." He told me I was *angenehm*—the German word for "cozy, pleasant, agreeable." I accepted the compliment, but told him if that were so, it was because he brought out the best in me.

I asked my German Pilates teacher, Sharyl, about the word. She said it is such a nice thing to say, Germans will rarely use the term to describe one another. Sharyl couldn't drive, and I suggested she sign up with Attila. "Do you really have confidence that I could learn to drive?" she asked, eyes downcast. It was that meek, uncertain female voice again, part of the chorus of the driving-phobic, issuing this time from a woman who was built like an Amazon warrior. "I have complete confidence that Attila can teach you," I replied.

I asked Attila if he had ever turned down a student. He told me he did once, a girl from an uptown address. "She jumped on me as soon as she got in the car. I told her, 'I don't even know you!'"

If this were an occupational hazard for him, the driving school did nothing to curtail it. The school, it turned out, sent most of its female students (who comprised 80 percent of its clientele) to Attila. I asked, "Do you have a theory about that?"

"Do I have to answer your question?"

I smiled the whole time I drove. He did too. He loved his job.

AS WE embarked on our second excursion to Bear Mountain, Attila told me, "You look gorgeous!"

"Thank you," I said, turning to him. "That's the first time you've let down your professional guard."

"Put your eyes back on the road. You can talk to me and still look ahead. Yes I did, for you. Ordinarily, I have to put up a wall immediately, on the first day," he explained. "A lot of people mistake this for a dating service. Marilyn, the receptionist, told me, 'You teach so many beautiful girls. Why don't you ask them out?' I said, 'Marilyn, this is my car, not my bedroom!' " Attila, with his silver jewelry and faulty English, was an instinctive gentleman, and I told him so.

On this same day—a waning one of autumn—the male toll-booth clerk grinned and greeted me with a big "Hello! I like your suit."

Attila said, "I've never seen that happen before."

Bear Mountain's showy colors of a few weeks before had mellowed into rusty tones, and the foliage had thinned. The domed peak resembled a cast-off crinolined ball gown, now faded and tattered.

"I was just thinking how the reds and golds of the leaves match the colors of your suit," he said. Noting my expression, he said, "Remember, I used to design textiles. Tricots, though, not wovens."

" 'Knits,' is how we'd say that here."

Sailing down the mountain, smoothly, this time, I told Attila I felt as if I were sprouting "wing buds" from my shoulders—an incipient, stirring feeling of freedom. Or else, I said, like a newly hatched bird whose feathers were crumpled and damp, but would soon dry, open, and spread. He said, "You're already beginning to walk out a little on your branch. And one day I will have to bump you off that branch and make you fly, by yourself."

"I don't want these lessons to end."

"You're getting too attached," he told me, very gently. He was right, and I thanked him. But I still could not imagine driving on my own.

I couldn't distinguish anymore what it was that I was really enjoying—the driving or the driving instructor.

"The combination," he answered.

THAT NIGHT, as I rode downtown to a *Vanity Fair*–hosted book party, I berated myself, Why can't I be like a normal student, and just learn to drive and be done with it? Why have I let this take over my whole life!

On a long trip up to Windham, New York, Attila again brought up my need to be "weaned," even though I was once more having trouble, getting so tense that the wheel wobbled under my fingers. "You're too dependent on me, you're not making decisions anymore." It was true. When I needed to act —about turning, about changing lanes, about speeding up or slowing down—I hesitated. Each hesitation was a silent question, a pause to be filled in with Attila's expert answer. And each hesitation was an invitation too—for him to take over (as he had on that first day when he grabbed the wheel and saved me from the SUV), for him to allow me to be dependent again, because I trusted him so much more than I did myself.

"Don't worry," he said, my thoughts transparent to him. "Attila will be here for you for a long, long time. Long after you become a driver."

I SAT in cars with other people—in taxis, on holiday—and observed their driving. I found it painful; I was silently correcting their errors, Attilacizing their actions—turns too wide, signals too late. This was exactly why Attila said he couldn't bear riding in a car unless he was the driver, or the teacher. The worst torture for him was the back—where he "hadn't sat for five years." He could never turn off his instructor's instinct to perfect and improve. Even when he was a pedestrian he was watching for flaws.

I asked during a quick drive through Queens (he had an errand to run near home), "How does it feel to be the best instructor in New York?" He was carrying the whole driving school on his sturdy back, booked twelve hours a day, seven days a week during winter, the slow season. The school's other instructors could fill only two to three days a week. He earned a Christmas bonus every year for The Most Referrals.

Attila stopped the car in front of a red building (he always left the motor running during such interludes), got out, and dropped a long envelope into a wooden mailbox near a windowed doorway. He then parked at his own address, a six-story garden apartment complex, circa 1965, whose evenly divided sections were named after the dormitory houses of Harvard College. Attila left for a few minutes, and came back down with his dog, who wagged his pointed black tail into a blur.

"This is Ajan," Attila said. I stroked the animal for a minute, and the two of them bounded back inside. Like his master, the mutt was a big, healthy, dark male—threatening at first glance, but fundamentally sweet-tempered.

Over the clang and rattle of the Queensboro Bridge's rush hour traffic I said to him, "You are like Superman." The steel girders crosshatched the towers of Manhattan and blotted out the day's remaining sunlight.

"Why?"

"Because Superman could stop time and halt disasters. And because you've passed through the defenses, the walls, that I've built around me."

"Yes, I know I've done that. But I don't think Superman could pass through matter."

"Actually, you're right. It was Flash, D.C. Comics. He did it by vibrating his molecules."

After that exchange I couldn't stop thinking of him as the caped comic-book hero whom I admired as a girl. With his forelock of dark hair, he even looked like Superman. I guess that made me Lois Lane, girl reporter. In fact, I learned I was not the first journalist to have discovered him. There was a feature on him in a local New York paper—*Newsday* or the *Daily News,* he couldn't remember which—in 1991, following the failure of one of his earlier businesses. Responding to his letter to the editor, in which he had vented his disillusionment with America, a reporter had interviewed him. This had then led to a booking on the TV show *A Current Affair,* which never materialized.

"I was on TV once before, though," he said. "In Turkey when I was sixteen, to demonstrate karate. I chopped a brick in half with my hand."

I combed the archives of *Newsday,* the kind of research I conducted as a matter of course for my articles, and came up empty-handed. I ended my search there—a renunciation that never would have occurred to me if I were working on a *Vanity Fair* story. Attila could not find the clipping either. "I lost it, or threw it out. It belongs to another life," he said dismissively.

It didn't matter—Attila by now had apotheosized for me from the sage of the superhighway to the oracle of the turnpike, from the colossus of roads to the God of Driving.

The recurrent nightmare stopped. In its place came a pleasant new dream, of driving well—a state of grace.

THE DAY before New Year's Eve, Attila took my daughter and me car shopping at the Volvo, Lexus, and BMW dealerships in the West Fifties. He encouraged me to test-drive an LX 300 (which my daughter loved for its backseat television), and when I returned from my three-block circuit in the SUV, he said, "You see, my dear, you can drive on your own in the city without me." But I was not ready to drive more than three blocks without him—any more than I was prepared to buy a car. When the Lexus salesman made his fast-talking pitch to me about financing, all I could concentrate on was his surname. How, I wondered, could such a Mediterranean-looking man have ended up with a name like "Mr. Smith"?

FOR OUR third trip to Bear Mountain it was unnaturally mild, clear, sixty-degree weather—one day away from the full moon. I hadn't driven for a month (a trip to Florida had cut into my lesson time) and I was horribly out of practice. Terror had crept back into my driving—a relapse. "Sweetheart, you're too busy in your head," he said.

"You're still passing too slowly and too closely," he said on 84. "When passing, you must make sure you can see the car's front bumper in your rearview mirror before taking your place in front of it," he reminded me. "If you're passing a truck, you need to see three-fourths of it in the rearview mirror before taking your place in front of it."

Twice on this day he said, "What are the chances I would ever meet someone like you? That's why I love this job!"

He invited me to have coffee with him afterward. At a handkerchief-sized pastry shop near the driving school, we sat facing each other for the first time. From the front he looked like a different man—less sternly defined, more mutable and complex. Over coffee, quiche, and chocolate cake (which he ate with refinement) he told me haltingly, brow furrowed, that he was in exile from Turkey. If he returned to his country he would be thrown into prison for avoiding compulsory military service. "I haven't been home in six years," he said. He took the check and left the waiter a 50 percent tip.

And soon after, he invited me to dinner at an East Side Turkish restaurant with a family of four from Ankara—a cosmetician, his wife, and their two daughters—all of whom had been his students. He dressed up in a dark blue jacket, gray woolen trousers, an azure tie, and freshly polished, custom-made black lace-up shoes—clothing presumably culled from one of his more affluent lives. In spite of the strict new citywide ban, all around us Turks were smoking. Tuxedo-clad musicians performed for the patrons, and as the maître d', jabbering in Turkish, led us to our table, Attila nodded to the keyboardist. "I used to play saxophone with him at another place," he said.

Attila and I resumed our places side by side—I to his left on the plush red banquette—and he ordered me a glass of Turkish wine. Practicing Muslims, the family didn't drink, and Attila, like a pilot, wouldn't even inhale alcohol if he was going to drive.

The Scissors Effect

On Attila's recommendation, we began stick shift lessons, which was like starting again from zero. I didn't mind the humiliation, or the frustration—it was a pleasure to become the clean slate once more. By this point, Attila and I had attained such a teacher-disciple rapport that he could instruct me, if he chose, without speaking. Sometimes we sat side by side in peaceful, companionable silence, and he directed me as needed by means of hand gestures—a fluent sign-language communication.

Interrupted during my third stick shift lesson by a cell phone call from the driving school, he said to Marilyn, the receptionist, "Just a second, dear." I was so conditioned by Attila, I reflexively downshifted to second gear.

I ASKED everyone—a trainer at the gym, *Vanity Fair* colleagues —"Do you drive stick shift?" Whoever answered "yes" smiled. If the answer was "no," I found instead an irritated incomprehension at the very idea of my bothering to learn such an obsolete skill.

The night after my fourth manual lesson, a fellow guest at a TV reporter's dinner party inquired, "What's the difference between driving standard and automatic?" My reply, which I had tried out earlier on Attila, was, "It's the difference between making the movie and watching the movie. With a stick you're part of the mechanics, more in control of the process." Mark, a hedge fund manager, interrupted me to boast about his own driving prowess. I guessed that he was feeling threatened, because, though he had just bought a Porsche Cayenne S, he was strictly an automatic transmission man. His wife, Patricia—an investment banker and the alumna of two Ivy League universities—had then interjected, "But Mark thinks *I'm* a cretinous, pathetic driver"—a verdict she unquestioningly accepted with a giggle. The whole setup (not at all the first one I'd seen like it) had infuriated me. Why did bright, accomplished women become so self-deprecatingly silly on the subject of their own driving—especially as compared with that of the men in their lives? And why did husbands and boyfriends bully them about their competence, bringing about the very mistakes they anticipated—a self-fulfilling prophecy? After that loaded exchange, Bill, a soft-spoken newspaperman, had leapt into the conversation. "Whenever *I* get in a car my testosterone levels soar," he announced. "I turn into an animal."

"That's called testosterone poisoning," I had said. "Or road rage, a bigger killer than alcohol."

Attila had taught me that the primitive, animal, territorial instinct took over when human beings sat in their cars. Sealed off inside five-by-eight metal carapaces, each driver became the alpha male of his mobile turf.

"It's the only place where most people ever feel they have any power," I had said to Bill, the journalist.

"Yeah, I know a woman who left her husband because of road rage," said Susan, a lawyer. "What's wrong with you guys? The only straight man I know who doesn't drive gave it up after he killed somebody."

EVEN WHEN I was having difficulty coordinating my movements with those of the manual Toyota (the clutch's friction point eluded me), the rhythmic sensation of shifting gears and the seesaw dance with the pedals were comforting, like a heartbeat. (Attila called the delicate, dynamic balance between accelerator and clutch the "scissors effect.") I commented to Attila that I felt as if I had done this in a past life. He said, "You must have spent a lot of time with someone who drove stick shift." Yes, indeed—very happy childhood recollections of riding shotgun with my father, and of sitting with my grandmother in her ladybug-colored VW Beetle. The vibrations, the motory aromas of her car came back to me.

Driving stick shift, I decided, was one of the great joys on this earth. There was something immensely satisfying about the harmony between flesh and machine—no messy emotions in the way, I suppose, as there inevitably were when two bodies met. I had to stop lessons midway, however, because the school's Celica broke down repeatedly. First the heater, then the clutch went. Attila was appalled by the school owner's indifference to a standard-shift car—if he wanted it fixed, Attila would have to pay for the repairs himself—and promised to resume teaching me as soon as possible.

I was in no hurry to master manual transmission—the

champion driver Alfonso de Portago entered his first race, in
Buenos Aires in 1954, without ever having learned to shift
gears. (He finished his inaugural run second overall, first in his
class.) Lately I had been collecting such automotive trivia—my
fashion and decorating magazine subscriptions were expiring
and in their place I had begun to read *AutoWeek, Car and Driver,*
and "Driving," a Sunday supplement of the *Times* of London.
And I had discovered that most men will listen raptly if you talk
motor vehicles with them.

So, with the Celica out of commission, Attila and I reverted
to automatic for a while—a breeze after stick. It felt like I'd gone
from germinating a third arm and leg back to a more manage-
able two. In the Acura he took me over the Brooklyn Bridge at
sunset. "I knew you'd love this, dear," he said proudly, as if he
had stage managed the spectacle himself. But I was so capti-
vated by the sight of the sun tumbling pyrotechnically over
Manhattan that I gazed at it too long in the thin black frame of
the rear view mirror—and lost my lane position.

"You're beginning to understand stick but I'm losing a good
driver. You're distracted, sweetheart—thinking about the book,
about me. Your learning curve is going into free fall."

And then we stopped lessons altogether. He did not want me
to spend any more money with the driving school. In my quest
to become a perfect driver, I'd already taken more lessons than
any other student in memory. I needed just about twenty-six
years to catch up with Attila. "You're able to attain perfection in
other things, Amy," he said as we sat with the hazards blinking
on Park Avenue. "You don't have to become as good a driver as
I am—it's not possible and it's not necessary."

We started driving around instead on his day off, Attila at the
wheel. Often we'd end up beside Grant's Tomb, the columned
granite monument above Columbia at 122nd and Riverside,

initially because parking spaces were plentiful. One day he studied the shrieking children on the swing sets of the playground behind the memorial. "When I was their age," he said, "I used to swing so high I'd go upside down, until the chains wrapped around the top bar—a three-hundred-and-sixty-degree ride. My mother would cry from fear. She loved me too much. That was in Naples, when my father was at the NATO base."

"You haven't changed at all."

"No, I haven't. 'A man is the same at seven that he'll be at seventy.' That's a Turkish saying. In Naples I also went on my first roller coaster ride, when I was six. I screamed the whole time."

"From pleasure?"

"No."

"I see. You actually were afraid. But I'll bet you weren't scared of the speed, only because you were not in control of the ride."

"You understand me well," he answered.

We drove back to my neighborhood, and he parked by the synagogue. "You can learn a lot by watching me drive," Attila said. "But what you really need is a rest. I'll decide when it's time to give your 'toy' back to you. It won't be too long—it never feels good to have a toy taken away. Then in May I'd like you to try motorcycle lessons. Let's talk a little later." As he peeled away, he honked good-bye.

LEFT HANKERING for more instruction, I decided to do the unthinkable—call up another school and try out another teacher, on the side. I had to find out if Attila was really the thaumaturgist he appeared to be. And I wanted to see what it would be like with someone else.

In midwinter a Filipino named Rick from a school across

town picked me up in a blue Toyota. Rick (who still lived with his mother) had an answer to my question about why Filipinos dominated Manhattan's driving-school business. "We're very patient," he explained. Rick lacked Attila's toughness, empathy, and vigilance; he was far less concerned with safety, much less sensitive to the menace of the street. Hardly a forceful presence, he was also less of a diversion to me than Attila. I wasn't straining to please him.

"Modesty aside," Rick said, "I have a very high road-test pass rate—ninety percent." Not bad, but not hovering near perfection like Attila's. Rick was booked only twenty-five hours a week, as opposed to Attila's seventy. Rick, alas, had no poetic images to aid in his instruction.

I strayed from Attila only one more time, in late March, when I was in California for *Vanity Fair's* Oscars party. The L.A. school, which I found through a phobic Hollywood friend (she, paradoxically, was also a car magazine junkie), sent me Len, a former accountant from Iran. "It's an easy job," Len said indolently, looking at me instead of the road. "I work six-hour days." Bored, he fiddled with the radio and came alive only when I asked him to reacquaint me with the protocol of the four-way stop. "It's first come, first served," he said succinctly, "or whoever is on your right has the right of way." The far-flung, sun-dappled mountains and fizzy sea along the Pacific Coast Highway and the Santa Monica Freeway were a tonic for the eyes, a bracing contrast to the closed, shadowy, vertical spaces of New York. Though Len clearly was not stimulated by his work, he did say that he "never tired of the southern California scenery."

Reform School for Drivers

After L.A., I registered for Attila's six-hour class, presented by him every two weeks at the driving school offices. Criminally bad motorists could be awarded a four-point reduction from their licenses at the end of the class, but could enroll only every eighteen months. So it became a reform-school limbo from which serious offenders (like the grumbling twelve-pointer who checked in early behind me) would never exit. Law abiders could shave 10 percent off their car insurance for attending. As I was buying my first car—not the gadget-packed SUV I had looked at with my daughter but Attila's careworn Acura Integra, which the school was about to replace with a Toyota Camry—that was my excuse for mingling with vehicular delinquents.

Attila, who had earned his certification to conduct the points-reduction course through a Queens College program, had spoken to me often about his class, which he enjoyed teaching. Hostile and obstreperous at first, expecting tedium if not actual punishment, his students invariably ended up entertained and impressed. They lingered after the clock ticked past the sixth hour, hovering around Attila, asking him questions and talking about themselves.

"Two weeks ago, a Russian man paid fifty dollars again to sit in on the class for fun," Attila said as he led me to Marilyn, the bubbly Filipino receptionist. ("Hello, Amy! I love your suit. You're buying a car? I'm so happy for you!") A vivid statuette of the Madonna gazed down serenely at Marilyn from a shelf positioned just above her permanent-waved head. Marilyn took my credit card and continued welcoming me while Attila (tonight covering his Superman forelock with a baseball cap) excused himself to organize his instructional booklets and videotapes. Marilyn's devotional effigy reminded me of a news item I had read earlier that week in the *New York Post* about motorists in Calugareni, Romania, who in lieu of insurance or lessons were asking priests to bless their cars for road safety.

I took a seat in the back row of the classroom and waited for the rest of the students to congregate. Imitation wood paneling covered the walls, and a lone plastic philodendron, its leaves discolored by dust, stood in a ceramic pot in the corner. I watched Attila survey the room expectantly from behind his battered metal teacher's desk, and thought of comedian Bob Newhart's classic 1960 *Button Down Concert,* re-recorded with modifications by Nick at Nite in 1995, which includes a routine entitled "The Driving Instructor." The premise of the sketch is that Newhart had scripted "The Driving Instructor" as a pilot for a new TV series. "There is a group of men," it begins, "who every day when they go to work never know if they'll return because they face death in a hundred different ways. I'm talking about America's driving instructors." *(Laughter.)* The driving student (female, of course), ditzy Mrs. Webb, starts off her first lesson by throwing her car into reverse in her driveway at such velocity that her hapless instructor, Mr. Adams, flies out of his seat, never to be seen or heard from again. The second instructor she hires panics too—not just because her wacky driving lands him in the police station, but also because complacent Mrs. Webb asks to engage him for another lesson.

I don't find this set piece particularly funny, I suppose because I identify too much with poor Mrs. Webb. I see fewer faults with her driving than with her teacher, who should never have raised his voice or lost his cool. To me, the very best driving instructors are an elite corps, an intrepid brotherhood, who not only "every day face death" but also save lives daily, as a matter of course, in a "hundred different ways."

"Americans," Attila was saying to his class, now numbering eight pupils, "would rather be in their cars than anywhere else. They spend eleven percent more time in their cars than they did just eight years ago. In this country cars are more than transportation—they are identities. What kind of car do each of you drive?"

I broke the ice by raising my hand first. "A '92 Acura Integra," I said.

"Well," Attila continued, "Americans love their cars better than their pets and maybe even their children. The average household has one-point-nine cars—and how many children?"

"One-point-five, I think," I said.

I was gathering momentum.

"How can you tell if you're in a truck's blind spot?" he asked, several minutes later.

"If you can't see the truck driver's face in his left mirror."

"Good, Amy."

"If your car stalls on the railroad tracks while a train is coming, what should you do?"

Attila had just finished reading about this very scenario from the emergencies section of his teacher's handbook.

"Run from your car in the direction that the train is coming from."

"That's right. If you run in the same direction the train is heading, you may be hit with debris when the train strikes your *wee-hicle*."

"Strikes your what?" asked a sullen, muscle-bound man with a do-rag on his head.

"Your *wee-hicle*," Attila repeated.

"If your car starts sinking in a body of water, how should you escape?"

"Through a window," I said.

"True—if you open a door, water will rush in, and the car could turn over on top of you. But if the car has already sunk, go into the backseat, where there may be an air pocket. "

Among my classmates were two stumpy ethnic men who during the full six hours removed neither their stocking caps nor their parkas.

"How many of you guys think you're pretty good drivers?" Attila interrogated the class after our break. I had fetched him a coffee (but not an apple) from the tiny patisserie where months before he had told me about his legal status in Turkey.

This time everyone in the room raised a hand except me.

"You with the twelve points, and you with the eight points too?"

They each nodded and told Attila in turn from their mismatched school desks that none of the accidents that had landed them in the six-hour class had been their fault. Attila broke down one of the eight-pointer's incidents—a rear-end collision—and explained how it could have been prevented by preserving a safe cushion around his vehicle.

"Eighty-three percent of all drivers think they're better drivers than everyone else on the road. What does that tell you?"

"That there's a lot of good drivers out there?" suggested a Hispanic man with a neckload of tattoos and a history of speeding tickets.

"How many of you think you drive better than your girlfriend or your wife?"

The seven young men fidgeted in their chairs.

"Well, forget the girlfriend or wife. How about your mother, your sister, or your aunt? You drive better than she does?"

There was a tide of bobbing heads, a little forest of upraised arms. I was the only female in the room and—for the second time that evening—the only one without a hand in the air.

"Men account for sixty-eight percent of all car accident deaths," Attila said. He was roughing up these fellows a little. And if I knew my instructor, he would then—when he pushed them to their limit—suddenly go gentle on them.

But before that moment arrived, Attila asked the question, "So, when you're driving, how do you get most of your information?" (Correct answer: from your eyes. We had just watched a video on the school's creaky VCR entitled *Using Your Vision Effectively.*) The homunculus with the twelve points said, "Uh, from television?" The sad man from Ghana, whose dream it was to become a cabbie, said, "Uh, the radio?"

Then Attila played some AAA safety-propaganda videos, and the white male talking head telling us about tailgating and tire pressure was a guy I knew a lifetime ago in Tennessee, a football hero, long forgotten, from my sister's high school class.

At that point, I came down with a terrible falling-out-of-the-chair case of the giggles and could no longer answer questions.

THAT NIGHt I ordered Attila a copy of *The Button-Down Mind of Bob Newhart* from Amazon.com, and I brought it to him gift-wrapped eight days later when we drove to the DMV in Queens to finish up paperwork on the Acura. There was a long wait just to get a parking space; we didn't bother to stick around to see if the lines inside were any shorter.

"You see what a big business driving is," Attila said, pointing his car back toward Manhattan. "And almost none of these drivers are properly trained. Oil conglomerates, insurance companies, car manufacturers, law firms, the medical establishment—they've got no use for better-trained drivers either. Car accidents generate billions of dollars annually. Why is high school driver's ed so bad, when car accidents are the leading cause of death for teenagers? Every month the equivalent of one jetload of teenagers dies in car wrecks. Driver's ed teachers take four students at a time for fifteen minutes a week. The kids sit in the back and do homework. Then those kids come to me."

If Attila ever got around to listening to the Newhart CD he probably would find it even less amusing than I did. The oddest thing about this auditory artifact is that the blurb on its cover reads, "The Best New Comedian Since Attila (the Hun)."

The Big Picture

Somehow in the course of our lessons I'd received from Attila an education in patience and peace of mind. He was right—whatever it was that he did inside the car had insinuated itself into the rest of my life. I had learned along the way, for instance, not to be cowed by anger and aggression—not mine nor anyone else's, neither on nor off the road. I had also learned how to become humble and trusting enough to ask for help.

Coming home via Queens one day—we were back on the stick shift for a refresher lesson—I was scared to make a left turn that Attila requested from me, because I mistook the road ahead for a one-way street.

"Trust me, Amy. Go."

I made the turn successfully.

"That was the very first time I ever trusted someone just because he asked me to," I said. "That phrase—like 'to be honest' or 'no problem'—usually means its opposite."

That night I asked him over the phone, "Where does all the fear that you take out of people go?" We had gotten in the habit of calling each other up every few days, and our conversations often became lengthy.

"I've wondered that myself."

"You don't absorb it."

"No, I don't absorb it. But can you imagine, if I put all of the fear that I've taken out of my students inside of a sack, what a huge, long bag I'd be dragging behind me."

As a result of my lessons, even my relationship with my daughter improved. I was more patient with her, and understood much better how to teach and soothe her. She trusted me more because I was now trusting myself. Learning to drive made me realize I could do anything as long as I applied myself, and gave in to time, rather than fight it, force it, as I had in the past.

I developed more tolerance, patience, and consideration. Strangely, many physical and psychological problems—back pains, for example—healed. When Attila extracted the driving phobia, he had pulled up other ailments too—the entire root system of the nasty weed. As Attila and I continued to speak and meet, I kept on losing and finding myself, through driving.

I conferred with my friend Robert, who at age forty-two had also recently vanquished his fears and learned to drive. I wanted to find out if his psyche had shifted too as a consequence of putting himself in the driver's seat. How much, I wondered, of my new state was the handiwork of Attila and how much was a natural consequence of taming a phobia? At Swifty's on Lexington Avenue, where we ate crab salad and tomato aspic, I said to Robert, "I used to think we were both neurotic, with our driving fears, but I've come to believe we were right to be afraid. It's a rational fear. What other everyday activity forces us to confront the idea of death so directly?"

"But to drive you have be in the highest state of denial," Robert countered. "You are at the wheel of a bomb, yet at the same time you are absent from reality, listening to music, lost in thought."

"I suppose the only sane approach to driving is to be neither completely afraid, like so many women and gay men that we know are, nor completely in denial, like so many straight men are."

"Have you noticed that cars—planes and boats too—are always designed with eyes, a mouth, a nose, and an asshole that eliminates waste products?" (Robert was an interior designer.)

"Yes, I have. Why do you think that is?"

"Whatever we create, we make in our own image—like God. Roland Barthes said, 'Cars are our cathedrals.' Why don't you drive up to Connecticut and visit me?" Robert had built a country house there, which I had featured recently in *Vanity Fair.*

"I still can't make a drive like that without my instructor."

"That's weird."

"Yeah, it is. I especially couldn't do it with my daughter in the car. But I will someday. I need practice. I just bought my instructor's Acura, because I feel comfortable in it—even though it's an old jalopy, with more miles on it than the starship *Enterprise.*"

"For the first year I could only drive the car I learned in, the VW Beetle," Robert said, signaling for the check. "What's great about finally being able to take one's life in one's own hands, to trust oneself to oneself, is—I've become more responsible about everything. I've become more prudent in some ways, and in other ways more adventuresome. Every time I drive it's a thrill all over again to know I'm doing something I thought I'd never, ever do, something that once filled me with terror. It's fun to drive."

"I know just what you mean. That's exactly what I'm trying to write about."

So learning to drive had been therapeutic for Robert too—he had been tutored by his boyfriend, Jeffrey. But I know he had missed out on the associated insights that came along with Attila's teaching. I would have to share with Robert some of Attila's driving aphorisms, all applicable to life—such as:

1. Don't look back to where you've just been. Keep your eye on where you want to go.
2. Create your scenario in advance, then act. Once you're in the scenario it's already happening, you don't have control, and it's too late.
3. Don't get caught up in the minor details and lose sight of the big picture.

Nor had Robert, for better or for worse, metamorphosed midcareer into a car-besotted gearhead. As my daughter told me—after I pointed out to her a seventies Caprice and a sixties Rolls parked along the street as we walked one afternoon to her pediatrician's—"You always take everything too far, and don't know when to stop!"

The Cadillac and the Car Show

I was happy to find in my mail one morning an invitation to the 2002 Gala Preview of the New York International Auto Show, a benefit for the East Side House Settlement. At last my two disparate worlds were overlapping—and at a party, no less. I was looking forward to attending (not alone if I could help it). But then I was stood up more times than I could count. My original date, Larry, contracted pneumonia from aspirating bat guano at his country house. So I next invited Attila, who was planning to attend the show during its regular hours, which would have required him to wait in line and proscribed him from sitting inside the cars. He declined my offer, I suppose because he did not want to distort further the already irregular boundaries of our student-teacher relationship.

At a big lunchtime meeting on the day of the party, I hit up three of the five queer men in the room. All their walker time had already been booked for that evening.

I resigned myself to going solo, but when I got home there was an interesting message awaiting me. "Amy, it's Ted. If you're

71

still planning on going to the car show, would you like me to send a Cadillac and driver to take you there?"

Ted and I had been hanging out together recently, during Oscars weekend. He was in L.A. promoting Van Cleef & Arpels, Paco Rabanne, and Helena Rubinstein—whose corporate mission it was to ply stars with merchandise. He was now asking Cadillac, whom he was also representing, to donate cars for VIP transportation to a New York City Opera fund-raiser I was cohosting. One last try, I figured, couldn't hurt. "Thank you, Ted, I'd love a Cadillac to take me there. It's such miserable weather. And I would like it even better if you would come with me."

"I'm sorry, honey, I can't. I have to go to an Hermès menswear event. But Tom and Shaun from the office will be waiting for you at the Javits Center. They'll take you around the show, and introduce you to the Cadillac people."

If I couldn't have a date with a person, I could at least have a date with a 2003-model car.

I tried calling Larry to see how he was feeling. There was no answer. Had he gone to the hospital, or only back to the country? I spoke to my agent, touched up my makeup, changed my dress, and picked up the phone when it rang, hoping it would be Larry.

"Hi, this is Ally, your driver. I'm running about fifteen minutes late. I'll be in a white Cadillac CTS at seven, right in front of your building."

So the driver was a woman. And the car—that's the one Attila suggested I test-drive, if I ever mastered manual transmission.

Thirty minutes later I was downstairs, outside by the fire hydrant.

A quick decision had to be made. Did I hop into the back, or into the front, of the Caddy?

"I thought you'd like the front," Ally said, "so you can see how it rides, and watch me drive."

I hesitated. "I won't be good company. I'll be on the phone most of the time."

"That's OK!"

Ally was blonde, with a beautiful hooked nose that looked as if someone had inserted a Tiffany diamond beneath the skin at its bridge.

"Are you an actress?" I asked, sinking into the front right seat.

"Yes, how did you know?"

"Just a hunch." She was too short to be a model, and too white and female to be a professional driver. "What do you do —TV, movies, commercials, theater?"

"I'm a stunt driver."

"That's exciting. I feel safe with you."

"I'm also Edie Falco's body double and stunt double on *The Sopranos*. You see her legs and arms, that's me. What do you do?"

"I write for *Vanity Fair.*"

"Annie Leibovitz just shot us for your magazine yesterday. I stood in for Edie Falco while Annie was setting up the picture."

Ally, who lived in Jersey City, was a girl of many parts. She had a nasal New York twang. The voice, the nose—it all started to come together.

"I'm also a singer."

"Do you sound like Barbra Streisand?"

"How'd you know? What sign are you? I do Streisand. I played her in a show in Miami called *Flamingo Follies.*"

Ally was one of four sisters, all jocks and good drivers. "My father wanted boys, so he made sure we excelled in every sport." They included, she informed me, lacrosse, basketball, softball, hockey, track. "I should have been a lesbian," she said.

We arrived at the Javits Center.

Inside the car show, I immediately found Tom and Shaun, handsome and handsomer, taller and smaller. They introduced me to Mike, who, happy that I had enjoyed my ride in the Cadillac CTS, offered to let me borrow one for a week. He didn't care that I hadn't mastered a stick shift yet. "If you're interested in purchasing one," Mike informed me, "our 'friends and family' discount is three percent." What kind of discount, I wondered, would an Oscar winner get?

This was the first charity event I'd ever attended where straight men outnumbered homosexuals, and where the guys were actually drinking beer from bottles.

The 2003 car models were mostly retro resurrections of designs from about 1930 to 1965. I fell madly in love with one car, called an Esperanza, which was custom-made in Atlanta and looked vaguely like a sixties Jaguar. I opened the door on the driver's side and positioned myself to enter.

"Hey, you can't do that," said an Esperanza rep. "This one's already been sold. Ninety thousand."

"You should lock the door, then," I told him, "and you should also remove the plastic from the seat." Shaun and I had already been cruelly whispering to each other that it looked as if the chair had been prepared for an incontinent driver. But I said something a little kinder to the man who had so rudely blocked my entrance to the vehicle.

"Your car's beautiful but it looks like one of those living rooms in which the sofas, armchairs, and lamp shades are permanently encased in plastic."

"Hey, you're right," the Esperanza rep said, wrinkling his nose but still not removing the offensive prophylactic.

"COME ON, let's go," said an impatient husband, tugging his wife's hand.

"There's one thing men like better than they like women," I said to the wife, whom I knew.

"Yeah, cars." She sighed. "I saw you with that Esperanza. Did you ever get inside?"

"No."

"That's too bad. They really should have let you. Cars are like shoes. You have to try them on to see how they fit."

"It's true. Car design has a lot in common with shoe design. Stylizing transportation."

"I'd say that's true of the foreign models, but not the American ones," the wife said, braking her bolting husband with her eyes.

"American cars are also like shoes—like sneakers," I said. And then, thinking of stalwart Ally waiting uncomplainingly with her Caddy for me outside in the rain, I felt disloyal. "But that new Cadillac CTS is pretty nice."

"What are you doing, guarding your silent auction item?" the husband said impatiently.

"Is that what it looks like I'm doing?" I said evasively.

"Yes. I know the symptoms. Which item are you after?"

"You're not bidding on anything? OK, the Verdura watch."

A voice over the loudspeaker ominously announced that the silent auction would close in ten minutes. Tall handsome Tom, who had become my de facto date, said, "I used to play hockey in high school. I'll guard your watch and jump in if anyone else dares to swoop down on it."

Tom performed his job admirably. I'd already stayed too long at the party. As Hedda Hopper used to say, "Go before the glow fades." But I wanted the watch, retail value $3,500, at a rock-bottom price, and so far nobody had outbid me. I got it for $750. My money would go straight to where it was needed, in the South Bronx, and there was no tax.

I popped the watch around my wrist, and saw on both its face and that of my old Cartier that it was now an hour past time to go home. Tom cell phoned Ally, who showed up to fetch me and nearly swooned over Tom.

"Tom, why don't you let Ally take you home?"

"No, thank you. You go with Ally. I need to stay longer."

Ally was disappointed, but I restored her self-esteem. "Tom's beautiful, Ally, but are you really sure he likes women?"

"I never can tell," she said regretfully.

"May I drive the car home?"

Ally looked at me doubtfully. "Your heels are high, it's raining outside. Let me do it."

"You're right. I also had a glass of wine." Attila wouldn't approve. "But may I take over when we get off the West Side Highway?"

Ally, who had been talking soulfully about dating, mother-hood, and marriage, pulled over by the Museum of Natural History. But she pulled out again when she saw a police car stopping another motorist.

"We don't want any trouble. Let's cross the park."

Finally she let me drive, two blocks from my house. A half block into the ride, I stalled the Cadillac in first gear at a red light. "I'm sorry. I'm making poor publicity for the CTS. It de-serves better." A long crocodile of angry, honking cabbies formed behind us. The light turned green, then red again. Once more, I stalled.

"Let's switch places," Ally said. More honking ensued as we traded seats.

"I can't believe they offered to lend me this car for a week and I can't even drive it."

"Hey, you did all right, Amy. I'm proud of you!"

I gave a good-night kiss to Ally, stunt driver and Streisand impersonator, and promised to look for her legs and arms on *The Sopranos*.

Attila's Apostles

Larry, my wise book editor friend (now fully recovered from his bat guano inhalation), sounded like a detective who had just stumbled upon an important lead when he phoned to say that a neighbor, Ophelia, had started driving lessons. "Ophelia says her instructor is a miracle worker. He has eliminated her fears, her whole outlook on life is changing. It must be the same guy! The only catch is that she calls this teacher Andrew."

Bingo. Out of all the driving schools and all the driving instructors in the world, Larry's friend Ophelia ended up with mine, Attila. This was very intriguing—the first validation that my conception of his powers might be more than the left half of a frontseat folie à deux. Larry read me the notes he had dutifully scribbled during his conversation with Ophelia. Her husband was scheduled for bypass surgery, after which he would be unable to drive for several months. In the meantime, how would they get to their weekend house on Long Island? Ophelia had a license, but for nearly thirty years she had been too fearful to put it to proper use.

Larry suggested introducing Ophelia and me over lunch. He also thought that I might observe from the backseat as Attila taught Ophelia, to see the process from a third-person perspective. Like a good gumshoe, Larry cautioned, "It's probably better that Attila doesn't know that the three of us are about to meet."

I informed Attila that serendipitously another friend of Larry's, Ophelia, was also his driving student. (I'd spoken to him often of Larry, the only friend of mine he ever requested to meet.) Attila was delighted to find that the dots connected, for Ophelia was his current favorite. "I told you about Ophelia. Remember?" he said.

Yes, of course I did, now—the older woman with the stick shift lessons. She was well traveled, intelligent, and—this rated high with Attila—had been to Turkey. "Larry's going to introduce us. We've made a lunch date." Withholding this information did not feel right to me after all. "Would that be OK?"

"Amy, you should meet Ophelia. And you should also come along one day to observe while I teach her."

"That's exactly what Larry said."

But when Attila asked Ophelia if I could watch her final lesson, she said no.

A WEEK later, Ophelia, Larry, and I convened at Michael's on West Fifty-fifth Street. Oddly, neither Attila nor Larry had mentioned Ophelia's beauty—she was a strawberry blonde with limpid green-blue eyes, a delicate nose, high cheekbones, a chiseled jawline, and a slightly distracted air. She was dressed more informally than I, in a grass green cashmere turtleneck, and, partial to the color on that day, she wore two emerald rings, one on each hand. She and Larry talked through shrimp salad and fried zucchini flowers about their world, their friends, their past. Not until dessert did Larry ask, quietly but pointedly, "How's the driving going?"

Ophelia, who had already glimpsed at her watch and murmured preparatory exit lines, suddenly became still and dreamy.

When she collected her thoughts she spoke ardently. "Andrew is an excellent teacher, and that is because you know with him nothing can go wrong. Nothing! Everything he says is the gospel. You believe in him. He's very good at keeping you calm."

That was a pretty good testimonial for the opening five seconds.

"He's a psychologist," she continued. "He knows exactly what your hang-ups are before you can name them. My dread of driving—I couldn't even begin to describe it or explain it. I didn't want him to know how extreme it was. It was too embarrassing. I have felt like a freak for years, and I was—the only person in the world who couldn't drive."

"Believe me, I understand." I knew that the humiliation surrounding Ophelia's driving phobia was as much of a problem as the fear.

"I can barely even say it," Ophelia elaborated, "but bridges horrified me. Do you know what I mean?"

"You have no idea how much I know what you mean."

"Well, the other day I went over a suspension bridge. By myself." She smiled—not for me but for herself. "One vital thing I've learned from Andrew is to drive with the gears rather than the brakes. It's the hallmark of a good driver."

"Did you start out on automatic and switch to stick?"

"No. It was stick from the start. That's what we've always owned."

"How strange, to think we've been driving the same car—the '88 Toyota Celica."

We looked at each other. It felt as intimate as discovering that we'd been sleeping with the same man on the same side of the same bed.

"Can you picture him ever establishing his own driving school?" I asked. Attila and I had begun to talk about his opening one, in partnership with me.

"Andrew is a maverick," Ophelia answered. "He's more likely to start all over again with something else, somewhere else. He's lived in Italy, Turkey, Germany. He's intelligent, fluent in three languages. His father told him, 'A man with one language is one man. A man with two languages is two men.' Andrew is three men. I think his German must be excellent. It's not as if he ever intended to have this job. So many times I wanted to ask him, 'Why are you a driving instructor? *Why?*' But I was afraid of offending him. At the same time, I can see that this is a calling."

"That is exactly what I told him," I said.

"Andrew's mother died in 1985," Ophelia said. "He was just a baby. Sometimes I really wanted to snuggle him. His father, the NATO general, never remarried. He learned American English from his father, who made Andrew and his younger brothers study grammar and vocabulary while other boys played outside. Andrew hated him for that, but now he is very thankful. He read Jules Verne, H. G. Wells, and Mark Twain as a child. Without studying he was a great student. Did you know he was able to attend school free because of his high test scores? He plays the saxophone and the guitar and has written his own music—have you heard his demo tape?"

"You learned a lot about him," I said with a pang. Should it bother me that he had confided these stories to another student—maybe to many others?

Larry, who had been intently following our conversation—

and perhaps my train of thought—noted, "A closed car is a good place to talk."

"And we often went on long trips, you know what I mean, Amy—to Bear Mountain . . ."

I certainly did.

"Did you understand what he meant by 'one thousand one, one thousand two'?" she asked.

"Not at first, it was like a math-class word problem. But I finally got it."

"I never did."

Ophelia said her husband had been "supportive," and was "proud" of her new proficiency. But one evening in the country when Ophelia boldly proposed to him, "Let me drive you to dinner," he disparaged her every maneuver. Ophelia said to us what she would not repeat to her husband: "Andrew would never talk to me that way."

"My whole perspective has changed as a result of my lessons with Andrew. I have a lot more self-esteem—I hate that word! I don't know if you understand . . ."

"You'd better believe I do!" I said for at least the third time.

"*I* decided to take this freaking course. I did it all by myself!" she said, tapping her slender index finger to her heart. "My husband had surgery, but it wasn't really about that. And it turned out he could drive after the bypass anyway. I wanted to please Andrew. I wanted to be a 'good date.' I wanted to be the teacher's pet."

"I think you were. I think we both were."

"Really?" she said brightening. "Isn't his accent adorable? 'You are t'inking about something else and not concentrating on the task of driving.' " She giggled. And then, curious and a little reproachful, she challenged me, "Why do you call him Attila? He is Andrew to everyone else."

I didn't answer. How could I tell her, "Because he asked me to, after the second lesson," without making her feel diminished?

She resumed her panegyric. "Oh, I'd pretend to be relaxed, I'd lean back insouciantly. But I couldn't fool him. He'd say, 'Ophelia, you're tense—your arms are so stiff you won't have control.' " As she talked, Ophelia drifted off somewhere far away, revisiting those pleasurable moments of self-discovery and self-reclamation, alone with the God of Driving.

"This man could become so famous," Larry interjected.

When her focus fluttered back to me, Ophelia said, "His last words to me were, 'Call me anytime—and drive, drive, practice as often as possible.' " Ophelia gave her phone number to me and ran off to her three o'clock appointment. I had one too, but I lingered on the sidewalk with Larry. "Thank you for setting up the lunch. It was riveting," I said. "A confirmation of everything I had been feeling these last few months. Now I know for sure that I wasn't deluded about Attila. I hope we weren't boring you."

"Not at all. I was mesmerized," Larry said. "You both talk about him the same way. This is a man who probably can teach anyone anything."

"It felt a little like two girlfriends of the same guy discovering that they had been taken to all the same places, and told all the same tales. What did it sound like to you?"

"Like Paul and Matthew discussing Jesus."

THAT NIGHT I phoned Attila. At 9:45 P.M., he was just unlocking his apartment door, returning from a workday that had begun at 6:30 A.M. He had not yet walked his dog, Ajan, nor had he eaten dinner. He had, as usual, also skipped lunch.

"What did she say?" he asked. One of his more human traits was his fascination with other people's opinions of him.

"Ophelia called you a psychologist," I told him. "You've heard that before."

"Did she mean by that that I am a healer?" he asked.

"Yes. You know that already."

We were both silent—this happened often during our conversations.

"It's kind of weird," he said (he pronounced the word *veerd*). "Why can't I just teach? Instead, I am detecting the virus [pronounced *wirus*] in people's brains. Then, I work very hard and long on the virus until it is out of the system."

When they did not derive from Turkish proverbs and parables, Attila's metaphors usually arose from the technical vocabularies of automobiles and computers. "Whatever I do, I always want to be the best," he said. "I am a perfectionist. But with teaching, it's gone beyond that. It has become brainwashing. I am manipulating people out of their fears; then what I have given to them becomes a permanent part of their hard drive."

"Ophelia has been telling her husband, 'Andrew told me this' and 'according to Andrew that'—your statements seem to have been seared into her brain."

"Seared?"

"Burnt."

He was intrigued and perplexed. "Ophelia is an older woman, in her sixties," he said haltingly. "She's intelligent, mature, and has led a full and interesting life."

"Yes, she is a fully formed woman," I agreed.

"And so it doesn't make any sense, how I am able to reach inside someone like that and change her."

We were both quiet again for a second or two.

"How did you know that it was time to terminate Ophelia?"

"It's not a guesswork," he said. "I am able to pinpoint the right moment to cut the cord." He transferred his thoughts to a newer student, who came through my referral network. "You know, Meredith really enjoys driving now." I was surprised that he was offering me a peek into the mechanics of his teaching; I would never have dared to pry. "I eliminated her fear in one lesson. I worry that I am too powerful at what I do," he said. "I can catch a student's eye movements, down to the dilations of their pupils, with such precision now that I know not only what they were looking at, but also what they were *thinking* about while they were looking."

"How do you mean?" I asked.

"At an intersection where Meredith had the right of way I saw that she was focusing on pedestrians. She was worried that they would cross the street at the instant her car was going through. So I said to her, 'These pedestrians are not going to walk. You are creating a situation that is not going to happen. You are not going to hurt anybody.' That's when she said, 'How did you know what I was thinking?'

"I see things before they happen—four or six steps ahead, not only with my students but with the other drivers on the road. It's just like with the numbers." From time to time Attila played the lottery game Win 4, straight, and had in fact won once. Several times a month—sometimes even twice a week—he got three out of the four numbers correct, or he got all four numbers, but with the sequence scrambled. Or else he chose all the numbers exactly right, but found out it was the winning number from the day before. The strange thing was it started happening to me too, beginning with the very first game that I played. I quit while I was ahead.

"I went to see Frank this afternoon," he continued. Frank

was his ex-student, the Turkish cosmetician with whose family we had dined months before. If he had a spare moment between lessons Attila liked to stop by Frank's little shop, located a few blocks from my apartment, to drink a quick cup of coffee and smoke a cigarette, or if he had a cancellation, to play backgammon. I'd gotten in the habit of dropping off stacks of magazines at the store every month, to keep Frank up to date. (Frank's real name was Muhammad but he did not think that would trip easily off his Upper East Side clients' tongues.) More than a few times when I passed by, Attila was there, in the doorway or out on the sidewalk with his Dunhill, as if he'd been expecting me.

"About what time were you at Frank's?" I asked.

"At two-twelve." Attila's information about time was accurate to the minute, like a train schedule. "Frank said to me, 'Atti, do you know how scared we are of you?' He had just sent a Turkish friend of his, a woman, to me."

"Why scared?" I asked.

"Frank said, 'Because everything you've ever told us is true; you are always right.' The school is sending me troubled students, full of fear, frightened by accidents. Many of these people already know how to drive, they just have become afraid to do it. I feel like I become their psychiatrist. Do you know how many students have said to me, 'I shouldn't pass the road test'?"

"Why do they say that?" I already knew why but I wanted to hear how he formulated his reply.

"Well, the students say, 'If I pass the road test, then I'm not going to have any more lessons with you.' I'm a driving instructor! They sign up for their twenty, thirty, thirty-five hours, to learn to drive, and then something else takes over. At that point they're looking for something else—so out they go.

"There always comes a day when you have to take the bottle away from the baby. Then, maybe the baby will start sucking his fingers because he misses the bottle. Students say, 'Can't you clone yourself?' "

"Why do they say that?"

"They want to clone Andrew so he can be with them at all times."

Attila sometimes talked about himself in the third person, just as he occasionally referred to parts of the car by the personal pronoun. ("You got off the clutch too quickly, Amy. You must make a scissors effect between him and the gas pedal"— then he'd perform some snappy staccato footwork on his side of the car to demonstrate his point.)

I think Attila must have known that this yearning for an Andrew clone was the same as an infant's wish for the symbiotic omnipresence of a good mother—a watchful, protective, caring, constant, reliable guardian.

"Part of me wants to get away from this, and part of me is in so deep there is no way out. There are pieces of me scattered everywhere, among all these people I've taught. The more I try to pull away, the more I'm drawn back into it. I'm fighting against some power that won't let me go."

Attila excused himself to answer his apartment's buzzer. It was a Colombian deliveryman with his dinner. In spite of the fact that Attila hadn't eaten all day, he let the meal grow cold as he continued to talk. "With Meredith," Attila said, returning to his analysis of his current most challenging student, "I want to find the breaking point. You have seen how I do that. Recently, I put Meredith in a situation that caught her so much by surprise she froze. I took her to a regular street in the Bronx, near the Havemeyer road test site. Right nearby this street is an expressway entrance. Meredith's driving along, doing OK, and at the

88

last second, I tell her, 'Go left.' 'Shit!' she cries. 'This is an *expressway!*' She couldn't move. The simple word 'expressway' can break someone down to pieces.

"You see, everybody has fears in his pockets. The question is, in which pocket is he hiding them? By looking for the breaking points, I find out what and where the fears are. Then, one step at a time, I clear them. Each individual has a different level of fear and a different level of hiding.

"Don't take any of this lightly," he said. "Driving is life. Everything behind the wheel can be applied to life. There is nothing more real than driving.

"Here's something else I did with Meredith: I noticed that she loves to have the windows up. Why do you think that is?"

"She doesn't want to know what's out there?" I guessed.

"True, she doesn't want to know what's out there. But what she really doesn't want is to hear *noise*. She was trying to trick me into thinking that raising the windows was about the air-conditioning. I knew better. One day I parked the car, left her in it, and ran up to the school for a moment to pick up something. Before getting out of the car, I deliberately lowered the windows. A few minutes later, when I returned, all the windows were up again. Without speaking a word, I lowered them again. She couldn't say nothing."

"She couldn't say anything."

"She couldn't say anything. We started driving up Third Avenue. The trucks were passing us and she was getting tense. After twenty blocks I said to her, 'I know you noticed that the windows are down.' She was silent. I continued, 'I want you to *hear* things. Ninety-five percent of the information you receive when you're driving is coming through your eyes. Where is that remaining five percent coming from? Do you want to ignore that?' "

The second-brake Socrates again.

"Meredith said to me, 'You are so slick. What are you going to do now, put on music?' "

" 'As a matter of fact, yes,' I said, and I did. You see, I want to make sure that she will be able to drive without me, under any conditions."

He paused again, long enough for me to infer that he was about to divulge something significant.

"On that first day when I put a new student in the driver's seat, I look at them straight in the eye and I see the baby inside. I see only the baby, not the adult." He pronounced the word *ba-BEE*, tenderly; it was not a taunt. "That is where my work starts. If that baby makes a mistake, I will cover for him; all mistakes are forgiven. Whatever I give that baby, that is what he will become.

"Everyone still has the baby inside him. Once you touch the baby side of a person, he will trust you, and he is yours. If you do something wrong to the baby, then he will no longer have any trust." He was quiet again.

I inserted, "And everyone, as a baby, had something go wrong at some time that caused him to lose trust, or become anxious, angry, and fearful."

"That's right. So you have to go back to the beginning, before his heart was scratched, and start all over from there. It is the end of teaching, the end of learning if you do not have the baby's trust. You have to gain and keep that trust."

How was it, I wondered, that he could speak more like an objects-relations psychologist than a driving instructor? I now had a better sense of how he got to me.

"Were you able to see this, to do this, when you first started teaching three and a half years ago?" I asked. "Or did this ability evolve gradually as you taught?"

"I didn't notice this at the beginning," he answered. "But I asked myself, how am I able to make people so comfortable that they trust me so completely with their lives? You see, a student has to know he is secure at all times, when he is at his most vulnerable—when his life is in danger. He is as exposed to harm as a helpless infant. It was from there that I figured it out."

"Are you able to see the baby in yourself, or only in other people?"

"That is a deep question."

"That's why I asked it." I tried another one: "On that first day, when you saw the baby in me, what was she like?"

He wouldn't answer. "It is amazing what I can feel," he replied instead. "I've been given a gift. Driving is just the tool. God has been good to me.

"Today I have eleven hours of work behind me. I have not taken a day off in three weeks. Ten years ago I would have said, going out to nightclubs, buying drinks for everyone, that is life. Compared with those days, my life seems so simple. It looks like I have a routine—I wake up, I walk my dog, I get coffee, I work, I go home, I walk my dog, I cook dinner, I go to sleep. But it is not at all what it seems. Every day I am deeply, intensely, imiti . . ."

"Intimately."

". . . intimately involved with five to seven different people. The prophet Muhammad said, 'Whoever teaches me a new word, I will be their slave.'

"Anyway, today I caught a motorcycle student in the air and prevented her from breaking her legs. I told her, 'Put your right index finger down.' I knew if she didn't put the finger down she would lose control of the throttle and the motorcycle would slip from under her. I see things before they happen. I knew in advance she'd be OK because I knew I would catch the motor-cycle. But if I hadn't known that, she would have crushed both her legs.

"In 1987 in Germany, I met a woman, a Yugoslavian novelist. She had written a couple of books. One day we were at a café, and this woman said she wanted to write a book about my life. I said to her, 'I'm only twenty-eight. In thirty years maybe you can write my life story, not now.' Do you believe this? This woman wanted to write my future."

So I was the second writer to imagine him as the hero of a book.

"Why do you think you and I have ended up together fifteen years later, doing a book?"

"How many times did you hear me say while you were driv-ing to 'expect the unexpected'? This is what my father taught me. He is a very wise man. But I didn't really understand what he meant until I started applying it to driving. So my answer to you for now," he said just before we hung up, "is, life is full of surprises."

TWO DAYS later I spoke briefly to Attila again. He called me on his way home from work. Again, it was nearly ten o'clock. He had been up since six, and had eaten almost nothing all day.

"Superman subsists only on water now?"

"That's all I've had today. But I'm going into the deli now to buy bread."

"What kind?"

"Pita."

"So—you are on a prison diet of bread and water?" Attila seemed hell-bent on punishing himself, for what sins I did not know. Several times he had said to me, "You know Amy, I'm no angel."

He laughed, I suppose because the joke struck close to the mark. "The funny thing is I don't feel tired at all."

"Not physically, not mentally? Not in your eyes?" Several weeks before, on the first of the month, his eyes had been dried out and hazed over, and he nearly collapsed from pains brought on by dehydration. By depriving himself of fluids, he had been trying to save himself the time of searching for a men's room and a parking spot.

"No. But I know I'll feel my exhaustion one day soon, and it will hit me all at once. It's a boomerang I've already sent out, and it's heading back my way."

"When is the boomerang due to land?"

"I can't predict that," he said. "I can forecast what will happen with other people better than I can with myself. But if I don't do something before the boomerang comes back, I will break down."

The following Tuesday we had planned another stick shift lesson. On a whim of Attila's, we wound up having no lesson at all. Instead I drove the school's automatic car, the navy Camry, to the Cloisters, the turreted sanctuary of medieval art perched at the northern end of Manhattan on the promontory of Fort Tryon Park, overlooking the Hudson River and the palisades of New Jersey beyond. He had navigated us there once before, in late winter, at sunset. Attila had never entered the Cloisters; I had interviewed for a job there half a lifetime ago, after college, and had returned more recently to show my daughter the Unicorn Tapestries.

"Curious to go inside?"

"Yes." Attila had never passed through the portals of the Metropolitan Museum of Art or the Museum of Natural History. He had been to the movies only once in five years; during my daughter's winter break he had taken us to *Jimmy Neutron: Boy Genius*.

But just as we did the last time, Attila and I stayed inside the parked Camry and talked. He hoped for rain so that his next appointment, a motorcycle lesson, would cancel. He talked about the business woes of a relative back in Turkey, whom he was trying to help out. "I am not a man anymore," he said. "I am a machine. If I lose my hands and I still need to dig, I will use my teeth."

A call came in on his cell from one of my referrals, Maureen—a shrill summons back to reality.

He hung up, and I swung the mood halfway back to where we had left off. "Attila, one more thing Ophelia had said to me was, 'I wanted to ask Andrew, "Why are you working so hard? Instead of going home alone to your dog, shouldn't you be taking out a beautiful girl?" ' "

"I am out with a beautiful woman," he replied gallantly. "But not at night."

ONE DAY I reached him in his car while he was shepherding a motorcycle pupil (who was riding ahead of him) to his practice site, off Seventy-ninth Street near the East River. "Amy, today I drove by four former students of mine on two consecutive blocks. They yelled out to me as I passed, 'Hey, Andrew! How's it going?' " Attila is conspicuous because of the school signboard projecting crosswise from the car's roof.

"Can you imagine an entire city populated by your former students?"

"That would be scary," he answered. "I'd have to move away."

"And then you'd make students of all of the next town's citizens, and then of the one after that. And pretty soon . . . no more unsafe drivers, and no more accidents."

"That would be nice."

Attila as the Johnny Appleseed of safe driving—urban folk hero and road warrior, mowing down death, not life.

"One thing I do hope to accomplish," he said, "is to change the image of the driving instructor."

"You already have."

ATTILA had had a series of setbacks. "Every two steps I take forward, I take three back," he said. I told him the myth of Sisyphus, but Attila's torment was not a boulder that could not be rolled uphill, but crushing debts he should not have taken on and a legal situation in Turkey that resisted solution. He was so discouraged he was saying that the last twelve years of his life, those spent in America, had been a waste.

"I am in bad need of a break. If I don't get one, there is only one place I can go."

"You mean, taking it out on your students?" He had intimated this before.

"Yes. Right now I am using this ability of mine to make them responsible, safe drivers."

"You would make quite a villain if you abused those abilities." I was seeing him as a comic-book fiend, the Mad Driving Instructor, evil twin and invincible adversary of the Superhero of the Highway, the God of Driving's diabolic doppelgänger.

"I don't have a criminal mind."

"But what were you thinking you would do if you broke down—methodically turn your students into dangerous drivers, destroyers of American road safety?"

"No, there are enough bad instructors out there doing exactly that already."

"You mean you would play around with their minds and make them go crazy?"

"Something like that. Do you know the definition of a safe driver?"

"No."

"A safe driver never gets caught by surprise. A safe driver knows the rules and the laws. A safe driver knows there are choices in any given situation. A safe driver makes the right choices. Everything to do with driving relates to life. I will not make the wrong choice.

"I have gone from one interest to another, one country to another. I could leave New York next week and start an ostrich ranch in Australia.

"My father says I am like a monkey. If a monkey is eating a banana, and you offer him an orange, he will accept the orange. And then if you give him a nut he will take that. I think I am finished being a monkey."

"You have found the best banana?"

"Yes. It is driving, teaching driving."

MARIO, the Costa Rican tennis pro who teaches from a court near our island house, had a riddle for my daughter and me, during our back-to-back lessons on the first weekend of June. What is the most popular sport in America? We could not guess. The answer was fishing. Mario's second question: What is the most popular spectator sport in America? Not football, not baseball, not basketball. Certainly not tennis. It was car racing.

If it hadn't been for Mario, I never would have bought my

highway driving package the previous fall. Mario coaxed me onto the court, and from there taught me not only the rudiments of his game but also that I could overcome my resistance to learning a complicated new skill, one I could master only through hard work. More important, he made me realize that I could accept being a beginner, and that it is more important to learn than to excel.

While the World Cup games in Seoul, Korea, were in progress, Attila in Queens and Mario on the island independently and simultaneously set their alarm clocks for 4:30 A.M. in order to watch the soccer match between Costa Rica and Turkey. I told my daughter about the two men's parallel actions.

"But which team are we for?" she asked anxiously. "We love both Attila and Mario?"

"I'd have to choose Turkey," I said. "But the game's already been played and it was a tie."

"Good!" she said "Did Attila play on the Turkish team?"

THE NIGHT after we returned to the city, Attila called me, his voice frayed with weariness. As he was commuting from Queens to Manhattan at 6 A.M., a tire on the school car, the Camry, blew out. The vehicle was towed to his local garage. The mechanic repaired the tire, and then Attila asked him to perform a full inspection. Both the axle and the brakes (which Earl, the school proprietor, had said had been fixed recently) needed work. Attila called Earl, who owned the car. Earl balked at the five-hundred-dollar estimate and boasted that he could find a better quote. So Attila waited around the garage all day while first Earl searched in vain for a lower price, and then the mechanic performed the necessary repairs. Attila lost a whole day's worth of income, which Earl would not make up to him.

"Aren't you angry that you wasted all that time while Earl tried to save a few pennies?"

"I can't even think that way anymore. Amy, I'm burned out."

"It's happened? Where are you feeling it?"

"Not in my body, but in my brain."

"We'll save that brain."

"How?

" I think the baby in you needs some toys."

"You know that's not going to fix my problems."

"No, but it will help prevent you from breaking down."

"True."

He knew the plan—we'd talked about it before. He would take a few days off, whether or not he believed he could afford to, and I'd rent us a mean muscle car—a red Dodge Viper GTS, an aggressive, noisy, male driving machine that can go from zero to 60 in five seconds. And then, after we took two day trips in that, I'd rent a behemoth of a motorcycle, maybe a Harley Fat Boy or a Ducati Monster.

"But I don't know what you'll do after that."

"I'm not thinking that far ahead."

"I am—as far ahead as the horizon."

"Remember, Amy—scan into the distance, but then bring your vision back to where you started."

The Bentley Boys

Before I even had a chance to secure the toys for Attila, I was sent a big plaything for my own use for a few hours on a sultry June night. My nocturnal adventure with the Bentley boys really got started the week before, when Jim took me out for lunch at JoJo. Jim and I had been friendly ever since we were paired up for the Oscar party in March. As handsome as many of the movie stars with whom we mingled that night, Jim was a black Irishman, with salt-and-pepper hair, luminous blue eyes, and the facial structure of an action hero. He had been invited to the party because the company for which he then worked, Vertu (which makes platinum and eighteen-karat-gold mobile phones), was at that moment one of *Vanity Fair*'s biggest advertisers.

At JoJo, Jim and I talked, naturally, about telephones. He promised to replace my gnarly, out-of-date Nokia with a better model, and teach me once and for all how to retrieve my messages. Jim was infatuated not just with cellular phones, but also with automobiles, so our conversation inevitably progressed to driving.

I repeated to Jim some of the car-and-driving lore I'd gathered from men and women, from drivers and nondrivers; he was a careful listener. I invoked for him the pithy formulation of my gay musician friend Frances: "No man ever considers himself a bad driver—just like no man ever believes he's bad in bed! We girls go through life waiting to be disappointed."

Jim exploded with laughter, tear-spraying gales of it. And I said, "But gay men are the exception to this rule. Like women, they have no problem describing themselves as poor drivers. Often they don't drive at all. Why is this?"

Jim looked at me. "You're right," he said. "I don't have the answer. But most of my gay friends, if they do drive, are quite nervous behind the wheel."

Jim thought that given my escalating, consuming obsession with cars and driving, I might like to attend a ceremony the following week during which the newest Bentley model, a lower-priced coupe, would be unveiled. His company, Vertu, was teaming up with Bentley for some sort of joint promotional endeavor, and who knows, maybe Bentley and I could strike up some kind of synergy with my book project? I gave him permission to pass on my number to Melody, a manager at Bentley Motors.

Melody called the next day, very happy that I could attend the preview party for Bentley's Continental GT Coupe, not officially for sale until fall 2003. I told her I was obligated to make an appearance at two other events that same night (actually there had been three, but I dropped one). Would it be possible to send a car so I could be sure to arrive at each one on time? She said yes, absolutely, Bentley would gladly send a Lincoln Town Car to take me wherever I needed to go.

"Thank you very much," I said. "A Town Car, not a Bentley?"

"Let me see what I can do," she replied. "I'm not sure if there will be one at our disposal for you that night, but I'll call tomorrow first thing to let you know. If there is, it won't be the new GT, of course. There's only one of those!"

Melody phoned the following morning and reported that a Bentley Arnage R and driver would be waiting at my apartment building on the appointed date at 6 P.M.

That evening I dressed with the first event, a benefit at an art gallery for the rain forest, in mind. The party to follow that was a political fund-raiser at a Sutton Place apartment. The Bentley unveiling would be the final destination on the evening's itinerary. I wore a tiny verdigris-colored lace halter dress from Geoffrey Beene (it was a steamy night), high damask Manolo pumps with rhinestone buckles, and a thick pearl-and-sapphire choker from Mish, my jeweler friend.

The clasp of that necklace was in the form of a laughing netsuke mask, mimicking the very mood I found myself in when I stepped through my elevator door and descended to the lobby. My daughter came down with me in the elevator so she could get a peek at the beautiful car that would whisk her mother away from home and bring her back again.

The smiles on the faces of my doormen were even broader and more mindless than the golden netsuke mask's. Theirs were the big, goofy smiles that animate a man's face when he's confronted with either a friendly blonde with big tits or a very hot car. My mirror told me several times a day that I was neither buxom nor blonde, and my daughter was only eight, so I had a distinct feeling that the Bentley must have already pulled up.

A thirtyish Filipino man, whose hair was as long as he was short, stepped into the lobby and said, "Hi, I'm Donald. I'll be driving your Bentley tonight." And there it was, a sleek navy blue vessel, gleaming in the fading sun, already attracting male passersby, moths to a resplendent flame. My doormen—who usually couldn't be bothered to perform their basic function of opening the building's front door (except at Christmastime), beat a path to the Bentley to crack it open for me. I kissed my daughter good night and slid in.

Imagine a foot that has never occupied any shoe except an old Reebok lowering itself into a Manolo pump, and there you have the difference between slipping into a taxi's backseat and sinking into the fleshy armchair of the Bentley Arnage R.

It took less than a block for Donald, the driver, to explain that he was not really a driver at all but a Bentley manager. He lived in New Jersey, and had not yet learned his way around Manhattan, he said. He did know his way around cars, however, because he had earned a degree in automotive engineering. Everybody else in his family was in medicine; he was concerned with auto bodies, they concentrated on human ones.

Our first stop was the C & M gallery, just eight blocks away, so Donald did not need a navigation system to get us there (the Arnage R is too haughty to have one anyway).

Out on the street, when I exited the gallery half an hour later, moths were flapping willy-nilly around the flame. As he released his velvet rope to secure my passage onto the sidewalk, the beefy, baldheaded bouncer said confidentially, "If I wuz you, I'd keep the car and lose the driver."

Donald and I rolled to our next stop, Sutton Place, for the political fund-raiser, where I stayed for less than five minutes.

"Not a good party?" he asked, surprised to see me again so soon.

"No, terrible. But now we'll make it in plenty of time for your Continental GT preview—in fact, we'll probably arrive too early."

"You really like to party, don't you?"

"Well, it's all more or less for work, and I never stay out too late because of my little girl."

"I really like to party, go out to clubs. Do you?"

"Not too much. OK, so you know exactly where the Bentley party is, on West Eighteenth Street, right?"

"Yes."

I sank back into that creamy leather chrysalis, plucked my Nokia out of my bag, and called Attila. He was the only person on my speed dial who would have any idea what a Bentley Arnage R was, and I wanted to share the fun with someone. Only twenty-four hundred were made a year, I learned from Donald, and they retailed for about $200,000. Most of them were purchased in Florida, California, and the greater New York area. Nearly every customer was a cash buyer. What I had never known about the Bentley before was that it was not just the more understated alternative to a Rolls. With roots in racing, it was also a performance car—a term I had just picked up from Donald and was using for the first time. Guys, I was learning, loved it when you actually encouraged their car talk. The Arnage R is a 5,699-pound auto but it can go from zero to 60 in under six seconds.

"That's about the same as the Dodge Viper," Attila said, referring to the muscle car that we were on the verge of renting for two days of rubber-burning fun. (He pronounced it *Wiper*, as in windshield.) So the Bentley was a soigné lady who could also sprint like a warrior. "Wouldn't you like to come with us to the unveiling of the new Bentley? We can pick you up in Queens. We're not too far away—Sutton Place—we've got time."

"No, thank you," Attila said. No matter how many times I invited him to glamorous galas, he always declined. But I kept asking him because I thought he liked being asked, and also because I enjoyed softening the stubborn resolve of his self-denial. If I really wanted company, I'd have asked someone upon whom I could have depended to say yes. What made running around town on one's own so exhilarating was the knowledge that anything could happen, and it did. "I've got to get up at five." Attila was reciting his usual litany. "I have my first student at seven. I used to be a fun guy, you know, but my life's different now."

"Hey, Donald, where are we going?" I interrupted Attila. Somehow, we had voyaged almost to the far end of the Queensboro Bridge. "We're not in Manhattan anymore! We're supposed to be going to Eighteenth Street. We're in Queens!"

"Oops. I made a mistake. Sorry, Amy. This is really embarrassing. I thought I was heading downtown, and somehow I ended up on this bridge. I told you I didn't know Manhattan."

"Forget it. I have no sense of direction either. But the guy on the other end of the phone lives in Queens. He'll tell us how to get back to Manhattan." By then we were penetrating deep into alien outer-borough territory.

"Attila! We're near you. We're in Queens. Are you sure you don't want us to pick you up?"

"Yes. But I'll tell you how to get out. The driver must have thought you were directing him to Queens, misunderstood when you *in-wited* me."

"No, no, he didn't. He's from Jersey, he's not a professional driver. Donald, you didn't think I was directing you to Queens to pick up my friend, did you?"

"No. No. This is really embarrassing!"

"OK, just follow my friend's directions."

Attila guided us back to Manhattan. Donald, now happily on track, phoned ahead downtown to the Bentley boys. "Get the cones ready!" he alerted his cohorts. Donald was not placing an advance ice cream order, but rather was instructing some of the Bentley staff to mark off a place on the street for safe parking. We arrived at the Altman Building (rented for the occasion), on Eighteenth Street, at seven-fifty, precisely when Melody expected us. Donald helped me out of the car. As soon as my feet touched asphalt, I was greeted heartily by James.

"James! You work for Bentley now?"

James is an agreeable British extra-man-about-town, whom I have known for years but had not seen since he left his manager's job several months before at one of Manhattan's grand hotels. I was very glad to see his familiar face in this strange new world of luxury automobiles.

"Amy, of course I knew you were coming and I'm very delighted you're here." James placed a glass of champagne in my hand and took me to meet Melody, on duty inside at the check-in table. The air-conditioning was cranked up to frostbite level, and with the cold drink dropping my body temperature even lower, I was shivering. Melody, sensibly dressed in a suit, looked at me pityingly in my naked lace dress.

"Sorry—this is not exactly the ideal accessory for your dress," she said, giving me a large plastic dog-tag ID to hang around my neck. "For security reasons, we also need to take your purse." I reluctantly surrendered my diminutive beaded LambertsonTruex evening bag. My anxiety in handing it over was not so much about parting with my phone, my lipstick, and my money. What I really dreaded giving up was the few manuscript pages, folded and refolded like an origami bird, that I had been editing in the backseat of the Arnage while chatting with Donald and Attila. The purse was my briefcase.

"Next, we need you to sign these forms," Melody continued. The papers in question were an oath not to reveal to a soul what

I had witnessed tonight, not to record anything I had heard, nor to take pictures of anything I had seen. In short, I was being sworn to secrecy. Who knows? I could be a spy for a competing automaker.

Showtime! An actor in an eye patch impersonating W. O. Bentley, the company's founder, delivered a brief history of the firm. Two beautiful cars, artfully angled like a pair of ballerina's legs, were stationed behind him, colorfully illustrating his tale. On the left was a Bentley Speed Six race car from 1928 and on the right an R-type Continental from 1952. I was hoping that the new GT, waiting for us behind the curtain, resembled this gorgeous postwar ancestor.

The curtains parted, and we were led into a room ringed by a dozen plasma TV screens. Projected on each screen was a still image of a tiger's face. The Bentley of the future waited in the center of this circle, covered, like a Christo object or a pagan virgin goddess, by a modest opaque white cloth. Donald—astute enough to recognize that the goose bumps on my arms and legs were not springing up in anticipation of viewing the GT—courteously helped me into his jacket. "I was too hot anyway," he said.

"Who are all these people?" I whispered. Most of the other guests seemed to be fifty- to sixty-year-old men with torsos neatly encased in sports shirts. "They're clients, or very good prospects," he whispered back. "The Bentley customer looks a lot different from what you'd imagine." A short-haired young woman in jeans and heels, leaning unsteadily on one of the guys, was the only female in the group besides Melody and me.

A hush swept over the room as the CEO of Bentley Motors, Alasdair, gave a speech and launched the video on the twelve screens. We listened as a female overvoice recited, more than once, William Blake's "Tyger Tyger" from *Songs of Experience*—

"Did he who made the Lamb make thee?"—and then, through some sleight of hand (invisible wires?), the white drapery lifted off the debutante, and among gasps and applause, the Continental GT Coupe was revealed.

My first thought was that for $150,000, this looked way too much like other cars—especially in silver, the obvious, ubiquitous color trend du jour. My second thought was, this car is crazy gorgeous and I want it, want it, want it. Alasdair walked around the car, describing how the GT's styling derived from the body of a tiger poised to pounce on its prey. He talked about the "latent power" intimated by the car's supple, flaring haunches, the dynamic tension implied by its sinewy musculature. He mentioned the aesthetic affinities with the 1952 Continental that we had just seen. The car looked as if it had been cut by a lapidary laser, not formed from a mold. "And the interior is composed of the three materials found in all Bentleys—walnut, metal, and Connelly leather." The Continental GT Coupe embodied the Museum of Modern Art design department's curatorial conception of the automobile as "hollow rolling sculpture."

"So what do you think?" Donald asked as we strolled around the car to see it from every possible vantage point.

"I think it's going to be knocked off immediately by everybody. You are going to have to keep changing the design to keep ahead of the pack." He nodded affirmatively and took two dainty champagne flutes from a circulating waiter. This had to have been his third; it was about to be my second. Donald was supposed to drive me home. Attila would not approve.

"Are you driving me home?" I asked.

"Would you like to drive the car?" he replied.

The preposterous idea scared and excited me. "Maybe," I said. "Just in case I do, I'll skip this drink. Would you like it?"

"Yes," he said, draining the tiny glass.

Donald said, "Are you ready to go?"

"Yes," I said. "I have to go home to my daughter."

"You're driving," he said out on the street, opening the door for me.

My God, and so I was. To be in the driver's seat of that Arnage R was like sitting in an angel's lap. Donald demonstrated how to work the seat and mirror adjustment buttons. Very good, Donald—that's exactly what Attila would have required that you attend to first. The metal seat levers, situated just behind the gearshift, were arranged in the shape of two little chairs. All you had to do was push or pull them in whichever direction you'd like your back or bottom to go. There was luxury in not having to see an overstimulating display of numbers and lights on the dashboard, just handsome dials. For up-to-the-minute technology to work properly for you, I decided, you don't have to see it.

Donald showed me how to shift—you needed to pull up on the stick in order to glide it from park to reverse to drive (all Bentley road cars, even the new GT, are automatic transmission). It was a very satisfying sensation, like pulling a smooth plant up by its roots.

"It's already on," Donald said. The engine was so noiseless I hadn't noticed. I executed the next steps fluidly—reverse, drive, and go!

I must have been nervous because I asked Donald for directions back to my own apartment. This was the very first time I had ever driven a car more than five blocks in the city without Attila as my copilot, without the protective backup of the dual brakes—and I was doing it not in a battered Acura but in a Bentley Arnage!

I looked over at Donald. I couldn't believe he was not only

trusting me to drive—who but Attila had ever done that before?—but trusting me in the saddle of his $230,000 thoroughbred.

"I wouldn't call you a beginning driver," Donald said.

Oh, Donald, thank you. His words relaxed me.

"Donald," I said, "this is really fun. I'm being extra careful because I don't want to make any mistakes or get pulled over."

"Oh, when you're in a Bentley cops never give you any trouble. They just wave at you and smile. Taxi drivers give you the right of way. Pedestrians in crosswalks let you pass. People give you the thumbs-up. Nobody's envious, they're just happy for you."

"This car must attract girls like crazy."

"You wouldn't believe it! It's incredible! You don't have to do anything. I took the car out to the Hamptons, and there they were—rich and poor, ugly and beautiful, classy, trashy, young, and old. The brighter the Bentley's color, the more they want to meet you. This dark navy Arnage wouldn't bring on quite as many as that lighter blue Azure that you saw parked on Eighteenth Street." The same rule of color, I thought, that governs aviary mating behavior.

Honk! A bus was barreling down alongside me, trying to pass. I had failed to see this fuming monster in my right side mirror. Attila would not have tolerated such negligence. But Donald, feeling his champagne and reliving his babe-magnet memories, hadn't noticed. Let's just get home before I do some damage, I thought.

I double-parked by my front door (doormen scrambled to the car with goofy smiles on their faces again). Donald said, "Well, anytime you need a Bentley to go out at night, I'm sure it won't be a problem."

This was a magnificent offer—but one I had better back into

carefully (so to speak). A Bentley was a big responsibility. "What would they send me—the car to drive, or a car and driver?"

"Oh, what I mean is whenever you're going out for a night of partying again, I'd like to do it with you. You know, I can drive the car in from Jersey and take you out."

"What a nice idea," I said, accepting his business card and shaking his hand good night. "Thank you so much."

As the bouncer back at the art gallery had said, keep the car, lose the driver. But just in case, I clipped Donald's card into my Rolodex.

Snakebite

Our June plans to rent the Viper were deferred until early July—Attila was working too many hours and taking no time off. He was running on empty—no sleep, no food, no happiness. Yet he was able to minister to his students as before—this was the period when Meredith, the pupil who feared open windows, passed her road test. He was also now visiting a hospitalized friend, a restaurant manager and part-time bouncer, every evening.

Except for the scattered breaks I was arranging for him, he was planning to carry on with this schedule for five more months, until November.

"Then I need to go to Australia and spend a month in the desert on a motorcycle," he said one night by telephone. "Something is calling me there, something is waiting for me. I want to go for such a long time without water that my lips crack open, to go where gas stations are five hundred miles apart—while I'm on a bike that uses up a tank after two hundred miles. Figure that one out! I want to be so alone that I have no echo. I have this weird feeling I've been there before, and that I need to go back."

I had a pretty good idea what might be waiting for him in the Australian desert—his appointment in Samarra. He would travel eight thousand miles to the other side of the globe to encounter head-on the fate that he tempted daily in New York. He had recently dreamt that his teeth were breaking, the premonitory nightmare that had preceded the deaths of several people close to him.

I also speculated that, left alone in the desert like a hermit saint, he might receive some message, undergo an epiphany, experience a vision.

"What do you think is waiting for you there?" I asked.

"I don't know."

"I have thought of two possibilities, one good, one not so good."

"Amy, I'm not going to go running after the next minute— the minute has got to come running to me. Otherwise I'm going backward. I only know that I've got to take a break, and clear my head."

"And empty into the desert all this fear that you've collected from your students?"

"Maybe."

"If you want to go that badly, you will."

"It's not much to ask for."

"No, it's not. You're not greedy."

"You know, I did not learn not to be greedy."

"You were born that way?"

"Everybody is born that way."

"You're saying people become greedy to make up for something they were not given in the beginning—as babies?"

"Yes, I am. It's the same with fear. I never had fear. And I thank my mother and father for that. Parents scold their children for trying to pet Ajan when I'm out walking him in the neighborhood. It makes me angry to see parents implement fear in their children. Is that the right word?"

" 'Instill' or 'inculcate' would be correct."

"From my job, I've come to understand people too well. Show me how you drive, and I'll tell you who you are. After an hour or two with a person, I know a student's frustrations, miseries, strengths, weaknesses, anger—everything. The opposite is also true: I can alter a student's whole personality by changing the way he drives. People are too easy for me to manipulate. They've become like dolls or puppets that I bend and twist— thank God I'm doing them good, not harm. I don't like feeling that way about people.

"The only thing keeping me going is teaching. Every time I pick up a student, I'm recharged. When I'm finished for the day, there's nothing left of me. My eyes started to close on the way home yesterday—something I never do, teach my students never to do."

"Get some sleep tonight, please."

"I've had my warnings. He always gives me a warning to let me know when I'm in danger."

SEVERAL nights later when he called he sounded even more spent. "Amy, this is the burnout."

"So it's finally happened." I was sitting on a raspberry Directoire armchair in my dressing room, with a glass of red wine in my hand and a spiral-bound notebook on my lap.

"I can't fight it anymore. My engine is gone. The brakes are shot. There's nothing left for me to do but coast downhill."

"What's at the bottom of the hill?" I asked.

"I don't know. I'll find out. Amy, this has happened before. I know myself and what I normally do when I reach this point."

"Leave, and start all over again somewhere else?"

"Yes."

"Where would you go this time?"

" 'A man who runs from rain will head toward hail'—that's a Turkish saying. This time I'm not going anywhere."

"Why not?"

"What will keep me here is a promise I made."

"To whom did you make the promise?"

"To you."

I presumed by this he meant his promise to work with me on the book.

"I hope this doesn't feel like a burden to you."

"A burden? I have never felt a burden in my life. I am a locomotive pulling I don't know how many cars behind me. If another car gets hitched on, or one of the cars gets weighed down with extra freight, I don't feel it. Amy, you are the only person I've met who has not become another car for me to drag along. You're on your own parallel track, keeping pace."

"I've been speeding along on that track for a long time, without knowing for certain what my destination or my purpose was."

"Mine is clear to me: to take away the burden from other people. Everybody comes to me for help. I am so aware of it you can't imagine. I have an unlimited capacity to give to other people. I can help anyone, but I cannot help myself."

"I'll help you help yourself," I said. "We have the Viper rental coming—that should give you some days to recuperate."

"I'm looking forward to that."

"When I was feeling low last spring, waiting for news about the book, you told me, 'Keep your sails up, and they'll fill with wind'—and they did. Now you put *your* sails up."

114

"There's the other Turkish saying I've told you: 'A pear does not fall directly from the tree into your mouth.' "

"That may be so, but I'm going to pluck one off a branch and give it to you."

He stayed quiet for a moment, and when he spoke again he sounded less weary. "I am an adventurer," he said. "You like a solid base beneath you. That's what makes us a good team. You provide the solid base; I give you the adventure."

It was Geoffrey Beene who, months before, had inadvertently instigated the plan of renting the Viper. "Do you know about Million Car Rentals?" he had asked one afternoon when we met for lunch. "They're expensive, but cheap in the long run. Whenever I'm convinced I can't live without some new car, I first rent it through Million—that's what I did when VW reintroduced the Beetle. After two days with a car I usually get it out of my system." The next time we had lunch, Geoffrey Beene handed me Million's price list, folded discreetly into thirds. I showed the stratospheric rate sheet to Attila one day after we had finished a stick shift lesson, and asked him to make his selection. He scanned the roster, and ignoring the obvious choices—the Ferraris, Porsches, and Lamborghinis—he tapped his index finger on "Dodge Viper GTS Coupe," at a cost of $700 a day, minimum two days' rental. "I'd like to try the *Wiper.*"

"Viper," I corrected. "You are saying *Wiper*, Attila. Like a windshield wiper."

ON THE eve of our rental, I asked Attila a few questions about the Viper—I knew nothing about it except how to pronounce its name. As I had hoped, the prospect of driving it was perking him up. "You will see when you sit inside of the Viper GTS," he said, "the difference between four hundred and fifty horsepower and the hundred and forty horsepower of the Acura. Don't feel bad if I don't let you drive it. If you don't know exactly how to control those horses, the car will be in spin in no seconds. When you tap the gas pedal you'll be scared by what you feel beneath you. It is that much of a beast. It does zero to sixty in under six seconds. If you hold the gas and clutch in the scissors for long enough you will start burning rubber and leave your signature on the asphalt. This is a ten-cylinder machine. This car is like a wild horse; if it senses you are afraid, you will never tame it. I'll see you at eleven-fifteen tomorrow, in front of your house."

Before going to bed I read about the Viper in a book called *Standard Guide to American Muscle Cars* and in another, Daniel Carney's *Dodge Viper,* new additions to my library. The beefy Dodge, I learned, was the brainchild of Chrysler executives and racetrack legend Carroll Shelby. The mission of these men was to mastermind a sports car as swift and sexy as Shelby's classic 1965 Cobra, but jazzed up with the latest technology. For Tom Gale, Chrysler's vice president of design, their vision corresponded to a middle-aged man's memory of his high school sweetheart. "In the mind's eye, we always remember her as perfect," he rhapsodized. "She was gorgeous, intelligent, courteous. Everything a perfect person could be. That's how the Viper had to be. In our mind's eye, the Cobra was perfect. So we had to design Viper as we remembered Cobra."

ATTILA MET me at my door in the Acura, which he had been storing for me in Queens. Either out of respect for each other or for the Viper, we had both dressed up for the occasion. Forgoing his customary uniform of jeans (which had replaced the cargo pants) and black T-shirt, he wore immaculate white linen pants, a short-sleeved plaid aqua shirt, slickly polished loafers, and no socks. (He had a military man's fastidiousness not only about punctuality but also about the cleanliness of his clothing and person.) I wore a short navy blue cap-sleeved Beene that unzipped down the front like a scuba suit, and blue-and-white Manolo mules.

We headed for the East Village, some seventy blocks downtown. To my amazement, Attila navigated us off course twice, first going too far west, and then too far east. I pointed out both errors to him, a disconcerting reversal of roles. "It's because I'm not teaching," he explained.

I was meditating on this chink in his armor as we traced a parabola back to the correct address. "I was discussing the book with Larry, and he thinks I ought to write about some of your failures."

"Why?"

"Why do you think?"

"Because otherwise I would seem too perfect?"

"Yes."

"Well, I do have a ninety-six percent pass rate. Maybe you should write about the Morellis. They're part of that four percent."

The Morellis were a symbiotic mother-and-son duo who took joint lessons with Attila, and had submitted themselves to back-to-back road tests twice. They both failed both times—but they had not given up on either their driving licenses or on their driving instructor, and he had not given up on them.

"I'm guessing that the problem with the Morellis could be solved if you separated them," I proposed.

"I tried that. On their last road tests, I scheduled them five hours apart, and they still both flunked."

"That's not enough of a separation."

"You mean I should schedule their tests on different days?"

"Different days for their lessons *and* for their tests. They seem to feed on each other's anxieties."

"The dad won't let them—and that's the problem. They are terrified of him. It's cheaper to do the combined mother-son lesson. Both of them are always saying, 'Oh, he's going to kill us if we spend any more money. Oh, he's going to kill us if we don't pass.' "

"So, Attila, you do tough-love family therapy as well individual therapy?"

"You betcha," Attila said.

This was a favorite phrase of his. It sounded like something he had picked up from a comic book or a TV show. He also liked "Don't try this at home."

"You could also mention Meredith's friend Vanessa," he suggested. "I understand she dropped out because she had problems taking orders from me, a male authority figure—something to do with her dad deserting the family when she was small, and blah blah blah. She wasn't ready for me yet. And Maureen didn't finish either—but that was because she ran out of money."

"Any others?"

"On the motorcycle there was Ray. He had been riding Harleys for eighteen years and thought he knew everything. His license had expired. We had just one lesson, before the road test. I told him, 'I know you're an experienced rider, but for the next ninety minutes you have to listen to me and do everything I tell you to do—if you want to pass. This is about passing the test, not about how good you are.' 'Yeah, yeah, I hear you,' Ray kept telling me, and I spoke sharply: 'Ray, I know when someone's listening to me, and when he's not.' He flunked his test, of course. I wouldn't take him back for a second try, because I will not teach anybody who refuses to do what I tell them."

I found our destination—a high drab compound that housed a parking garage and tire shop as well as the rental agency. Leaving the Acura in care of the garage, we went into the rental office to sign off on the Viper paperwork. The proprietor of Million Car Rentals was a South American called Sol, a man so suspicious that when I extended my right hand to him he offered me his left, and when he shook it he couldn't look me in the eye. Sol nonetheless had managed to surround himself with a bevy of young, pretty assistants—good-looking women, I was learning, congregated wherever expensive cars were found. And Sol's girls were as exotic as his cars. Mary, the one helping me, had dark wispy hair, an aquiline nose, secretive almond eyes, olive skin, and a foreign accent that made her sound as if she were speaking with her lips pressed against a mirror. After paying my deposit, I asked her if I might use the rest room. She pointed to a battered white metal door across the garage. But a sign barred me from entering. Hand-lettered in the kind of serried uppercase writing characteristic of folk artists and anthrax terrorists, it read, "Out of Service."

"Mary," I said, walking back into her shoe-box-sized office. "I cannot use that bathroom. Do you have another one that works?"

She said, "Oh, didn't I tell you? The toilet works just fine, it's just that we don't want people coming in off the street to use it."

"What a good idea. I should hang a sign like that on myself."

While we girls were giggling in the rental office, Attila had slipped away. Passing back into the dank garage, I discovered the source of his distraction. An attendant in a jumpsuit was bringing the Viper down from its nest; the snake was about to meet its charmer.

From the photos in my books I had expected something crude and vulgar. Instead, I found that the Viper in the flesh bore a family resemblance to the fantasy wheels of my early childhood: James Bond's suave Aston Martin, Adam West's predatory Batmobile, Barbie and Ken's Dream Car. Its body was like a horizontal exclamation point, and it was painted the most primary shade of male American red. Two silver racing stripes streamed like bands of liquid mercury from the Viper's roof down over its hood. Inside, the bucket seats, steering wheel, and dashboard were upholstered in cognac leather, and the gauges were almost retro in their circular simplicity. The stick shift and emergency brake were sheathed in skin too, whipstitched along the seam. The effect was more than a little anatomical.

"The car's beautiful," I said to Attila. He was earnestly orbiting the car with the attendant, now bearing a clipboard and pad on which he was scribbling notes about the condition of the car's exterior.

"Do they usually come back in bad shape?" I asked Mary, who had stepped out of her Formica-lined cubicle to join us.

"Much better than you'd think," she answered. "The damage is usually just to the body—dents and scratches. People drive it too fast, and then don't know how to control it."

"You'll get it back from us looking even better than it does now," I boasted.

I stepped back to contemplate the front view of the Viper. Its headlights, high set and slitty, were angled toward each other like a pair of accent marks. The grille was a slim grimace, and the nose a triangle, curved at the corners like a billiard ball rack. I felt that at any instant the Viper would flick out its tongue.

"Its face looks just like a snake's!" I gasped to Attila.

"That's the idea," he replied.

The hood ornament, a shieldlike badge, depicted the head of a viper baring its fangs menacingly above an erect, muscular neck.

WE DROPPED into our seats and spun out into the daylight. With Attila I never asked where we were going—he told me whenever he was good and ready. Surprisingly, there was plenty of legroom in the Viper. My legs were extended straight out in front of me, like a doll's.

"This car's pretty feisty," Attila said, accustoming himself to the Viper like a man adjusting himself to the body of a new woman. "The clutch is set a little far to the right. And the center console is wide. Second gear is odd. It works better if I double-clutch it. Are you uncomfortable? Sports cars are not usually comfortable—because, basically, your butt is dragging along the asphalt."

We headed uptown on the East Side.

"This car feels a lot less boxed-in than a European sports car," Attila observed.

"Well, that's America for you—wide open spaces, and everything larger than life."

"You know, I was disappointed when I first came here—I thought all Americans were going to be very tall, like cowboys. But I'm as tall as most of the men here."

Two girls in sleeveless sheaths stood on the corner of Eighteenth Street and Park Avenue South, in front of the restaurant where they had just lunched. I could lip-read the wail of one of them as we whizzed by: "I want that cah!" she cried.

"You've got to watch every bump, every irregularity in the road," Attila noted as he swerved around a pothole. "Otherwise you might need to buy a new set of rims or tires. We're lower to the ground than we'd be in any passenger car."

It felt as if we were skimming along Park on a toboggan, or else (when the surface below us really buckled and warped) a cardboard box.

"The sweet thing about this car," Attila said as we coasted through the intersection of Fifty-seventh and Park under the 30-mile-per-hour speed limit, "is you know you have the power, but you don't have to use it. The car is show-off enough already. It's good to hold back."

"Attila," I said, "you're all about holding back."

Much of Attila's magnetism, I had figured out, derived from his ability to contain his feelings, mute his words, check his actions, restrain his expressions. This was quite different from garden-variety male impassivity because with Attila you could detect a rich emotional life churning beneath his still surfaces—a teeming reef flourishing under smooth, cool, inviolable waters.

"If you have self-control, you can control anything," he said.

Attila was using only his pinky and his ring finger to manipulate the stick. ("Don't try this at home.") These fingers, girdled by silver bands, and his forearm above them were bronzed from driving with his students in the summer sun. They were the same shade as the Viper's leather interior.

"Did you see how it took me three to four minutes to get oriented to the car?" Attila asked. "Every time I get on any new machine—whether it's a car, a truck, a motorcycle, or a computer—after a few minutes it's like I've known it forever. I understand its language, and it understands mine. This is a well-made American car. I love it." I was thrilled to hear these words. The ad hoc Viper cure was already taking effect, and more quickly than I had hoped.

On the Park Avenue meridian at Fifty-ninth Street, identical long-haired male twins, about twenty-seven, bracketed a leggy blonde. As the twin to the left followed our Viper with his eyes, he licked his lips.

We were on our way, I learned, to Long Island to take a look at the Harley Fat Boy we would be renting the following week from a dealership in Huntington Station. En route we passed through Queens, slowly circumnavigating Astoria Park, an arcadian greensward situated beneath the colossal arched stanchions of the Triborough Bridge. Attila had his reasons for our detour around Astoria Park. Lately, whenever we had spent any substantial amount of time together in a car, he had made a point of revisiting scenes from his thirteen-year history in America. Usually I could only half guess a place's meaning to him—sometimes, thinking aloud, he would supply a clue. I sensed he was systematically rekindling memories in order to extinguish them, as if he were planning to build something new upon their ashes.

"Many years ago, I spent a lot of time in this park with my friends Russ and Desi," Attila said.

"What did you do here?"

"We hung out, talked," he answered laconically. "Everybody's looking at the Viper," he noted. "But they respect it too much to make a commotion like they did with the Excalibur. This is a great American car. It's the best stick shift car I've ever driven. This is a real pleasure for me. Thank you."

"The pleasure is all mine." My smile felt like a long elastic band stretching from one side of the car to the other. "So, what does a driving instructor do for fun on his day off?" I asked, setting him up.

"He drives," he answered, picking up speed.

WE WERE now on the Long Island Expressway. "The tires are so wide," Attila explained, "they grab at every little mark on the road." As if by suction, they pulled us here, then there, to wherever trucks had worn down grooves and depressions in the grainy macadam. Two Hispanic men in the front seat of a Honda Civic (license plate: NEVR2BIG) grinned at us, nodding approvingly, like bobble-head dolls. As we passed, they punctuated their endorsement with the double thumbs-up sign. It intrigued me that they were so excited to see a man in a superior vehicle. A female eyeing another woman in jewelry more opulent than her own would be more likely to look at her with envy than with camaraderie or complicity.

"Maybe it's because they see me as a regular Joe, not a snob," Attila proposed. The Viper, he informed me, retailed for about $75,000. "But you can get a used one for thirty-five thousand. And you have to be an athlete to drive this. Men admire athletes. If a machine doesn't challenge me, it doesn't interest me. Put your hand on the metal rod of the stick shift."

It was burning hot.

"That's not from the sun, it's from the friction. Do you see how I'm not using the brake at all? I'm using only engine compression when I need to slow down—downshifting to third is like putting on the brakes. Then, when you upshift, this car leaps right from under you. It has the pull of a motorcycle—a Japanese one, not a Harley. And we're not even going sixty. We could easily go double or triple that. I like doing fifty in this car. It's a good feeling to conserve power," he said.

"You're talking about yourself as much as the car."

"Yes, but I didn't use to be like that. In the past, I used all my power at once. The intensity scared people."

As we approached the Huntington Station exit, I called the Harley dealership for directions. Still unable to find it, we pulled into a Mobil station. The voracious Viper had burned up close to a quarter tank of premium fuel on the thirty-seven-mile drive to Long Island.

In my abbreviated Beene, stepping out of the car posed a bit of a challenge. Not only was the car extremely low-slung, the metal doorsill over which I had to pitch my legs was extremely wide, and blazing hot. As Attila took my right hand to lift me to my feet, the roasting metal branded the backs of my bare thighs. This car was strictly for trousers, for men. Further proof of that fact was the absence of a vanity mirror on the flipside of the passenger seat's sun visor. There was no expedient way to perform a lipstick check. Inside the gas station's convenience store, Attila addressed in Turkish the two salesmen from whom he was buying cigarettes and water. They responded in English.

"What's wrong, did you forget your first language?" he demanded in Turkish.

Obediently, they switched tongues.

"You people are everywhere," I remarked as we settled back, pilot and copilot, into our seats.

"The one with the shorter hair was named Atilla too—but he spelled it differently."

"Two *l*'s and one *t*?" I asked. Attila had taught me the distinction between these two spellings back in November, after another Atilla had introduced himself to me in the green room of the New York State Theater, during the intermission of *Abduction from the Seraglio*.

"Yes," he nodded. " 'Atilla' the way he spells it is much more common in Turkey. You are more likely to find my spelling in Hungary."

Following double-*l* Atilla's directions to the Harley dealership, we turned into the parking lot just as the shop was closing for the day. The last customers and the staff—a tattooed regiment of men wearing silver-and-black skullcaps (half-measure headgear that looks, depending on your point of view, either like a GI's combat helmet or an upside-down stainless-steel mixing bowl)—were departing on their bikes. "We'll be back next week," we told one of them, a fellow named John.

I could tell by the purposeful set of Attila's face that he had a second, nearby destination in mind. We flowed back onto the LIE. "What I would like to try after this is the Viper Venom," Attila said, this time mastering the tricky double *V*'s. "They are customized Vipers that have been pumped up to seven hundred horsepower."

"Is it going to be hard to turn this back in when we're finished?"

"No—enjoy the toy, and go home."

As we neared Port Jefferson, Attila said, "I know a little place somewhere around here where we can get something to eat—it's been about six years, but I'll find it."

"You have a little place everywhere."

"Yep."

Two motorcyclists on Yamahas darted up to us, retreated, then buzzed up to us again like a pair of bloodthirsty mechanical mosquitoes.

"They're playing with me," Attila said. "They know I'm the only car on the road that can keep up with them. This car can go so fast that this horse van, that Nissan, would think they're standing still."

Along the route we passed another Viper, in basic blue. Its driver held up two fingers to make a V. A few minutes later a trucker barreling in the opposite direction signaled his enthusiasm with a fraternal blast of his horn.

"It is amazing how I have become one with this car," Attila said.

"Like a mother with a baby," I said.

He laughed. "But what a workout it is to tame him. I feel like I've been in a boxing match with Muhammad Ali. My hands are blistered." He took the right one off the wheel and held it palm side up to show me. I stroked my index finger over the chain of translucent white bubbles that had popped up on the fleshy pad of his hand. "The engine is frying my right leg." I leaned over at a red light to lift the cuff of his crisp white pants. The right side of his bare ankle—paler and more hairless than I would have expected—was strawberry red.

"It looks as if it were badly sunburned," I reported.

"Does it really?" he asked, pleased with this evidence of his exertions. And then he rotated his elbow toward me. "My right elbow is skinned from the center console." It had, in fact, been abraded. "It looks like a rug burn," I said. "You need an elbow pad." He smiled. "Well, it's a muscle car, all right. You really feel its muscles at work."

"What exactly does it mean to feel a car's 'muscle'?" I asked.

"It's the torque that you're feeling—in this car, five hundred pounds of torque."

Torque, I had learned, refers to the amount of force that the engine delivers to the driveshaft; muscle cars are an American phenomenon, dating from the early sixties.

"This car really deserves a big applause," Attila continued.

"I'm proud of this country for producing such an extraordinary piece of machinery. I never cared much for sports cars before. You noticed that even though the rental list had Porsches, Ferraris, Lamborghinis, I had no interest in them? They're too *schiki-micki* for me. The reason I've always preferred coupes to sports cars is because I like to share. Cars with just two seats are—"

"Selfish." I completed his sentence. "My grandmother used to call them 'selfish cars.' "

"The only problem with this car, besides the weak AC, is the shoulder belt. It hits right at the—"

"Collarbone," I completed his sentence again. That's where it was chafing me. "Isn't that just where you broke it, on the right?" He had shattered his collarbone eight years before, he had told me one day on a long stick shift lesson, when he leapt out of a helicopter onto a Turkish mountainside with a snowboard strapped to his feet. He took my finger and glided it over his large bone, letting it linger on a knotty bulge. "That's the way it fused," he said. "That's where the seat belt is irritating me."

He found his way to the waterside restaurant he was seeking. We ascended an open-air staircase to a second-story deck where a band played Van Morrison loudly, making conversation difficult. I ordered a shrimp cocktail and Attila had shrimp scampi. While he delicately picked out little flakes of minced garlic with his fork and knife, he explained that he had last visited the seafood café with Malik, his best friend from Turkey. Attila had not seen Malik since then because in the interim his friend, an import-export entrepreneur, had developed a fear of flying. The harbor view from our table made him nostalgic for his family's beach house in Bodrum, on the Turkish coast. "Although you can hardly compare this to the Aegean," he said. I had not quite realized until then how homesick he was for his country, his family, his friends. "Are the Hamptons sort of like this?" he asked, changing to a less painful subject.

"It's bigger out there, and prettier," I replied. "And much more expensive."

Whenever we sat down together at a restaurant after driving, Attila's demeanor altered completely. He relaxed, softened, and seemed fondly surprised to find himself in my company. After spending so much time side by side, it was always a small shock for both of us to see each other face-to-face. I still prefer his profile.

At the seafood café, I was feeling just a little let down, as if our dashing Viper ride had come to an anticlimax. There was so much I wanted to say, but it was too effortful to speak over the din of the band. So I just listened to him talk, and let him offer me some of his food. I suppose my inchoate sense of disappointment came from knowing the day would end.

"Let's go. It's too noisy in here," he finally said.

"What did you think of the band?" I asked as we climbed down the outdoor steps to the parking lot.

"It's a bar band," he said, self-evidently.

Both of us seemed more at ease back in the car. Maybe it worked best for us when we were three—he and I, and a machine. It didn't even have to be a car; it could be a telephone.

WE HAD glorious weather again for our second day out. This time, we both showed up dressed informally. I wore the newest addition to my wardrobe—blue jeans—a white T-shirt with a ruffled neckline, and blue-and-white floral Manolo mules. Attila was dressed in a striped stretch T-shirt with a zipper up the neck, warm-up pants, and sneakers. We drove to the West Side Highway, and on to the Taconic Parkway. It didn't take long for the Viper road rites to begin again.

A young man with large chocolate eyes stuck his head out of his Jeep. "How does she handle?" he shouted across the lane.

"Beautifully!" I yelled back.

"Was that the right answer?" I asked, turning back to Attila.

"It was," Attila said. "There's a woman tailgating me. Same as yesterday. Women are more aggressive with this car than men."

"Why do you think that is?"

"Maybe they had boyfriends with Vipers?"

"Maybe they had boyfriends period," I said. "Don't you think a lot of American women have lost their femininity?"

"If American women have lost their femininity," he asserted, "American men are to blame. What goes around, comes around."

The Viper—a gleaming red knife slicing through a verdant landscape—catapulted us far out of Manhattan, deep into Dutchess County. "I'm not minding the color of this car anymore," I said, hypnotized by its flashy, elliptical hood. "It's the perfect complement to all this bright green around us."

"And I was just thinking," he replied, "that I don't mind the gray stripes anymore. They match the color of the road. What a great car this is! It sits on the highway like a *surfbrett*."

"You mean surfboard?" He was slipping back into German, a habit when he was relaxed or tired.

"Yeah, a surfboard. Listen to the valves," he said, ears cocked like an orchestra conductor's. "They could be a truck's." The valves sounded like a gaggle of children sticking out their tongues and vibrating them wetly between their lips. "I would love to drive this car in Europe."

"Where to exactly?" I knew he wouldn't say France, a state he despised nearly as much as New Jersey.

"We would take the Viper on a boat across the Atlantic to Amsterdam. Then from Amsterdam we'd drive about one thousand kilometers to Italy. At Trieste or Venice we'd put it on the ferry, sail on the Adriatic Sea past Greece to Turkey, down to Bodrum. We'd drive to my family's beach house and from there . . ."

"Be careful what you ask for, Attila. I just may make this happen." Every time Attila conjured up a new pipe dream, I felt commanded to give it substance, and I often did.

"I know that by now," he answered. "I can't believe I am so one with this car," he said. "With the Viper, every time I get back in, it's new all over again."

"That is love," I said.

"Yes, I have fallen in love with this car."

"You look like a man in love," I said. He turned away from the road, driving only with his peripheral vision (a stunt I had seen him perform before—"Don't try this at home"), and he faced me. "With the car," he said concisely.

For a daredevil, he was a careful man.

"Did you bring CDs today?" I asked.

"Yes, but it's hard to hear them over the noise of the car."

I was curious to see what he had stashed in the glove compartment. I guessed an Ozzy Osbourne album might be among his selections, but otherwise I was ignorant of his musical tastes. Whatever he played I would end up enjoying in spite of myself. He had packed just three CDs, it turned out: Ozzy Osbourne's *Down to Earth*, as expected, Tom Petty and the Heartbreakers' *Greatest Hits*, and Jimi Hendrix's *Are You Experienced?*

"I bet you didn't think I liked Tom Petty."

"I didn't think you didn't."

We listened to his music for a while without talking. Sometimes Attila sang along with it. He had a sweet voice (as I had learned when I played the demo tape he had given me months before). Attila was partial to Osbourne's song "Dreamer," which I had heard only once previously, when I was in L.A. three months earlier. I had phoned him from my hotel room one night and when he answered, the song was booming anthemically on his stereo. Under the influence of Jack Daniel's (which he scrupulously avoided on workdays; I still had never seen him drinking) and the music, he had said, "With you, Amy, I have on all my brakes. My hand brakes, my emergency brake, my foot brakes."

"What would happen if you released one of those brakes?"

"It won't happen," he had said. "My brakes are also my security system. Here is another Turkish saying you should know: 'A man who has burnt his tongue on hot milk will find himself blowing on yogurt.' "

HE EJECTED the last of the CDs and began to look for a restaurant, one of his "little places," which, he informed me, fanned out beyond the Northeast into the South and the Midwest. Attila needed to rest; his fingers were cramping from the strain of handling the Viper, and the abrasion on his right elbow was hardening into a callus. On the way, he turned onto a dirt road that opened into a pasture. We stopped and took some snapshots of each other and the Viper with a disposable camera I had brought along for that purpose. Attila liked photographic keepsakes; he had an almost primitive belief in the truth of Kodachrome, and he was capable, like a tribesman, of being astonished by the sight of his own recorded image (especially one that brought out his virile beauty).

We had reached the location he was hunting, only to find

that the restaurant had been replaced by a gas station. He seemed vexed that it should have disappeared from the landscape but not from his memory. Deprived of our dinner, we turned around, bound for Manhattan. We were both savoring the melancholy pleasure of the end of the trip. Overcome by a sensation of peace, I felt tears of happiness spring to my eyes. What had induced this blissful state was simple—the rocking rhythms of the car, the warm summer wind stirred up by the onrushing Viper, the sweet aroma of freshly cut grass, the feeling of the sun lowering and fading, and the solid, dependable masculine companionship. For a fleeting instant I was transported back in time, far away, to a road somewhere else, to the idyllic countryside of Bucks County, Pennsylvania. I was seven or eight and I was sitting beside my father in his red Corvair convertible, on a wooded road in the fragrant July heat.

"It's amazing what memories can be awakened just by the movement of a car, and the scents in the air," I said.

"Nothing else does that like driving," Attila replied serenely. He had been floating through his own time-trip reverie. Whatever pieces of his past he had briefly retrieved through sense memories had caused his eyes to glisten too, and the corners of his mouth to turn up to the cerulean sky.

WE ENDED the day by going to dinner at a tiny Turkish restaurant on the Upper East Side. Everything he ordered, especially the eggplant fritters, was delicious. I asked how they were made, and he responded with the refrain of all good cooks: "It's easy. Anybody can make them." We ate and talked, studying the front view of each other's face with curiosity—dark sides of the moon. I drank a glass of red wine, which emboldened me to say, "Attila, one day, when you stop being a machine—a stone—and turn back into a flesh-and-blood man, I will tell you some things about myself."

"I'll be all ears," he said. "But you know that the only thing that concerns me is who you are when you're with me."

Whatever I thought I had urgently needed to say to him no longer seemed to matter.

Instead we got around again to the subject of female tailgaters.

"American women are angry," he said. "They feel underpowered."

"You're right," I said. "What do you think is the remedy—besides learning to drive well?"

"More reverence from men."

"That's it?"

"Well, they also have to know how to accept it," he replied.

On the short ride back from the restaurant to my house, Attila said, "Amy, I have found the baby inside me. I thought he had been lost."

"He was never lost," I told him. "The baby was sleeping. You just needed help waking him up."

"Thank you for doing this for me."

"The pleasure was all mine."

And we said good-bye on the street with a kiss on the cheek and a hug.

THAT NIGHT, he called to thank me again. "For five and a half years I have been a man in a coma. These last two days, I have rediscovered life. I feel my valves opening up. I believe in life again."

"Are you familiar with the fairy tale 'Sleeping Beauty'?"

"Yes."

"Well, then you know that Sleeping Beauty was a princess who slumbered in her castle for a hundred years. This is your story, except you have been the Sleeping Prince."

"Yes. That's me."

"And now that the spell's been broken and you're wide awake again, the trees outside the castle are sprouting leaves and bearing fruit—pears. The flowers in the gardens are blooming, and the streams and fountains are flowing."

"All true, and none of it would have happened without you. And you know what else? I have to concentrate on my work as an instructor, and maybe even on opening my own driving school. With your help if you like."

It made me happy to hear his words; these were the realizations that I'd hoped he'd come round to, ones he had to find for himself.

"If you were my driving student, I would terminate you now," I said.

"Why?"

"Because nearly everything you needed to see is visible to you now. But just as you have kept me on even though you finished with me as a student, I'll stay with you even though you don't really need me anymore. That is, if you'd like to continue working together."

"My answer for you is another Turkish saying—'The machine that keeps on working will continue to look brand-new. The machine that isn't used will break down and get rusty.' There is so much we can do together. New York shouldn't be a town full of people full of fear. There are three phases to getting what you want from life: dream, plan, and execute. In the past I was too impatient. I made the mistake of skipping phase two. That's where we are now."

135

REVIVED BY his Viper tonic, Attila went on to refurbish his bachelor's flat in Queens—he laid down a new kitchen floor and ripped out a thirteen-year-old carpet and installed a fresh one. "I feel like I just moved into a new apartment," he said. "My head's clear, in order, and so are my surroundings."

If Attila had been rehabilitated, for the moment at least, where did that leave me? Certainly not in the driver's seat. Reverting to habit, I had ceded that place to him, as I invariably had to the men (and women) in my life. On the Viper trail with Attila, I had lost sight of my primary mission—learning to drive on my own. I was backsliding, and consequently, the old nightmare returned in new forms. One night I was at the helm of a Mini Cooper (a car similar to my father's Morris Minor), losing control. Another night I was desperately trying to back an enormous trailer up a steep muddy hill. And then I dreamt I was driving a red Viper—an achievement of which I was very proud, until the machine bolted away from me and smashed into a pedestrian, who turned out to be my Costa Rican tennis pro.

Diva at the DMV

When I shared with Attila my concern that I had once again become car-shy, he said, "Maybe what you need now is a different experience of the road. Soon it will be time to start your motorcycle lessons, and when the time comes I want you to be ready—you've got to get your motorcycle learner's permit." This was a finite task, I felt, one that I could manage. I allotted myself a week to study, and on a Wednesday, following a Michael's lunch with my agent, I skipped off downtown to the Department of Motor Vehicles branch office across from the flagship Macy's on Herald Square.

The DMV on Thirty-fourth Street had no there there. What I did find there was a vertical shopping mall—with a Modell's, a Mrs. Fields Cookies, and a cardboard sign in a metal stand by the front door that indicated: "DMV," *arrow-arrow-arrow.* Then there were more *arrow-arrow-arrow*s, which led to a cul-de-sac and an elevator bank. The last lift was the DMV's express ride to the eighth floor. When I stepped out of the elevator, there was no spatial or architectural sense of arrival, only a long line leading to an information window. Visitors had to stop first at this

137

paned station in order to be sorted by a clerk into another line in the next room. It was an absurdist bureaucratic hell, but once I decided to be a tourist in purgatory, the experience started to become interesting. For ten minutes the line didn't budge, and the standees (some eating their paper bag lunches), were getting restless. Then all at once the line started moving briskly. Another "Information Services" window had opened.

I arrived at the head of the line, a green form from Attila's school and a driver's license in hand (a New York State driver's license is an ID worth six points, the DMV's highest ranking). The man whose head and torso filled the window frame was an extreme example of a suffering white functionary. His face was sunken and dented like a badly peeled potato and he was covered with bandages of all kinds—adhesive tape on his right ear, Band-Aids on his face, a sling on his arm. He resembled a cartoon caricature of a car accident victim, freshly discharged from the emergency room. He greeted me miserably and directed me to the test takers' area, a collection drain for car, motorcycle (class M), and maybe even truck learner's permit candidates.

One by one we submitted our forms to an Afro-coiffed clerk, then posed for pictures. (No class photo for us, just individual portraits.) I was elated to be granted this second chance for a license photo. If I succeeded in earning the new license, it would be good for both cars and motorcycles, and therefore would supplant the present, very poorly illustrated document I held.

With expectations of an improved ID photo clouding my thinking, I headed to the next place where the space logically flowed—it was a kind of funnel effect that whooshed me into the room to my left. But a uniformed man halted my progress. "Hey, where you think you goin'?" he barked. Oops. I had wandered into the test-taking sanctum sanctorum, where a few terrified souls hunched over one-armed desks, making pencil marks on slices of cheap computer paper. I smiled at the ungentlemanly DMV officer and retreated to the pen where I belonged, defined by wooden pews segregated behind a glass partition. Nearest me was a group of Asian girls, probably seventeen or eighteen years old. Their heads were bowed over manuals, all written in an impenetrable language. My God, the brochures I had studied already read like Chinese. I could only absorb the information about motorcycle driving in an abstract sense, as rote material devoid of any practical meaning or context. I worried about whether I would be able to read highway signs correctly in English. Could these girls even read them at all?

Spurred by their diligence, I leafed through my driver's and motorcycle booklets (I was to be tested on both subjects) and the crib sheet of 110 questions, fifteen or twenty of which were likely to appear on the car segment of the test, supplied by Attila's driving school. It was a ten-page Stanley Kaplan–esque educational aid, and access to this sample exam alone justified the price of a deluxe package of driving lessons (not too dear anyway).

The previous batch of test takers were evacuated from their cell, and we filed into the room from which I had been banished, replacing them. On the way we passed a box over which hung an ominous notice: "Leave all driving manuals in this carton before entering room." There was no way that I was giving up my highlighted, Post-it'd, and dog-eared manuals, let alone my driving-school cheat sheet. They were my war trophies, my source material, my reference texts! I stuffed them into my purse and snapped its metal clasp shut.

I knew all too well why the sign and the booklet receptacle

were positioned there at the antechamber of the DMV's exam room. When I had taken my written test for the driver's license permit two years before, the monitor had noisily accused me of consulting my manual, which lay on the floor by my desk. She threatened to flunk me. The box discouraged not just cheating but also false accusations.

The knot of Asian girls, a blonde white teenager (looking a little like a corkboard because of the pushpins of varying size inserted near or in every visible orifice), a swarthy pockmarked man draped in golden chains, and I were herded single-file to a counter. We were asked in what language we would prefer to take our tests. The five Asian girls requested the DMV's Korean edition. "We only have four Korean tests left," the bureaucrat behind the counter droned. The least pretty of the girls (the one whom I saw studying most assiduously on the wooden benches) was instantly weeded out by her friends. She looked despondent as she was directed to her desk. The pockmarked man asked for a Spanish test. He got it. "English," I said. "Motorcycle?" she replied, raising her eyebrows as she handed it to me. I was actually starting to quiver.

I heard the clerk say, "English—motorcycle," to a latecomer behind me. I turned around and saw that the one other inmate of the testing room who was seeking a class M permit in the national tongue fit the stereotype of a biker only slightly more than I did. He was a wholesome-looking, middle-class, State U–ish kind of guy.

We were shepherded to our desks by the same guard who had upbraided me for walking into the room prematurely. His task completed, he took his seat on a high metal dunce stool in the corner. Laminated on each of our desktops was a colorful page showing an array of highway signs—the skull-and-bonesish RR crossing sign, a stop sign, a speed limit sign, and so forth. It was very attractive to see them all laid out this way. It was highway Pop Art, and could be a standout at the Whitney Biennial.

More signs above the counter indicated that mobile phones had to be switched off and that talking was forbidden. The Korean girls were prattling. I wondered once more, did they read English?

"If any of you talk again, you all flunk," the female clerk bellowed.

I was trembling.

"You have exactly fifteen minutes to complete your test," she continued. "Motorcycle test takers: On your sheets, questions five through nine are about motorcycles. The other questions are like everybody else's. You are only allowed to get two motorcycle questions wrong. Otherwise you flunk the whole test. Everybody: Questions fifteen to nineteen refer to the road signs that you see on your desk. If you miss more than two of those questions, you flunk the whole test. You may start!"

It was multiple choice. Miraculously, every question so far had its perfect twin on the driving school cheat sheet. My early surge of confidence ebbed—I'd come to the motorcycle portion of the test. And then my concentration broke. The man on the stool and his colleague started conversing and chortling merrily, as if they hadn't seen each other for weeks. One of their cell phones started ringing shrilly. Nobody answered it.

5. Where is sand and gravel most likely to gather on a highway?
6. When traveling in formation, how should a group of motorcyclists take a curve?

7. With a properly adjusted mirror, exactly what should you be able to see?

I answered this one quickly, then erased my response and carefully changed it.

8. Which of the following is correct: Lean left, push left, go left. Lean left, push left, go right. Etc.
9. On a wet road, it is safest to: Apply the front brake only. Apply the back brake only. Apply both brakes. Brake as quickly as possible.

The State U guy was the first to hand in his test. This awakened dormant competitive feelings. The multipierced blonde was next to stand up and surrender her test. That did it. I submitted my test and returned to my seat. Suddenly, I was overcome with exhaustion. I put my hand to my forehead, a gesture I never make. I was filled with remorse about how I answered the "Lean left" question. I wanted to change my answer. It was too late. I acted out the scenario physically: "Lean left, push left. . . ." I got it wrong. That made me even more tired.

"Time's up!" the lady announced.

The stragglers gave up their tests. Then the woman read off our first names, one by one. It took forever for her to reach mine. "Amy!" she said sternly. At the counter, I watched her, upside down, scribble a *P* on the sheet. As she continued writing, the *P* became *P 100*. She looked at me, impressed, and then became a block of cement again. I was hit by a long, sick wave of déjà vu. Years and years of school, college, graduate school. The nervousness, the push to be the best student, the perverse kick of getting the top score, the A-plus—the anticipation, the stress, the triumph, the perfectionism . . . for what?

Attached to the test there was a small slip of paper with another number, *A 123*. This was a ticket assigning me a place in the next line. I exited the test-taking room and went into a railroad-station-like waiting room, where I would receive my temporary permit. The wholesome motorcycle man looked at me. So did the father—or was it the grandfather? maybe the pimp?—of the pierced blonde. She seemed happy.

I picked up someone's discarded *Times* from the bench. I read one article, then I hit the speed dial of my cell phone, which, as had already been demonstrated jarringly, worked just fine in the vertical mall.

I reached the voice mail for Attila, most likely on the road with a student. "Attila? It's Amy. You are the first to know that I have passed my motorcycle test with a score of one hundred."

Larry, the book editor, was next. I left a similar message.

Next came my agent.

The first human voice I reached belonged to Robert, my trailblazer, who by brave example inspired me to quit smoking five years ago and more recently to learn to drive.

"Darling, how awful, the DMV! What are you doing there?"

I explained everything.

"What unnecessary stress you've put on yourself, trying all your life for perfect scores!"

The number A123 was announced.

"I'll call you later. The lovely DMV lady needs to see me now."

The young woman behind the desk beamed at the compliment.

"How about this?" I said, shoving my papers to her.

"That's the first hundred I've seen since I started," she replied.

"Do you think I'm crazy, getting my motorcycle learner's permit? Motorcycles are so dangerous. I've got a little girl . . ."

"How old's your little girl? It's not the most dangerous thing you can do."

"No, I could be shooting up heroin."

"I should get my motorcycle license. I'd like one of them jackets."

"Yeah, the clothes are great. It's worth doing it just for the gear."

Her machine spit out a temporary motorcycle learner's permit. It was big and bulky, and didn't fold easily.

"So where do I keep this thing while I'm taking lessons?" I asked her. "I can't carry a purse on a bike, can I?"

"Honey, you can't be no *diva* on a motorcycle! You gotta be a *bad girl!*"

Permit in hand, I smiled all the way down the express elevator, back to the first floor. I stopped at the Mrs. Fields concession and got four miniature cookies—oatmeal, chocolate chip, M&M, and macadamia–white chocolate—to bring back to my daughter. I ended up eating them on the taxi ride home.

In the cab, between bites, I checked my messages on my home answering machine. Larry was recorded saying, "I'm not surprised you passed your written test, Amy. I'll be impressed when you pass your motorcycle road test."

He was right, but he sounded like my father. "An A? Not an A-plus?"

Ten days later the permanent class M permit arrived in the mail. The new picture was a vast improvement over the one on my driver's license. It looked like the "After" shot in a magazine makeover.

MY FIRST motorcycle lesson was still a distant uncertainty. The God of Driving had a very busy schedule. Yet he refused to hear anything about Geoffrey Beene designing my gear. Over lunch Mr. Beene had imagined customizing leather biker gloves for me with his pinking shears.

Luckily for Attila, Mr. Beene had had a change of heart. He sent me a fax retracting his offer to style a motorcycle costume. "I am interested in fragility, not toughness," he explained.

Could I be fragile and a bad girl at the same time?

The Queen Seat

Only once before in my life had I ever actually been on a motorcycle, when I was sixteen. It belonged to an older, red-headed boy whose name I can't remember. I don't recall much about that inaugural ride either except terror, not so much of the motorcycle, which wasn't very big or fast, but of the boy. It embarrassed me to do something so intimate as hold on to his waist. He transported me home, and I never heard from him again.

The only mercurial redhead in my life these days was my eight-year-old daughter. So what induced me, when I still lacked confidence as a driver of cars, to set a date for a motorcycle lesson? The one-word, one-man answer to that question was, of course, Attila—who may just have piqued my desire to try it out by making me wait so long for an appointment. And once I made the commitment I had to follow through because *Travel + Leisure* had commissioned an article from me on the subject of learning to drive a motorcycle for its October Style issue.

Getting on a motorcycle would not necessarily make me a better driver, Attila explained. But it would turn me into a better observer of the road. This was the strong medicine I needed to be cured of my hazardous tendencies to zone out, forget where I was, and lose myself in thought behind the wheel.

I told everyone I encountered, wherever I went, that I was about to start motorcycle lessons—not so much to poll them for their opinions but to convince myself it was true.

"I'll kill you if you start riding a motorcycle!" exclaimed my dentist, plunging his novocaine needle into my upper left gum. "Do you understand me? I don't want it on my conscience that I *ever* said that it was OK to ride a motorcycle!" And as he drilled, he told me a cautionary tale about how he and his best friend nearly became roadkill one summer on the Long Island Expressway.

Cathryn, an entrepreneur, recounted for me the chilling story of her wipeout in a rainstorm on the Merritt Parkway. After that accident she gave up on both motorcycles and the biker boyfriend.

The stories only grew more horrific from there. "But that eez 'ow my first love died at seventeen," said Philippe, a French artist who insinuated love and death into every conversation.

Kate, a blonde bombshell from Texas, drawled, "Aaymy, a very experienced bahker told me that there is at least one serious accident in every motorcycle."

"But what about the clothes?" I asked, attempting to appeal to her sunnier nature. "Don't you love the gear?"

"Aaymy, you don't need to rahd a bahk to wear a black leathuh jacket."

Lars, a fashion designer, grew very quiet when I brought up the subject over lunch at La Grenouille. "What's the matter?" I asked. "Are you worried I'm going to hurt myself? I have complete faith in Attila," I said, maybe a little too defensively. "With him, I know I'm safe."

"No, that's not it," replied Lars, who all along had shown sympathy for my driving phobia, because he shared it. "I was just picturing the motorcycle outfit I would design for you—a silk jumpsuit lined in sheared mink. I'll make a sketch for you."

I reported these conversations to Attila, who was not amused. "I'm going to cancel your lessons if you're planning on wearing designer outfits. You have to get serious gear. You need protection, not style."

ATTILA had now booked me for twenty hours' worth of lessons. "And when you're finished with me you'll attend the three-day seminar they offer in Woodhaven, after which you will receive your license. It'll be better for you than taking the motorcycle road test in the city. It's called the Trama School."

"*Trauma* School?"

During lunch at Le Cirque, glamorous Jill, whose boyfriend owns several BMW bikes, said, "You hadn't heard of the Trama School, founded by Gasper Trama? Well, there's also a famous study on motorcycle safety you should know about called the Hurt Report, compiled by Harry H. Hurt Jr. !"

I started inspecting motorcycles parked along city streets. Suddenly, they seemed ubiquitous, like pregnant women when you're expecting. I studied them, identified their parts, tried to imagine myself straddling them. One day, while walking home from the hairdresser, I saw a red Yamaha Roadstar Warrior, a fiery chariot worthy of Mars, parked on the hill behind the Sixty-seventh Street armory. Every man who passed this gleaming hunk of metal swiveled his head furtively once, then twice, for a double take.

At dinner one night, Nathan, a decorator, told me that he had been struggling to overcome his lifelong anxiety about the ocean by taking swimming and surfing lessons. "It's the guys in their Speedos that motivate me. You'll get the cute motorcycle guys in their leathers! These daredevil dudes have fears too," Nathan reassured me. "They're just not the same as ours. How relaxed do you think *they'd* be at a fashion show?"

FOR MY first motorcycle lesson I selected my black leather pants with ruffles down the legs, a tiny silver Geoffrey Beene T-shirt, and some old black boots from Manolo Blahnik. My daughter approved of the getup. "You look like a spy," she said.

Attila met me in his driving school Camry. "Where's your jacket?" he said by way of a greeting. "You'll scrape your arms if you fall." I ran back home and put on a customized jeans jacket that I had acquired in Dallas.

"That's better," Attila said as I made my second descent onto the street.

In the car he said, "Show me your boots."

I triumphantly lifted my foot to his eye level.

"I'm glad to see that they don't have stilettos. But the soles should be thicker and harder, preferably rubber," he said as I lowered my foot. "A motorcyclist's boots should be like a second pair of tires. But they'll do for today."

We drove to the spot where the driving school's motorcycle, a red Honda Nighthawk 250, was parked, in the East Sixties. To me, it seemed huge and nasty, a chimera about to spit fire. "Follow me in the car," Attila commanded.

He put on the driving school's helmet and hopped on the bike. We pulled out into the street, Attila heading up our little motorcade. Under his strapping body, the bike shrank to the proportions of a Shetland pony. It could have been a tricycle.

There was a long alley tucked under the FDR Drive near Seventy-ninth Street where Attila trained his motorcycle students. It was safeguarded from intruding traffic by a low elevation and by high retaining walls on three sides. Except for a discarded mattress, the smooth runway was entirely void of objects and people.

"You know how to ride a bicycle?"

"Yes, but I haven't been on one in at least twenty-five years."

"First, the right helmet." Attila removed from the backseat of the school's Camry small, medium, and large models.

The cheek pads of the small, in white, squeezed my face like an overly affectionate grandmother. The large, in red, wobbled around on my head like a gyroscope. The medium, in black, fit just right—a protective embrace for the head. I saw my image reflected in the car's window. On me the helmet resembled one of André Courrèges's bubble hats from his 1964 Space Age collection. I could see from the way Attila evaluated me rapidly through narrowed eyes that the helmet was flattering.

"Take your earrings off," he said.

I handed him my little white-gold-and-diamond Mish flowers.

Attila then gave me the ten-cent tour of the bike, much of it familiar from diagrams in my study booklet, the motorcycle operator's manual—gearshift, clutch, throttle, front brake, rear brake, kickstand, emergency engine cutoff switch.

"How do you mount this? From the left?"

"Like a horse. You've done that before?"

Not since summer camp, on a horse named Hercules, and I was no more a natural equestrian than I was a born driver. I hopped on the vehicle from the left, kicking my right leg higher in the air than necessary.

"Now, stand up with your feet on the ground and rock the bike between your legs like this." He stood facing me, demonstrating how to shuttle the metal monster left to right, right to left, thigh to thigh. Though the motorcycle weighed about 220 pounds, dry, it was not too hard a stunt to perform, thanks to Sharyl, my Pilates instructor.

"OK, that's enough. You don't have to swing the bike so low to the ground."

Yes, I was showing off—because I suspected this would be my last opportunity to do so. Evidently, the purpose of this exercise was to gauge the strength and length of my legs.

"You wouldn't believe what a workout this can be for your arms and legs. Now you may sit down."

"Almost every beginner opens the throttle when she means to close it. Hold it just with your palm and two fingers."

Simple enough. Forewarned is forearmed.

He switched on the ignition.

Feeling that motorcycle throbbing beneath me was an almost naughty thrill. It felt like a hot rocket about to fire. Attila held the bike by its right handlebar, as if it were a stallion on a short lead.

"I've fixed the bike so you won't have to switch gears, and so it won't go faster than fifteen miles per hour. Pick up your feet off the ground, place them on the footrests. Now go!"

As the Honda catapulted into the long cul-de-sac, it started listing severely to the left, nearly parallel to the ground.

Attila, who had been running alongside the bike, yanked it rightward, upward, toward himself. He flipped the emergency cutoff switch. The bike stopped. I was erect again, feet on the ground.

"Are you OK?" he asked.

"Are *you* OK?" I asked.

"Yes, if you are."

"What happened?" I asked.

"You weren't looking where you were going. You were focusing on the gauges."

I had no memory of seeing them, or anything else.

"We're going to try again. But this time scan ahead and look up, not low."

I hopped on the Nighthawk again, raised my feet to the foot pegs again, and let the missile surge forward. Attila ran alongside me, again holding on to the right handlebar. In my mind's eye, I was absolutely vertical, perfectly centered, strictly perpendicular to the ground. There was no way I was going to lose my balance this time. I looked straight out into the distance. I felt composed and sure.

But the whole shuddering machine started tilting precariously to the left again, sinking sideways like a waterlogged toy sailboat. Once more, Attila righted the Nighthawk and activated the emergency cutoff switch.

"Why did that happen again?" I asked, when my feet were back on solid ground. Attila unbuckled my chin strap and helped me remove the helmet.

"Maybe you'd like a cigarette?" he replied, rolling one for himself with one hand. He had exchanged his Dunhills for do-it-yourself Drum tobacco and papers. This archaic smoker's rite fascinated me.

"I just may have one."

"Oh, no you don't," he said flicking his match to the asphalt.

"Let's get out of the sun," I said, stepping into the shadow of one of the apartment buildings rising above us like battlements.

"Why don't we sit in the car instead? You take the driver's seat. Amy," he continued, taking a final drag on his homemade cylinder of tobacco, "some people are cut out to ride motorcycles, and some people aren't. Recently, I started to anticipate that you would have problems. But I first had to demonstrate to you how serious, how dangerous, and how difficult a motorcycle can be. Are you disappointed?"

"No. Are you?"

"No. I feel very proud about the way you drove the car. That was your first time driving by yourself in the city. You made good observations, excellent lane changes."

"Attila, I never dreamed of becoming a motorcyclist. It was never one of my fantasies. I tried it only because you suggested it, like when you suggested the stick shift. I'd been seeing this more as physical therapy for my brain—an exercise to wake up the part of it that never could understand anything mechanical or spatial."

"I know. I am aware of that, and I respect that. You don't realize how close that motorcycle was to falling on you. It could have crushed your leg, or worse. You don't realize your fragility; you could have lost a lot more than your balance. This was very hard for me to do. I don't mean the physical effort. I do that every day. What I mean is, I didn't like putting somebody I . . . like so much at such a risk."

"Attila, thank you. I'm very grateful. Thank you so much. But while you're sitting here reflecting on how you saved my life, I'm thinking about how to save my story! How am I supposed to write an article for *Travel + Leisure* about learning to ride a motorcycle if I flunk out after one lesson? One hundred percent on the written test, zero on the practical side. Well, I was always good at book learning."

"I know that."

"All right, so tell me, what did happen?"

"Amy," Attila explained gently, "you panicked—you were so stunned that you weren't even there. You were somewhere else."

"Did the panic register on my face?" I asked, remembering how serene I felt.

"No, your fear was so deep it didn't even show on your face. Only in the actions of your body. You were disoriented."

As Martha Graham said, "Movement doesn't lie."

We were no longer alone. A little boy, about six, accompanied by a husky male baby-sitter, trundled into the alley on a bicycle. The child rolled up to the left side of the car, where I sat in the driver's seat by the open window, at the dead end. He waved to us. We waved back. The child did a U-turn and pedaled back up to the mouth of the alley, and then back down to us again. He paused once more by the open car window, once more raising his hand in salutation. And then, instead of waving at us, he started striking my face, emitting little grunts with each blow. The baby-sitter reprimanded his ward sharply.

"Are you OK?" Attila asked, for the second time.

"Yes, yes, but that little boy . . ." Tears sprang to my eyes, for this mixed-up, impulsive, autistic child—and (as no tears are purely selfless) for me as well.

The baby-sitter stooped over the car door to address us. "Could you move the motorcycle, please?" He was afraid of the boy inflicting further damage.

"It's all right. We're leaving now," Attila said softly. And driving the Camry, I shadowed him out of the alley, to the East Sixties,where he reparked the motorcycle.

"Did you notice I was riding in the center of the lane?"

I nodded.

"Do you know why?"

I remembered this from the motorcycle operator's manual.

155

"So no cars could invade your lane—to protect your safe cushion." Attila wouldn't be asking me this question, would he, unless he was considering further motorcycle lessons?

"Let me think some more about what happened," he said. "Maybe one day we can try again with a lighter bike. I need to break it all down in my mind—analyze not just what took place but why."

WHILE I was away in Boston for the weekend, I learned from an article in the *Boston Globe,* delivered to my Four Seasons Hotel room with breakfast, that 9 percent of Harley riders were now women, up from 2 percent 15 years ago. The median family income of a Harley rider had risen to $78,300, and the average owner's age was forty-six. If you fit into this demographic, hard-core bikers might label you a Rub, a derisive acronym for "rich urban biker."

Back in New York, I resolved my journalistic dilemma. As learning to ride a motorcycle before my *Travel + Leisure* deadline was now out of the question, I would instead write about the more passive (and some say more dangerous) experience of riding on the "queen seat."

"For that, we'll need to rent a bike," Attila said. "A big one. And we have to get some gear." (Several years before I met him, Attila, presumably for financial reasons, had divested himself of his Suzuki and his leathers.)

My first stop for motorcycle clothing was the cult store Chrome Hearts, which has expanded the definition of biker gear to include black leather condom cases, phallus-shaped bongs, and Goth bottled water. "We also sell boots, jackets, gloves, and pants," said Chrome Hearts' publicist, Della. "But no helmets."

"Amy, you've got to go to a basic biker's shop," Attila said when I called him on the way out. "Not a movie star boutique with four-thousand-dollar leather jackets. There's one on Eleventh Avenue."

At Gearhead Accessories, the establishment in question, Attila pulled down from a rack a men's XL mesh polyester black summer jacket. Its exterior label read "Joe Rocket Ballistic," and its shoulder padding was commensurate with a quarterback's. There was further cushioning at the elbows (the equivalent of the couter in a medieval suit of armor), and down the back as well, where it became segmented and articulated like the plates of an armadillo. Attila also chose an XL Arai helmet, in black, and Joe Rocket fingerless gloves, in some equally superhuman size. In his full regalia he looked like a futuristic, mutant knight in shining armor. Betty, the salesclerk at Gearhead Accessories, selected a lady's size 8 Vanson perforated-leather summer jacket for me. It was short and tapered, with a peplum and several secret interior compartments. Miraculously, the jacket fit as if it were cut on my own personal dress form.

"You look like a Shoei girl," Betty said next, lowering a Japanese carbon-fiber helmet over my skull. It felt lighter than the school's helmet, more like an aureole than a vise.

"She needs goggles too," Attila said.

He chose a pair whose yellow lenses and black rims gave me the crusading appearance of the sixties cartoon bug Atom Ant. "They look very stylish," he said. I felt as if my whole being were undergoing reconstruction, from the DNA on up.

Attila went outside to drop more quarters into the parking meter.

"Betty, I don't even know how to ride a motorcycle," I confessed. "All I have is my learner's permit. My one and only lesson was a disaster. How long have you been riding?" She was dainty and pale, but she sure knew her way around biker equipment.

"I don't know how to ride."

"Really? You don't? You fooled me!"

"Well, I've spent a lot of time on the backseat."

"Boyfriend?"

"Ex-husband. I was in the garment industry, but my company closed down after 9/11. My landlord found me this job."

Attila reentered the shop and leaned over the horizontal display case with me while Betty rang up our sale.

"So what made you decide to ride a motorcycle?" Betty asked me, bagging the merchandise.

"The guy to my left," I answered. She studied us with a puzzled smile. We were an improbable pair, all right, but that's why it worked.

"This is the first time I've had gear but no bike," Attila said outside on the street as we loaded our packages into the car.

On the West Side Highway, a throttle-happy motorcyclist hovered for a moment beside us and then whizzed away.

"That is just a picture to you, Amy. But to me—a biker without a bike—just hearing that sound is enough to tear my heart apart. A motorcycle is not like a car," he added wistfully. "Every time you get on it, it is new all over again."

THE *New York Post* ran a Thursday supplement called "Ride," with a lead feature about girls and motorcycles. Eight percent of the state's forty-one thousand motorcycle license holders were now female, the article stated, and the largest regional motorcycle school was owned by a woman.

"You didn't have to tell me that," Attila said that evening via cell phone. "Half my students these days are girls. I had one this morning who was zero mileage."

"A beginner? How'd *she* do on her first lesson?"

"Really well. Look, Amy, I told you some people are cut out for it and others aren't."

"Well, what kind of girl was this zero-mileage student, who did so well on her first day?"

"South African. Her boyfriend is a biker. They recently sailed from Africa to the U.S. in a boat, living only on water and the fish they caught from the sea."

"For fun?"

"Yes, of course for fun."

I was way out of my depth.

Two-Up

Attila rented a purple Harley Fat Boy from Lighthouse Harley-Davidson in Huntington Station, Long Island, where we had first driven in the Viper. The soft-tail Fat Boy (Arnold Schwarzenegger drove one in *Terminator II*) had a twin-cam 88.0-cubic-inch engine, nearly three times bigger than the school's Honda Nighthawk, and weighed six hundred sixty-six pounds, nearly triple its weight. On a sweltering, hundred-degree July day, Attila phoned to say he was on his way to my house to give me an introductory ride. Minutes later, I beheld him standing beside the Harley outside my front door. He was rigged out in his new gear, his helmet in his hand and his jacket zipped open over a sweat-soaked tank top. He looked more relaxed, happier, and larger than I'd ever seen him. He resembled a warrior with his steed.

"You look complete for the first time since I've known you," I said.

"I'm glad you can see that."

I could hardly wait to get on board.

I jumped on the backseat and we rode north to Ninety-sixth

Street, sliced through Central Park at the transverse, headed south a few blocks, crossed back east again on Eighty-sixth Street, shot up Third Avenue, and then came to a halt at my front door. I could not reconstruct anything about our short itinerary until after the fact because, on the bike, time and space were suspended. The wind was strumming us, the park parted for us like a billowing green sea upon which end-of-workday pedestrians milled, children bobbed, ballplayers darted, music pulsed. At a red light—a pause button that brought this phantasmagoria to a fleeting standstill—I murmured over Attila's shoulder, over the blasts of the Harley's engine, "You don't know how much I am loving this."

He turned his helmeted left profile to me. "I do. I can feel it."

I did not feel shy about holding on to his waist.

Outside my building, when I removed the helmet (detaching a blue topaz Mish earring from my lobe in the process), I said, "I want to do that again. And again."

"You will. But because this was your first time, I kept it short and sweet."

"Too short. Too sweet."

"That was only ten minutes, and just thirty miles an hour."

"I loved the click-click-click noise of the gears changing. It's like music."

"That's timing, my dear. A rhythm you must have inside of you." And he took off.

I then noticed that the earring was missing. I found it fifteen minutes later, inside my underclothes.

OUR FIRST extended ride came a few days afterward. In retrospect, I understood why Attila kept that first taste of the motorcycle bite-size—it was just enough to whet my appetite, but not enough to scare me off. Our mission on the second time out was to extend the rental period of the Fat Boy at the Long Island dealership—a trip of about an hour and a half's duration each way. I put on a pair of brown pants, a brown cashmere camisole, and some Blahnik boots. Into the secret compartments of the Vanson jacket I zipped my cell phone and a tube of MAC Viva Glam lipstick. Slinging the helmet upside down around my wrist like a purse, I met Attila three blocks from my house, at Frank's, the Turkish cosmetician's.

We exited Manhattan via the Queensboro Bridge. In traversing this bridge I was also somehow crossing the threshold of my motorcycle tolerance. What threw me into the first panic was the magnified sight of the crayon-bright Roosevelt Island tram scuttling along on its high wire so close to the bridge. The disorderly network of tram cables, bridge girders, and roads seemed to be bearing down on me, collapsing all around me, ensnaring me. It was a replay of the old driving anxiety, which I thought had been eradicated for good. I held on to Attila more tightly, pressing hard enough, I imagined, to leave two handprint-shaped bruises on his midriff.

From there the terrors proliferated and grew. Everything on the highway became hypervivid—each bump, each groove, each painted line, each driver in each car, each road sign. I couldn't edit out anything. The environment was too live, too strong, too real—there was no background, only foreground. Every time we zoomed through an underpass I felt that my head would not make the clearance.

Then a thought lodged tenaciously in my brain. I was going to black out from dehydration—the sun and the wind were cracking my lips and parching my skin. I felt as if I were losing gallons of moisture with each RPM. If I fainted, I would fall off the bike. I was so convinced that I would pass out that

I concentrated all my energy on persuading myself that this wasn't going to happen, which only made me focus on the fear more.

And just as this obsessive fixation began to grind itself away, a new anxiety emerged. The wind started to lift the helmet from my head and fling it backward. The sun visor—which in proper position should project at a right angle from the brow—was shooting straight up from my forehead like a tiara. When we slowed down I tightened the chin strap and knocked the helmet back into place. But then as soon as we picked up speed the helmet started flying away again, now with the chin strap digging painfully into the underbelly of my throat. My neck and shoulder muscles were going into spasm from the force I was exerting to restrain the recalcitrant helmet. I prayed for our exit to come before I lost the helmet, fainted, and fell to the highway with an unprotected head. I thought of my daughter motherless. Finally we decelerated enough for Attila to hear me.

"Is it exit 40, or 49?" he asked.

"It's 49," I replied. "Huntington. I'm having problems with my helmet. It's flying off my head."

"The sun visor's catching the wind," he said calmly but not particularly sympathetically. "And you're holding your head too high—keep it down. Have you noticed," he said, changing the subject, I presumed, to deflect my anxiety, "that as soon as we hit thirty the wind becomes cool?"

Positioning the head lower made a real difference. Now all I needed to do was quench my thirst.

"Do you see how I scan all the way into the distance to the cars at the end of the curve?" he said at the next slowdown. "I start downshifting when they start braking. I do not wait to see what the car in front of me is doing—if you wait that long, then you're already too late."

When we coasted into the parking lot of Lighthouse Harley, I said to Attila, "I will never look at the road the same way again. I noticed everything, maybe too clearly."

"That's good," he replied. "This will really help you with your driving. But you don't need to lean your body every which way to look around. Every time you shifted your weight I had to compensate for it by shifting the bike in the opposite direction—tough work on a six-hundred-pound machine, and not safe."

"But if I don't lean around you, all I'm seeing is the back of your helmet."

"To see, you only need to pivot your head on your neck slightly, and slide your eyes from side to side. Don't fidget so much. To ride in the back, you have to become one with me."

That was the statement that did it.

"I'm never getting on the backseat with anyone but you," I vowed.

"You'd better not," he said gravely. "Don't leave that there, Amy!" he said, taking my helmet off the Fat Boy's handlebar, where I had just hung it. "That's your gear!"

At Lighthouse Harley we drank some water, renewed our Fat Boy rental, looked at the new Harley V-Rods for sale, and took off.

The ride home was an altogether different journey. This time, I was so at ease I was barely holding on to Attila. Sometimes I even rested my hands on my thighs. My helmet stayed in place, my neck and shoulders were relaxed. It was like a longer version of the first ten-minute spin—but for me it was still not long enough. In the reflective black hemisphere of Attila's helmet, I could see a new sight—me smiling beatifically, nonstop. This ride was the best high I'd ever known—better than champagne, a little closer to love. Attila corrected me only once, warning that I should be careful when stretching my legs away from the foot pegs. "If I take off while your feet are still on the ground, you could fall."

When I dismounted in front of my apartment building and removed my helmet and goggles, he peered into my eyes and said, "Amy, you are high from this. Now you know what it's all about."

"I do feel drugged," I said blissfully. "When do you come down from this?"

"Never."

"When can we do this again?"

"Tomorrow, but just for a brief run around town. I feel like the cylinders are in my head! This Fat Boy is a real workout, a beast—and it's a furnace too, because there's no radiator. It's air-cooled. I've lost at least a pound in water weight."

THE FOLLOWING day I put on black snakeskin pants, a purple cashmere camisole, black Manolo boots, and the Vanson jacket, of which I was becoming quite fond. I zipped into its interior pockets a credit card, lipstick, and, instead of a phone, this time a pen and notebook. I carried the helmet like a handbag, with the goggles inside. I stopped at the neighborhood Mail Boxes Etc. An attractive brunette girl waiting in line beside me stole a few glances, then said, "You look really cool!" I went to my Pilates class, and thanked Sharyl, the teacher, for making me strong enough to hang on to my seat. "It's all in the inner thighs," she said. On the way out of the studio, I was stopped by a woman whom I've known slightly for many years.

"Amy!" she accosted me. "Are big shoulders back? Should I put pads in my jackets?"

"This is gear," I replied.

"Oh," she said. "I thought it was fashion."

On a Lexington Avenue sidewalk a boy who could not have been more than fifteen brazenly gave me a once-over. What is it about motorcycle gear?

RIDING AROUND the city was in certain respects even more of a kick than highway cruising. It couldn't just have been the cloudless, sparkling, seventy-five-degree day that gave our jaunt through Manhattan such an otherworldly clarity. I was seeing the city, where I have lived for twenty-four years, through reborn eyes. Architectural details on buildings, invisible from a car, imperceptible on foot, popped out with a hallucinatory sharpness. Every block sped by like a flawlessly directed, fast-forwarded movie. Enigmatic sights thrust themselves into view, then quickly receded. A girl's gauzy summer skirt swirled around her legs like jellyfish tentacles, two mothers pushed identical empty prams, a shirtless young man gesticulated to a companion in suit and tie. It was like looking at the world through a freshly cleaned window, seeing without eyelids.

We stopped by Gearhead Accessories to exchange Attila's Joe Rocket jacket, which had shed one of its industrial-strength snaps. Irresistibly, we were drawn into the parent shop, Motorhead, where the real hardware—the motorcycles—were for sale. I followed Attila around while he surveyed the bikes and asked questions.

"You're really loving this," he said. "How would you like to buy a bike together, fifty-fifty?"

This suggestion was pure folly, but there was only one possible answer I could give.

"I'd love to."

We browsed some more, and he settled on a Yamaha Roadstar Warrior, a cruiser–sport bike with a seventeen-hundred-cubic-centimeter engine.

A leviathan of a woman, stuffed into a logo-adorned biker's jacket, swaggered over to us. "What do you ride?" she asked me, thumbs hooked into her metal-laden belt.

"Right now, a Fat Boy, but on the backseat."

She seemed a little amused by this girlish declaration. "That's *my* bike out there, honey," she said, pointing to a ferocious yellow behemoth on the sidewalk. "And that, baby, is My Dick!"

Politely, I responded, "Do you drive anything besides motorcycles?"

"Oh yeah, I drive a bus."

"That's your job?"

"Yep. I'm a city bus driver."

Ron, the Motorhead salesman, made a play for our attention. "We can get the Roadstar in titanium for you in a week. Is that too long a wait?"

"Not at all," Attila and I said together.

"You two are different from most of my customers. Everyone wants to drive their new bikes out of the shop on the same day."

"We're patient," Attila said.

THAT WEEKEND (while I was out of town and Attila was working) I noticed I was a little irritable, like a smoker who had recently kicked the habit. I realized I was in withdrawal—I needed to get back on that bike. I was counting the hours until Tuesday, when we would take our final trip on the Fat Boy, to Bear Mountain. On the designated day, Attila picked me up after lunch at Michael's on West Fifty-fifth Street. A cluster of book and magazine editors (who had already received their first frisson when I walked into the restaurant in my gear) assembled on the sidewalk to watch Attila spirit me away.

On that last day I discovered that on a motorcycle—just as in a dream—neither past nor future existed. There was no present either—only a pure, in-the-instant-and-gone being. The senses functioned in some other warped dimension. The odor of skunk along the highway was a memory an instant before it was even smelled. Maybe it had something to do with the wind.

We swooped and glided upward through winding roads, a free-form stage for Attila to demonstrate his cornering and leaning skills—which involved, I had read in my new book, *Proficient Motorcycling*, intentionally destabilizing the bike in order to negotiate curves and turns smoothly and safely (not easily accomplished on a Fat Boy with its low-lying footboards). With a graceful, precise motorcyclist like Attila, it felt as if you were taking the earth up skyward with you when you leaned—a gravity-defying cycling sensation with affinities to stunt piloting or figure skating.

When we reached the topmost observation area of Bear Mountain, Attila produced a can of Red Bull from his backpack, which he had toted along for me as a dehydration preventative. The panorama of majestic valley, sparkling river, fertile farmland unfurling far, far below us was sublimely peaceful—so still after all that motion.

"This is such a beautiful place," Attila said slowly, gazing outward. "For five and a half years I've been wanting to come up here by motorcycle. Everything I ask for, he gives me. I have only had to learn patience." He lit a cigarette, and placed one foot on a boulder. I took a seat on a rock beneath him, and looked up at his profile, thrown into high relief against the infinite vista.

"Life is so amazing if you understand it even this much." He placed the pads of his right thumb and forefinger close together as though they were holding a pinch of sugar between them. "Most people pass through life without understanding anything at all, and they are miserable."

I felt inexplicably alive and happy—as if a warm, golden, honeyed light was filling me up and flooding into the space between us.

We were both quiet.

"We made it up here in an hour and a half," he said, turning to me at last. He was tempering the mood, as he invariably did whenever feelings became potent.

"Was I crowding you?" I wasn't really sure what I meant by that question. Maybe I was wondering if he would have preferred to make the trip alone.

"What do you mean?"

"On the bike."

"Oh. Yeah. You need to sit higher up. You were too low down on the seat, sitting too close against me. That's why I had to stretch out my legs so often."

"I guess I took a little too seriously your advice that I had to 'become one with you.'"

He laughed. And then he gave me his succinct opinion of each person he had met on the sidewalk outside Michael's, every comment a perfect little jewel of observation. I was still sitting on my rock staring up at him.

THE NIGHT before, over the phone, I had told Attila that among the thousand images of him that I had retained from the past nine months, two stood out indelibly. The first one was the sight of him leaning against his Acura, arms crossed, waiting for me at my corner, on the day I met him—day one of our driving lessons. The second was the vision of him standing expectantly outside my front door beside the Harley Fat Boy, his helmet in his hand, his undershirt beneath the motorcycle jacket, and his hair, drenched with perspiration.

"When I was drifting off to sleep," I said to him, rising from my rock, "I thought more about those two persistent images of you, and I figured out why among all others they stand out so distinctly."

"And?"

"And the reason they stand out is that in each instance you were offering to show me something I'd never done before, to introduce me to somewhere I'd never gone before."

"And I will continue to do that for you."

"And I will continue to come along."

We descended the mountaintop and returned to the city.

"IF WE do share a bike," Attila said that night by telephone, "you will own the back wheel and I will own the front."

"Because I'm on the backseat?"

"No. I'll explain. On a motorcycle, the front wheel supplies the braking power—that's me—and the back wheel is what pushes the bike forward. You, Amy, have supplied the force, the energy that has made me grow."

"And you'll keep growing because I can give out more energy. But really, do you think it's a good idea to get a bike together?"

"Sure. Why not? It's just another merge."

"Two lanes into one?"

"I don't know how many lanes into one."

"Well, if we do, I don't want anyone else going two-up with you. Even if you buy it on your own. A lot of people are going to be asking you for rides."

"Then they can wait until their next lifetimes, because you will be the one exception. Otherwise, I ride alone."

Mercedes Joe

Just when I was wondering what my follow-up to the Fat Boy would be, Jim, the same friend who had sent me to the Bentley boys, dropped Joe into my life. "Joe's in the PR department at Mercedes," Jim said. "Mercedes is relaunching a vintage brand called Maybach. An early production version of the new Maybach car will be coming over on the *QE2* from Southampton, England, in late June. Joe's looking for a journalist to accompany the Maybach on its maiden voyage to New York. Would it be OK if I gave him your telephone number?"

When Joe called, he pitched me hard on everything—the Maybach, the transatlantic crossing, and, without really intending to, himself. It was an instantaneous rapport, and before we hung up Joe and I had already analyzed a few reasons why. A bachelor aesthete in the macho bastion of the auto industry, he was thrilled to have found a kindred spirit who shared both his camp sensibility and his passion for cars and driving. Likewise, I was overjoyed to discover a partner with whom I could zigzag back and forth between my old and new worlds—someone who could not only recognize a Geoffrey Beene dress but also introduce me to such arcane automotive terms as "suicide door." (It hinges open the opposite way, the better to hurl yourself into eternity.)

I declined Joe's QE2 invitation, but I did consent to greet the Maybach when it made its triumphal approach into Manhattan. Hoisted from the QE2's foredeck by an Erickson Air-Crane, the automobile sailed through the sky to Wall Street—rather like Fellini's helicopter-borne statue of Jesus in the opening scene of *La Dolce Vita*. And so it was at the Wall Street Regent Hotel's grand ballroom, where the car was displayed for the day, that I first encountered both the Maybach and Joe. Both of them, it turned out, were dark and elongated, over twenty feet in one case, almost six-foot-three in the other.

Wilhelm Maybach—the early-twentieth-century German engineer for whom the vehicle was named—"was an automotive innovator, an unsung Henry Ford," Joe lectured me (he spoke rapidly.) "He drafted the blueprint for the first modern passenger car, with the engine up front, driving the rear wheels." In 1901 Wilhelm Maybach designed the original Mercedes, named for the daughter of his patron, Emil Jellinek. In 1921 Wilhelm's son Karl began producing engines and chassis on cars with the formidable double-M Maybach logo; his customers included opera heartthrob Enrico Caruso, boxing champion Max Schmeling, King Paul of Greece, and Emperor Haile Selassie of Ethiopia. The revived Maybach I was ogling beneath the hotel's coffered dome was a sybaritic, three-hundred-fifty-thousand-dollar, custom-built dream machine, not available yet to U.S. consumers, but already on order in Europe for such clients as the royal family of Holland.

Even though the vernissage of the Maybach had more or less ended—drained champagne flutes and crumb-strewn buffet trays were littering the ballroom—the four men sprawled in-side the only Maybach in the New World showed no signs of moving.

Joe rapped on the car's enormous double-paned window. "Amy would like a turn inside," he announced. All but one of the men gave up their spots. We took over the two backseats, Joe on the right, I on the left. Joe demonstrated how the grand napa leather chairs could recline like recamiers, or hospital beds cranked up to a TV-watching position. And in case the need for a television fix arose, embedded in a frame before each seat was a flat-screen television with DVD players. There were also slick folding desktops, a telephone, and a second set of dashboard gauges, on which backseat drivers could monitor speed, time, and temperature. Arcing over our heads was a mul-lioned skylight, which modulated, at the flick of a switch, from opaque to transparent. And tucked into a cupboard between our plump chaises longues was an icebox, stocked with cham-pagne bottles and silver goblets.

"Would you like a glass of champagne?" asked Brian, the light-haired man in the front seat who had not evacuated on Joe's request. Brian turned out to be a Mercedes manager, and eyeing my bare legs extending from my short, slit, polka-dot Beene, he said to Joe, "We could use her in a Maybach ad to show how much legroom we have. So, Amy," he said, turning back to me, "how do you like the opera lighting?" He was point-ing to a trio of chrome sconces, as flawless in their form as teardrops. "How about the Dolby Surround Sound system? We've got twenty-one speakers."

"Amy will really appreciate the cabinet work on the doors and dashboard," Joe interjected. "It's Indonesian aboyna root, and three-dimensional. See how the profile projects? Go ahead, touch it. What do you think?"

"It's so perfect it seems fake," I said.

"You could order it in cherry, burred walnut, or piano lacquer instead, even granite if you don't want wood," Joe ticked off. "Just about *anything* can be custom ordered, the same as if you were building a house."

"Or a yacht," Brian said.

"Could you match the exterior paint to a swatch of fabric from a dress?"

"Yes," Joe said. "And remember you have two choices, if your Maybach's two-toned."

"Well, then it's the car version of couture."

"You completely get the idea of Maybach, Amy," Joe said.

"Intelligent design seems to be happening in cars these days, not fashion," I said.

"And on top of that," Brian continued, diverting the conversation to more manly matters, "the Maybach's got a five-hundred-and-fifty-horsepower, twin-turbocharged, V-12 engine, six hundred and sixty-four pounds of torque, and it does zero to sixty in five-point-three seconds." This, I was told, was faster than a Porsche Boxster S and equivalent to an Aston Martin Vantage Volante—neither of which was a three-ton Tessie (the Maybach tips the scales at over six thousand pounds), much less a "lounge on wheels" (as Maybach promotional literature phrased it). But, Brian explained, armored with eighteen airbags, back and front seat belt pre-tensioners to prevent passengers from submarining beneath the harnesses in a crash, and six protective brake calipers, the mighty Maybach was as safe as it was powerful. And unlike most cars, which typically have been driven by twenty people before the buyer even inserts his key into the ignition, the Maybach is shipped in an inviolable vacuum-sealed container that keeps the machine immaculate—at least until the owner has his way with it.

"I can't imagine why anyone would ever want to fly any-where in a plane if they could be driven in this car!" I ex-claimed. It had happened again. I had fallen madly in love with yet another car—without ever having seen it move. It was exciting, this new tendency to get crushes on automo-biles.

"Amy," Joe said, shaking me back to my senses, "time to get out. Unless you want to end up with the car back in Sindelfin-gen, Germany, at the Maybach Center of Excellence. They'll be coming soon to take it away." Because it operated on some kind of cat's-paw-like hydraulic-pneumatic system, the door glided open noiselessly, exactly to the angle we desired.

THE NEXT time Joe called, shortly after he had inducted me into the mysteries of the Maybach, it was to share his passion for yet another expensive automobile, Mercedes's new AMG performance car, the SL55, still not available for sale. He had just driven it from Chicago back to the East Coast, where only seventeen roamed the roads.

"The SL55 is the nearest thing to perfection I've ever experi-enced in a car. Why don't you see for yourself? I want to show you. Can I run by and pick you up in it now?"

If the Viper waiting outside my door earlier in the month was raw viscera—more blood, guts, and muscle than metal—then the SL55 was an ethereal streak of silver shining energy. Lanky Joe stood in front of the car in mirrored sunglasses, whose re-flective surfaces were shooting off cool spikes of sunlight. Be-neath them, he was grinning giddily.

"Before you get in—watch how the top comes down."

Joe pressed a button hidden in the anthracite interior, and the roof—cantilevered on calligraphic double hinges—was swallowed up in two bites into the rear of the car. It was a sur-real performance, a metamorphosis worthy of Ovid.

After waffling for a moment, Joe decided he'd let me drive —that's how badly he wanted a partner in his newfound fana-ticism. "Did you check your side mirrors?" he admonished tensely as I adjusted the seat and started to pull out. There was not a thing wrong with them, except the reflection in the right one of a car coming straight toward us. That threat to his $120,000 bauble flustered Joe, but not quite as much as the abrupt realization—when he paused, midprattle, fifteen min-utes later to survey his surroundings—that I had piloted his precious SL55 far uptown, into a rather sketchy neighborhood.

"Amy, you're going to get us carjacked! Do you know how to get out of here?"

"This route's pretty familiar to me," I reassured him.

"Why, is your crack dealer on this block?"

In fact, I knew the general area from countless driving les-sons. "And I earned my driver's license not far from here in the South Bronx," I added cheerfully, like a tour bus guide. "There's a great fried chicken place somewhere nearby in case you're hungry."

"You were driving a '92 Acura then, Amy, not an '03 SL55! Can you just get us out of here?" He shut his eyes, wishing him-self out of the area, sealing himself off from the source of his pain.

"The SL55's so discreet, nobody's even paying attention. We're not as visible as you think."

"Well, then it's a good thing they didn't send me the SL55 in Magma Red with a Berry interior!" he replied, flopping back helplessly onto his head restraint.

When we finally hit a familiar street—Central Park West—

Joe heaved a sigh, sat up straight, and resumed his chatter. He told me about how he entertained himself as a child—first in England, and then in L.A.—playing with his collection of toy cars. "They're still in a suitcase under my bed. I played with them until I was embarrassingly old—about fifteen. The cars were my friends. When I lost my favorite Corgi—it was a Mercedes; isn't that weird?—I dreamt about it every night for two years. I just have always felt happier with cars than with people. I'd really like to find somebody to settle down with. But the truth is, I feel best when I'm alone, driving long distances in a car."

"Well, the things you seek are usually the same ones that you flee. Joe, you and Attila have a lot in common. You've got to meet. Were you your mother's favorite?"

"I'd say it's pretty intense between the two of us. I think my mother and I are working out some unfinished business leftover from a previous life. And I imagine it's going to take us a few more lifetimes to figure it out."

"Well, then, isn't it fairly simple? You're in a perpetual state of flight from Mom—trying to separate, in this lifetime anyway, but at the same time drawn right back to her. That's why you love driving away, fast, but are also good at forming tight friendships quickly. Look at us. How's that for bargain-basement psychoanalysis? I would apply the same principle to Attila."

I had gradually pieced together that Attila, the firstborn and the family pet, was poised for flight from the moment he could walk—bolting from the family dinner table, escaping into the driver's seat of his parents' friends' cars, declaring at eight that one day he, like his uncle in Germany, would leave home. He went so far as to join a Turkish folk dance troupe (the boys were costumed in embroidered vests, knee-high lace-up boots, flowing blouses, and pantaloons), with the intention of defecting during a tour abroad. He quit, however, "because too many of the dancers had lost eyes and fingers, from the sword and shield routines that were part of our dance. We beat out rhythms and lunged at our partners with them. Our group used to welcome tourists on cruise ships. I think our performances scared them more than they entertained them."

Just as Joe and I were gaining confidence in my handling of the SL55, it was time to go home. I parked the car across the street from my apartment building and we stood around the SL55, hands on our hips, awed into silent admiration; the car was as much of a pleasure to look at as it was to drive.

"Isn't the back view of this car extraordinary?" Joe said, almost lasciviously. "It's got a self-satisfied little smile, like the Cheshire cat's."

"You're right, it's an inward, enigmatic smile, like the *Mona Lisa's.*"

While we were studying the SL55's sphinxlike rear end, a beefy blonde cabbie popped out of his yellow taxi, and—indifferent to the traffic light as it winked from red to green—he shouted, "Hey! Congratulations! I am German. That SL55 AMG is the best Mercedes to come out since the 280SL in 1969. Nothing like great German engineering!" He waved farewell, jumped back into his cab, and drove away, uncorking the block-long traffic jam that had formed behind him.

"That was the first German taxi driver I've ever seen," I said, "and a whole different type from the guys who admired the Viper. What do you think of the Viper, Joe?" Dodge and Mercedes were now both members of the DaimlerChrysler brotherhood, so Joe was bound to have a piquant opinion.

"I think the Viper is vile, the most loathsome car on the planet," Joe replied, crinkling his face as if I had just waved an open container of rancid cottage cheese under his delicate nostrils. "I would not be seen with one in public."

He might as well have blasphemed my best friend—I felt that hurt. Trying not to reveal the extent of the blow he had just delivered, I asked, "Why do you hate the Viper so?"

"Well, put it this way, Amy—if at gunpoint I were *forced* to drive an American muscle car, I would take a Corvette over a Viper."

"But why?"

"How do I explain this to you?" he said with the impatience of absolute belief. "If the Corvette is Vegas, then the Viper is Reno."

"Oh," I said, crestfallen. Maybe Joe and Attila wouldn't become fast friends after all. But I still could not understand. Wouldn't anyone who lives to drive love the Viper?

And then, thinking it over in fashion terms, I figured it out for myself. Two women could live for *la mode*—and one of them could be a Pucci loyalist, the other a devotee of vintage Grès. Neither lady would be wrong.

"Different tastes," I said to Joe. "I respect that." We hugged each other good-bye.

"Hey, I love that you let go last," he said. "And Amy," he added, calling out after me. "If it makes you feel any better— the Camaro Z28 is Atlantic City."

JOE PHONED again soon, with another exciting proposal—to attend a Mercedes AMG event with him, either at the end of July on a Milwaukee racetrack, or at the beginning of August somewhere near Washington, D.C. "This will be more fun for you than the *QE2* would have been," he promised. "You'll get to do laps in our top-of-the-line, current-model Mercedes performance cars—the AMGs—with professional race car drivers instructing you. There'll be some classroom time, and you'll also learn some defensive driving skills. The AMG Challenge is really for our AMG consumers, not the press—but I'll get you in."

"Are you coming, Joe?"

"Of course, sugar."

"How about the God of Driving? Can he come too?"

"Write me an official memo requesting that Attila come, and I'll see what I can do. It's time I met him, anyway."

Joe received corporate approval for Attila to participate in the AMG Challenge, and he chose the D.C. venue for us over Milwaukee. "Gorgeous, the Wisconsin accommodations turned out to be too squalid for words—shared bathrooms and other indignities. You would never have survived. I reserved three suites at the Georgetown Four Seasons."

"So fill me in, Joe," I said to him over the phone, "now that we're all committed. What are we getting ourselves into? And what on earth is AMG?"

AMG, Joe explained, was an aftermarket company founded by two German engineers, Hans Aufrecht and Erhard Melcher. "*G*," he said, "stands for Grossaspach, Aufrecht's birthplace. They collaborated with Mercedes originally to make race cars, and later, road cars. In 1999, Mercedes bought AMG, which now constitutes the company's performance-car subsidiary."

In the nine-car Mercedes AMG lineup, retail prices started upward of $100,000, and only about a thousand of each model were produced annually. The SL55 with the beguiling backside that I drove uptown with Joe was the latest AMG showstopper.

"I've decided," Joe said magnanimously, "that I'll let you and Attila drive the SL55 down to D.C. and back, but *don't* let anyone else you meet at the event know—remember, the car's not yet for sale to the public. They're all fanatical AMG customers and they'll be so jealous it could start a riot."

Bell Jar on Wheels

Every August I move out of the city to a house on a tiny island off the Connecticut coast, and one of my objectives when I called to book my inaugural highway driving session with Attila's school was to learn how to conduct myself back and forth to this beach retreat. On July 31 the Acura's monthlong residency at the garage beside Million Car Rentals would be expiring, just in time for me to make my migratory drive for the very first time.

"Would you like to come with me to get the Acura the day after tomorrow?" I asked Attila, over the phone. "I need to pick it up, fill the tank, and wash it before I go away."

"No. I don't have time. That will be a long day for me, and I'll have to get home to walk Ajan. Thirteen hours is his bladder's limit, you know—he'll be peeing out of his eyeballs if he has to wait any longer." Attila had a way of blocking further discussion on a subject—it had something to do with the calm certainty of his tone. A lead door closed, a dead bolt slid shut, and that was that. Attila had also refused to accompany me on the drive to the island, so at the last minute I conscripted my daughter's baby-sitter, a competent driver, to sit beside me in the passenger seat.

Downtown at the garage, the attendant insisted that I had exceeded my month's lease by one day, since it was now the 31st and not the 30th of July. To pass the time while he went off to fetch the Acura, I visited Mary and Sol in the Million Car Rentals office. This time they offered the Viper to me at a reduced rate of $1,400 for three days, with an option to buy it later for $60,000. I declined.

Without Attila to animate it, the Acura, a rind stripped of its fruit, looked vacant and forlorn. It seemed more dented, scratched, and flyblown than I remembered. Was this the result of the garage's neglect, or had it always been like this? Adding further insult to its undignified state were the bird droppings splattered all over its hood, doors, and windows.

"They must have parked this in the pigeons' toilet," I observed, humiliated, to the woman beside me, who had a moment ago complimented me on my pink pants. "And on top of the monthly rate of three hundred and sixty dollars, they charged me a surplus thirty-five dollars for the extra day in July. It was Julius Caesar who came up with that calendar, not me."

"Hey," she replied, "I figure it this way—whatever it costs, it's cheaper than having it stolen. And they all come down from the top coated with bird crap, because there's no roof up there."

I felt like the parent of a child that only a mother could love—*my* Acura, I thought defensively, my first, my only car. Too bad if it looks like a driving-school discard, a beaten-down hunk of junk. Yet once I sat inside and started to drive uptown (by myself!), my hard pride softened into a glow that emanated, it seemed, not just from me but from the Acura's interior itself. Getting in the car was like sinking into a soothing, scented bath. So many happy moments had accumulated over the last eight months in this car—it was as if they were all still there, thickening and sweetening the atmosphere. This was the cocoon that had regenerated me, the forge of Attila's and my curious friendship, the incubator in which the book had gestated. The car's familiar aroma, a faint cocktail of Bulgari cologne and Morning Fresh car deodorizer, worked on me like a balm. The car, I was discovering, was a bell jar on wheels. Here was the clipping I had given Attila from the *New York Post*, there was the compact black umbrella with which he had once shielded me from the rain. Inside the glove compartment was the snapshot of Ajan as a puppy, which he had brought to me on our fourth lesson, and had never taken back home.

There too were odd bits of driving school detritus—a pencil stub stamped in white with the school's name and number, a credit card receipt for Meredith's last package of lessons, and in the trunk, magnetic Student Driver signs, black against yellow. I was going to be sorry to leave the car behind on the island; I would miss it. But if I kept the Acura in the city, within a year I would be paying its cost to me all over again in garage fees.

So it was in a kind of nostalgic reverie that I rode from the East Village garage up to the East Side Car Wash and Beyond on Ninety-first. I made one mistake only—inadvertently cutting off another driver when I realized I had overshot Ninety-second Street and needed to change lanes quickly in order to make the next right turn, onto Ninety-fourth. The driver cursed, spat, and completed his feral display by giving me the finger—assuming, of course that my clumsy maneuver had been a willful, aggressive taunt. Each vehicle on the road seemed to be a tinderbox, ready to explode at the slightest provocation. I thought of one of Attila's refrains: "It's a hostile environment out there." I felt grateful for the relative composure that by example he had instilled in me.

At East Side Car Wash and Beyond, I filled the tank and sent the car through the automated bath, both new experiences. I remembered the place from having visited it once before with Attila—it had a fifties-style retro logo, and as the sign promised, they served good coffee.

The detail man stepped up to vacuum and scrub the interior. Attila had also inculcated in me the impulse to keep the car tidy—I had absorbed from him the idea that a clean automobile reflected well on its owner, especially if it had little else to recommend it. After all this primping (I was thinking of Dorothy receiving her mechanically assisted makeover at Emerald City), the Acura was still not squeaky clean enough—but it certainly was squeaking.

"What's that noise?" I asked the detail man, a long-limbed African from the Ivory Coast.

"Maybe something wrong with you back right tire? Go to tire check."

I took the car to the tire center, where the mechanic cranked it up on the lift. No, there was nothing wrong with the tires. Then what was causing the noise? I felt crushed suddenly by the overwhelming burden of owning a car, daunted by my new responsibility, miserable at my utter helplessness and abysmal ignorance. When my anxiety subsided, I opened the door to step back in—and it swung right off its hinges. So very near to tears was I that three other slender Africans, speaking to one another in French, came rushing to my aid. While they fiddled with the door I wandered into the convenience shop to search for more Morning Fresh car deodorizer and a car vacuum. I found neither, but when I returned to the Acura, the door had been successfully reattached. I tipped the guys and drove to the garage closest to my house, trying my best to ignore the attendants' unveiled expressions of disdain. They could not even see past the '92 Acura to get a fix on me.

REGARDING the trip I made the next day out of Manhattan onto I-95, through Connecticut, and up to the coastal town where the ferry leaves for the little island, I can remember three things distinctly. I had clear, written directions, which I followed like a fundamentalist text. I had a tranquil and alert co-pilot in my daughter's babysitter. And I was in such an altered state of consciousness the whole time, I experienced the trip as if it were a film with a single frame, repeated with cumulative, numbing monotony over a time span of four hours (something like Andy Warhol did in his movie *Empire*). The heavy traffic on this weekend "getaway day" (Department of Transportation lingo) nearly doubled the normal length of the trip. Interstate 95 from New York to New Haven, the route I was traveling, was designed in the 1950s to accommodate seventy thousand vehicles a day; now it carried upward of 150,000. But Attila had taught me, again by example, not to let an overcrowded highway upset me.

Every now and again I would surface long enough from my altered state to realize with amazement what I was actually doing—a secondary, watching-yourself-from-the-outside awareness similar to "lucid dreaming" (when you remind your sleeping self that a dream's "just a dream"). When we reached our destination, the ferry pier, I backed the car onto the boat, an act of faith, for the ferryman forbade me to look either into the rearview mirror or over my right shoulder. "Look straight ahead at me and follow my hand signals," he commanded. My legs felt wobbly, like a sailor's sea legs—except now I was on a boat, not on land, and an ocean wind, instead of the stale, canned breeze of the air conditioner, fanned my face.

THE PHONE was ringing when we walked through the crackled green front door of the house, burdened with luggage. It was Attila, checking that I had arrived safely. "This gives me great happiness," he was saying. "And now I can let you know that I could easily have come with you to the garage last night. I didn't because it was time to cut the cord. I had to drop you into that Acura by yourself. You had to deal with the garage, the car wash—and the drive—on your own."

"Your timing, as usual, was perfect," I said. In fact, I was marveling that he hadn't knocked me out of the nest long ago.

"You made a mistake or two while you were in the city?"

"Yes."

"That's OK—you needed to see what a hostile environment it is out there. But don't underestimate your achievement—those four hours on I-95 are tougher than anything you've done before, harder even than the drive you made to Windham with me on the stick shift."

"Really?" I said, dazed. "But I had someone else in the car helping me."

"That's good."

"Now I'll have to try riding back in the other direction, by myself."

"Amy, you did it. Congratulations. You'll do it again."

For the rest of the day I had a headache, a shoulder ache, and a neck ache so monolithic I felt that the top third of my body was one solid, stiff, fused concrete slab. My body was telling me what my mind had been hiding: I had been in a state of extreme, unrelenting tension for four hours. The aches went away after a glass of wine and a very long and deep sleep.

Bird of Prey

A week later it was time to interrupt my beach holiday— swimming and tennis, al fresco brunches—for Joe's AMG Challenge. I was beginning to reconsider the whole idea, and for inscrutable reasons of his own, so was Attila. If he came at all, Attila was telling me tersely over the phone, long distance, two days before our departure date, he would have to leave the AMG Challenge early.

"Joe put his job on the line to get us into the program," I reminded him.

"So, that means I'm chained to his schedule?"

"No," I said, with the sinking feeling that in order to mollify Attila I might have to disappoint Joe. I didn't even know why he was resisting. Hadn't he told me he always wanted to try race car driving? Next, Attila retracted his offer—if the AMG challenge was still on—to pick me up from the train station in New York (I was not prepared to make that drive again so soon). So I was on the verge of being doubly let down, at a moment when I was about to help him turn two of his dreams into realities. Was that the problem? No matter how I attempted to disguise them, Attila could always read my moods as clearly as the gauges on his dashboard. He sensed my disappointment in him.

"Right now, I am feeling all my screws tightening," he said flintily. Attila the man had retreated, yielding to Attila the flinty machine.

"Then I will help you loosen them."

The man sprang back. Moments later Attila was inquiring about the prizes that would be awarded at the end of the day at the AMG Challenge.

"Joe," I said the day before I left the island. "You can exhale. Attila and I are both coming. But I've decided I'm only going to observe you two, and take notes. I'm not ready for the racetrack yet."

"Sweetcakes," he replied, "you *cannot* write a book about driving and sit back and watch other people! You've got to participate!"

ATTILA parked his dual-brake Camry in the garage near my apartment, trading it up for the SL55, which Joe, as promised, had dispatched to my doorstep. Before leaving town, however, Attila and I had some business to attend to—and this concerned the second dream I was helping to make come true. After our days with the Fat Boy, we had never quite abandoned our plan of buying a motorcycle together. The V-Rod, we decided, was too much money. We had conferred with Tony, owner of American Motorcycle Leasing, and a friend of a friend, but none of the bikes in his inventory appealed to Attila. And then Attila learned that Motorhead, the shop adjoining our gear supplier, had just received a brand-new, special-edition 2003 Suzuki Hayabusa—an obsidian black 478-pound fiend, dry. Named for a Japanese bird of prey, the Hayabusa was a four-cylinder, 1,299-cubic-centimeter hyper bike—one of the fastest on the market. Attila was infatuated; nothing else would do. His enthusiasm was catching.

On a hot Thursday afternoon, Attila and I had stood with his Brazilian friend Arturo and my daughter in a West Side warehouse, which smelled deliciously of fuel and leather, watching workers uncrate the glossy giant. We then repaired to a diner to discuss whether, and how, we would proceed with the purchase.

Arturo, who operated a flourishing Manhattan dog-walking service (his hourly fee exceeded that of a driving instructor's), came from an extended family of motorcycle buffs. "My mother is sixty-seven," he said at the diner, "and she still rides. She just got a brand-new bike. My nephew, who's two, is already learning. That's how old I was when I started. In our family, we start as soon as we can walk."

"What about your dogs? Do they ride motorcycles too?" my daughter asked.

"Yes, of course," Arturo said, his aquamarine eyes fixed steadily on her. "It's not so hard to train them. When a dog is a puppy, first you try him out on a bicycle, to see if he likes the wind. If he doesn't, he will never be a motorcycle dog. If he does, then you advance him to the motorcycle. He sits on the gas tank, with his paws on the handlebars. The majority of dogs end up loving it."

"Do they wear helmets?" she asked.

"Sure, you can put helmets on them."

We ate burgers—Attila had begun to transgress his vegetarianism of the last four years. "So, Amy, what do you think?" Attila asked, when—after a little skirmish with Arturo over the check—he paid the bill. (First he had to wake up the waitress, who, having pulled a large, incorrectly hung 9/11-era American flag over her face, had fallen asleep on a nearby banquette.)

"Has anyone ever said no to you?"

"Do I have to answer that?"

So on that day we began the preliminaries—credit applications, insurance forms—for the Hayabusa.

THE PLAN was to drop in at Motorhead on the way to D.C., put down a deposit, and finish up our paperwork. But during that first week of my August beach holiday, doubts not only about my participation in the AMG Challenge but also about the purchase of the motorcycle—and yes, about Attila himself—began to creep up on me. By what means had he mutated from instructor to book subject to partner in a major acquisition? Tony, the motorcycle leasing man, opposed the idea, on the grounds that the Hayabusa was not a bicycle built for two. "You'll have to crouch on the backseat, practically in a fetal position," he cautioned. "And at the speed that bike goes, you're likely to be thrown."

Only Larry, my book editor friend, sanctioned the plan. "Do it, Amy. Why not? It'll be fun."

I figured I couldn't go wrong listening to Larry.

Just in case, I made sure to take out the maximum policy on everything—theft, liability—during our stop at Motorhead on the way to D.C. Even Stanley, the dealership's insurance broker, thought I was excessively cautious. Why was the whole process of buying and insuring the motorcycle making me so nervous? I knew Attila would be good for his 50 percent share, and I was even more certain he would drive the bike responsibly. But if something went wrong—say, if somebody tripped over the bike on the street and broke his foot—I could be sued. After all, everything was going under my name—I had the better credit rating.

"Excuse us for a moment," Attila said to Stanley. We stepped outside the broker's office, into the showroom. Attila looked at me directly, eyebrows rippling into a peak of concern. "Stop worrying, Amy," he said. "We don't have to go through with this."

"I already told you yes. It's just that it's all so new to me. Let's finish up, so we can get back on the road."

We returned to Stanley's paper-stacked office and completed our business. As we rose to leave the insurance man said, "What a nice-looking couple you two make."

"Thank you," I replied. Attila's response was less intelligible. His eyeballs glazed over coolly, as if he were coating them with a nictitating membrane—the interior, third eyelid certain animals use for self-protection.

But his eyes cleared and brightened again as soon as we stepped outside into the August sunshine. We lowered the SL55's top and streaked out of Manhattan.

There was no traffic to speak of on the New Jersey Turnpike, and the SL55 smoothed the road before us like a satin ribbon.

"When we reach D.C.," I said to Attila, "you're going to end up with a blonde."

"I am? Why?"

I pointed to the sun overhead, and the polished blue sky, relieved here and there by clouds so dainty and puffy they could have been shot from a pastry gun. "I should be wearing a scarf over my hair."

He laughed, and put on some music. He had brought along

the same hard rock selection he had chosen for the Viper, as well as one jazz CD, a gift from a student. I pulled page proofs for two articles out of my purse (one was the *Travel + Leisure* motorcycle story, and another for *Vanity Fair* on Hilary Knight's new Eloise book).

"Remember my dyslexic students," Attila asked, after a long silence, "from my first year teaching?"

How could I forget them?

"One of them, Donna, saw me on the street last week. She stopped me and gave me a hug. 'Andrew!' she said. 'You can't believe how much you've changed my life. I don't just mean by teaching me how to drive. *Everything* has changed for me—and for my brother too. He's divorced now—we're enjoying ourselves so much! I've got to call you and tell you what has happened!'"

"I know what she's talking about, Attila."

"Sweetheart, the fear that eats away at people is of no use at the end. The fear that you have of bees is not going to prevent you from dying of their sting."

"You have a way of looking at things from the longest perspective."

"I am able to do that. You see, I do not fear anybody or anything. I don't fear death, and I don't even fear God. I love him, but I do not fear him."

We arrived in Georgetown, put the top back up, and checked into our suites at the Four Seasons. I phoned Joe, who had preceded us to the hotel by half an hour. We made plans to meet for dinner at eight at the restaurant downstairs, Seasons.

"I've got some news for you that you might not like hearing," Joe said.

"What is it?"

"The racetrack is not anywhere near Washington."

"Where is it, then?"

"It's in West Virginia—at least an hour and a half away."

"West Virginia?"

"You heard correctly. And we need to be there by seven-forty-five so we have to leave at six tomorrow morning."

As much as I adored Joe, I wanted to kill him. How could he have been so misinformed? My least favorite thing in the world is waking up early. It's a simple physiological fact—I cannot function on less than nine hours of sleep. It's a handicap that has ruled my life, dictated my college course work, determined my profession.

"Joe, that means I have to go to sleep right now! I'm serious! On five or six hours' sleep I'll pass out. My blood pressure plummets. My brain doesn't function—I feel schizophrenic. It's a real problem! I didn't even wake up early to give birth! I dread sleep deprivation as much as I ever did driving—more. The combination of those two that you are proposing for tomorrow is deadly! And besides, I'll look like hell. What will I do?"

"So you're backing out?"

"No, Joe, I can't do that either. But you're going to have to make sure that dinner doesn't go too late."

When I hung up the phone, it rang. It was Attila, inquiring if I would like to come to his room for a drink. I walked down the corridor to 706 and knocked tentatively. Shyly, he let me in. He had cranked up both the air-conditioning and the TV—his room was both too loud and too cold. In my room, I had switched off the cold air before the bellhop arrived with the bags, and I wouldn't have known how to turn on the television even if I had wanted to.

Attila showed me the sofa, and I reclined on it, my legs stretched out along its length. This was the first time we had ever been alone in a room together. I accepted his offer of a Heineken.

"I'm guessing you'd like it in a glass?" He was drinking his from the bottle. I told him about Joe's abrupt revision of our plans. Attila knew well my abhorrence of dawn reveilles.

"You'll be all right," he said, eyes trained on me. "I'll power you up."

I had faith that he would. As we graduated from Heineken to Dewar's (this he drank from a glass), Attila brought up the subject of Claude, his ex–business partner, with whom he had patented several inventions, including the reusable, adjustable dress patterns. The Four Seasons suite reminded him of his years as a high-rolling entrepreneur in Germany.

"I lived in hotels for seven years," he said. "Claude and I used to sit and talk and drink in rooms like this for hours, lining up the empties as the night wore on. We'd end up with a row of empty bottles as long as this wall. Sometimes he would pass out, and I would have to carry him to his room. He never had to carry me. We'd go out together to the same restaurant night after night, order the same thing every time, and get the best service. Everybody knew us. And then suddenly, for no reason, we'd stop going to one restaurant and move on to the next. We were rarely apart, and when we were together, even though we looked like we were having fun, we were always working. I was sketching, inventing, he'd be talking, planning. He had a chateau in France, a villa in Italy. My German is better than my English because he was constantly correcting and improving it."

"It sounds like us!"

Attila's face darkened. "Don't ever say that, and don't ever think that, Amy." His mobile eyebrows shot up, then crimped in pain. Because the right one was set so much higher than the left, this expression made the two sides of his face shift in opposed directions like tectonic plates. "Claude relied on me to get to people. Do you do that?"

"No."

"So it's not the same thing, is it?"

"No, it's not. You would know." I was not quite convinced by his argument. "It sounds like he was in love with you," I said.

"No, we didn't go there."

"But he did love you."

"Yes, he loved me. I believe he learned from me that it is possible for a man to love another man. It was his daughter who was in love with me—because I was the only man her father respected."

"What happened to her?

"I don't have an answer."

It was quarter till eight. "We need to get to dinner. I'd like to change first."

"I'll come get you in fifteen minutes," he said. "You've never seen me drink before, have you?"

At Seasons, the hotel restaurant, I sat between Joe and Attila. Minutes after their introduction, the two men were already clashing over the comparative merits of the SL55 and the Viper. "I like to feel the clutch," Attila was pontificating, "to feel that my left leg's an extension of the machine. Sure, the SL55's got the bite of the Viper, but there's too many fancy electronics. The SL55 doesn't peel up the road like the Viper—it drives itself. In the Viper, you're an American hero—in the SL55 you could be just another big-money schmuck."

After Joe's Reno-Vegas analogy fell on deaf ears, he backed off and the two of them halted their combat as quickly as they had started it. By the second bottle of pinot noir, Attila had taken command of the table—a role he assumed with surprising ease for a barely invited guest conversing in his third language. Joe and I both leaned forward, spellbound, when he divulged that "years ago, I used to own a Smith & Wesson .38." Neither Joe nor I dared to ask why. "Were you a good marksman?" I asked instead.

"What do you think?"

"I'd guess you hit the bull's-eye pretty regularly."

"That is correct. Historically, in Turkey," he said, in lieu of an explanation, "the right to carry a gun was passed on to the old-est son."

Attila excused himself to go to the men's room. Joe exclaimed as soon as he was out of earshot, "What a character! I totally un-derstand your fascination."

Joe's turn at the washroom came next. In his absence, Attila said, "Joe is a good man. I really like him. We're creating a nice circle of people around us, Amy."

At my prompting, Joe told Attila about how he once pushed up a friend's car to 150 in Pennsylvania. "You're lucky you didn't lose your license," Attila reprimanded him in his instruc-tor's voice. But I knew Joe had won his respect. Attila then re-galed him with tales of racing on the autobahn in cars, and on motorcycles. He also spoke about the Hayabusa waiting for him in New York, which he would be riding out of the shop in two days.

"It's the speed I like most," he was saying. "I'm addicted to it."

"That's sick," Joe said.

"Yes, it's a sickness," Attila agreed.

I insisted they break it up so I could get to bed.

Joe arranged for room-service breakfast to be delivered at five-fifteen, long before its official start time. I had drunk so much wine, and enjoyed the two men's company so much, I was no longer worried about falling asleep, or about waking up. We said good night to Joe, who was lodged in another sec-tion of the hotel, and then something—maybe the liquor or a childlike feeling of dependence—made me take Attila's hand as we walked toward the elevator. He squeezed it lightly, and carefully let it go. He took me to my door, where we said good night. For a change I didn't need an Ambien to bring on sleep for those few hours of the night that remained to us.

Rednecks Steering Left

The Georgetown Four Seasons switchboard operator awakened me, as I had instructed, at 5 A.M. While I was showering, the phone rang again—it was Attila this time, calling to make sure I was up. "Yes, and I'm half bathed and dripping wet." I kept waiting to be sabotaged by the dizzy, queasy fainting spell that always comes over me due to my morbidly low blood pressure, when I do not get a full night's rest, but nothing happened. I didn't even have a hangover, or dark circles under my eyes. I made up and dressed for the racetrack—black T-shirt, black trousers, black flats, and sunglasses. The only thing I forgot to put on was sunscreen. At six sharp, Attila came to my door.

Joe was waiting for us nervously in the lobby—he had fully expected me to oversleep and to bombard him with complaints. We took off in his CLK320 for Summit Point, West Virginia, stopping first at Starbucks for coffee and at a drugstore for Rolaids. "I should have known better than to mix beer and scotch with red wine," Attila said.

The drive took us seventy miles west of Washington, deep into lush rural hills. Scooped out of sleepy farmland, the Summit Point Raceway, we conjectured, was about to receive its first-ever carload of a Jew, a Muslim, and a lapsed, Cher-loving Anglican. Under a festive white tent marked "AMG Challenge," where breakfast had already been devoured, forty participants were siphoned off into three color groups—blue, green, and yellow. I was sorted into the yellows, Attila into the greens. AMG officials snapped color-coded bands around our wrists. "But we have to be in the same group!" I protested. "Joe, can you switch Attila?"

"It doesn't matter," Attila said to Joe.

"Yes it does!" I did not want to be left to my own devices in this alien setting.

A man volunteered to trade places with Attila, and Joe joined our group as well; now I felt more secure. Our fellow students were mostly middle-aged men, the majority of whom were wearing khaki shorts and the AMG baseball caps that had just been distributed. I was the only girl in the yellows. Not counting the catering staff, there were only two other women under the tent. One of them, an athletic-looking brunette, was, like me, a participant. The other female, whose curly hair slithered down to her derrière, was the petite girlfriend or wife of one of the men, and was there as a spectator. She held her guy's hand, and every time she looked up adoringly at him, her long brunette coils shook like Medusa's serpentine headdress.

"Do you have any scissors?" I hissed to Joe.

"God, do I hate hair that length!" Joe spat back.

This uncharitable exchange seemed to soothe our jolty nerves.

Next we were introduced to the pros who would be our group leaders, instructors, and classroom teachers. Mercedes had rounded up some pretty impressive hotshots; the yellows' intrepid leader was Adam Andretti, whose uncle was the race car legend Mario. Adam herded the yellows straight out to the track, where, he explained, we would each get two turns driving around the loop, with a pace car setting the speed and an instructor at our side coaching us. Adam, who shielded his eyes from the sun with a pair of iridescent aviators, gave us some basic pointers, none of which I comprehended. Out of nervousness, I began to whisper to Joe again, like an obstreperous schoolgirl.

"That ambulance is a nice touch," Joe whispered back. Seeing my eyes widen in alarm, he added hastily, "I'm sure it's there more as a deterrent. They really don't expect to use it."

". . . Make the turn as wide as possible," Adam was saying, under the clear blue country sky. "Don't apex too early."

"Did he say, 'Don't climax too early?' " I asked Joe.

"Yes, Amy, he's talking to these guys about premature ejaculation."

I watched Attila, standing apart from the group, elevated on a small slope, listening to Adam as if he were delivering the Sermon on the Mount.

"Use up as much of the track as you can on these turns," Adam continued. He had a relaxed, easy way of speaking, the same kind of lullaby cadences that airline pilots use on their passengers. "This track is one mile. The main track," he said, indicating the speedway up the hill where logo-smothered cars were zooming around, shattering the air with their man-made thunder, "is two miles. None of these AMG cars are stick shift. You brake in a straight line. Not on a turn. Look ahead to where you'll be going. Your mind gets confused if you look one way and you want to go another." This was beginning to sound like Attila's own driving school catechism. "All right, everyone, climb in, two to a car this time."

Attila and I were assigned to an S55 AMG, a 355-horsepower

car that accelerates from zero to 60 in 5.7 seconds—a "limousine with an athlete's heart," according to the AMG publicity pamphlet. Our instructor, who sat in the front passenger seat, was a crusty seventy-two-year-old veteran named Bob, from Maryland. "Normally I race a Camaro and other V-8 muscle cars," he said. I climbed into the backseat, directly behind Attila, who, thankfully, volunteered to go first.

He began to slalom around the track as if he had last done it yesterday. I rocked and swayed behind him, clutching my stomach, praying I would not barf on his neck. I didn't know if it was the swaying motion of the car itself or the rushing, bending view of the road out the windshield that did it, but I felt as if I were on the upper deck of a storm-tossed boat—lashed to the mast. As I turned paler and then greener, Bob chuckled with pleasure and narrated for my benefit each of Attila's actions. "You see how there's an orange cone placed at the apex of every curve? Watch his lines. He knows the fastest lines to follow." Lurch, lean, turn, brake, speed up, throw up. "He's really good at this," Bob said to me over his shoulder. "A real natural." He turned back to Attila. "You've never raced before?" Attila was drinking up this praise like a parched house plant. He looked even happier than he had on the Harley. "All right, pull into the pit."

"I feel like I've been doing this all my life," Attila said wonderingly as we switched places. I gave Bob a little speech, one I would repeat several times before the day's end. "I'm a new driver, Bob. I only recently got my driver's license. I'm here trying to conquer a phobia."

"That's just great, Amy. Now go!"

I had two attentive instructors in the S55 with me, Bob on the right, Attila behind me. Bob talked me through my moves,

Attila refined and corrected them. They made a great team. I tried to be a student worthy of them both.

"Brake here, before you turn." I was fascinated to see how much lapping technique, paradoxically, depended on braking. I had expected it to be all about acceleration.

"Hit the apex."

"Pick up speed here."

"Now you're on the straightaway. Go faster."

"Let him pass you."

"You apexed too early there."

"That's great, just great."

"Just tap the brake and let it go."

"Look far ahead, not directly in front of you."

"Use as much of the road as possible."

I went around once, two times. Twice I burnt rubber.

Bob was chortling.

"Sorry!" I said.

"That's what you're supposed to do here!" he replied brightly.

"I'm only going seventy."

"You're here to learn technique, not how to speed."

"Use up all the track."

"You're doing great," Attila and Bob said together.

In the driver's seat, I did not get seasick. What I did get when I stepped out of the car was the sensation that I had rocket fuel coursing through my veins. My blood was on fire, burning and rising to the cortex of my brain, lifting me up and away. I had never felt so alive.

"This does something to your blood," I said to Attila.

"Yep. Just wait until you ride on the Hayabusa. You'll feel all your white blood cells shoot up your spine. And you start shivering at the same time from heat and cold."

"It sounds like a fever."

"Not really."

"A fever without disease?"

"Yes."

"Did you learn anything?" I asked him.

"Oh, yes. I learned I was braking too soon. I think I've got it figured out now."

I was being called back into the next car, a CL55 AMG—a two-door, 355-horsepower four-seater. Attila took this as his cue to drop me. I knew he was going to make me separate from him sooner or later—for my own good, mostly, but also so he could stop teaching and be a student himself for a change. Still, I couldn't help but feel a little abandoned, especially when Bob invited Attila to climb into a car with him.

"I can't go in that CL55," Attila explained. "I won't sit in the back of a two-door."

This was interesting. "Because you can't get out easily?"

"Yeah. I feel trapped, claustrophobic." Of course. Attila always had to be in control, able to escape, run away. I had found his Achilles' heel—his Attila's heel—the clay foot of the God of Driving. Somehow that made me feel better about being tossed out by him.

"So now I know you do have one fear. And I can even name another—a fear of being told what to do. You would have had to face both in the military."

"I sure would have. I have another fear you don't know about."

"What's that?"

"L.A."

"L.A.? Why?"

"I don't know. I've never been there."

"Ha. Now I know exactly how to torture you."

"Do you want to torture me?"

"Only if you're a bad boy."

"Amy, get in!" Joe cried. "The instructor and the other student are waiting for you!" I gave my novice's speech to the new instructor, Tom, and when he asked if I minded if he coached as I drove, I begged him to talk, please, the more the better. So he kept up a running, singsong patter like an auctioneer's. "Smooth S curves," he kept saying, snaking his hand in the pattern he wished me to follow. From the two-mile track on the crest of the hill I could hear the vroom-vroom of the real race cars. Their sound lent a certain authenticity to what I was doing on the lower track; sometimes the noise of the stock cars was in sync with my own driving, so that every now and then I felt it was I who was spitting out that percussive fire.

The high was less extreme this time—the kick of novelty was gone—but strangely enough, when the buzz subsided, it was replaced by serenity. What had happened was that the concentration on the daunting task of lapping was so intense, so absolute, so total, that all petty, annoying, worrying thoughts were blasted right out of my mind, vaporized into nothingness. Surprisingly, I also discovered I had more courage on the track than on the highway—for the simple reason that I did not fear the other cars. "Statistically, the track is three times safer than the road," Adam said, "because the drivers are better." All this time I had thought it was only my poor driving that scared me, when, in fact, what was crippling me even more was terror of anonymous, capricious strangers.

Under the shade of a small baldachin, Joe and I ate some power bars, drank water, and watched the other participants as they fumbled and screeched all over the track, like the Keystone Kops fumbling a chase scene.

"Joe," I said, "I have no idea what I'm doing."

"Nobody does."

THE YELLOWS were rounded up and sent indoors to the classroom, where Bill Cooper, a veteran of three hundred professional races, presided. The lecture was impenetrably mathematical. I glanced over at Attila, who had taken a seat across the aisle, apart from Joe and me. He was following the lecture raptly.

Once Bill moved away from physics and engineering, much of what he said resembled a refresher course for Attila's driving lessons—useful to hear.

"Be smooth," Bill said. "Never do anything that surprises the car. Always give it a hint of what's coming. Treat the controls like they're rheostats, not on-off switches."

"Be consistent," Bill continued. "Have a systematic approach when you drive. Your hands should be at nine o'clock and three o'clock, with your elbows bent. Put your rear end back in the seat, so you can feel the chassis. Work the pedals with the ball of your foot.

"And concentrate. Anyone here a doctor?" Bill's classroom shook its collective head no. What did these guys do for a living? "I relate a lot to surgeons," Bill explained, "because they really have to focus, one hundred percent. You have to block out everything—the stock market, the kids, the wife—cleanse yourself, relax, and let go of everything."

In preparation for the yellows' next activity, the skid pad, Bill went on to talk about vehicle dynamics. He lost my attention again, regaining it only when he introduced us to the semiotics of racetrack flags, which reminded me of the heraldic banners of Siena's Palio races. The checkered flag, I learned, signified "end of race or session," and was the opposite of the green pennant, which meant "start of race." And so, concluding our class, Bill sent us back into the heat, toward the skid pad.

The skid pad, I found out, was a loop that had been doused with so much water that as soon as you opened up the throttle, the vehicle started losing traction. If you didn't catch it in time, the skid would escalate into a 180-, 360-, or even 720-degree spin, as it did once for Attila. It was so sunny that the skid pad dried up every half hour or so and had to be resoaked. The yellows assembled under yet another white tent, stocked with water, soft drinks, cookies, and energy bars. Adam announced, "We'll follow the protocol of the track. Ladies first! Amy you're up!"

Attila's and Joe's propitiating smiles propelled me forward, into a CLK55 AMG Cabriolet. My skid pad instructor was Mike, an affable man with a baby face, a button nose, and an eagerness so infectious that I instantly felt safe with him. I recited my litany for the third time; like any rote prayer it was beginning to lose meaning from repetition. "That's great!" Mike exclaimed, practically wagging his tail. He was as happy as a puppy who had just been handed a fresh stick of rawhide. "I'm a local yokel," he drawled, giving me his hand to shake. "I race Corvettes." We started round the doughnut, slowly. "Speed up, speed up!" he crowed, nearly bouncing off his seat with anticipation. There wasn't much to it yet except keeping the steering wheel turned to the left and the accelerator to the floor. I thought of a description of stock car racing I had read in a magazine: "a bunch of rednecks steering left." As the car plowed headlong through the deepest, richest puddle, delicious plumes of water sprayed musically to either side, as if we were an act in an automotive aquacade. And then the car started to hydroplane, spinning abruptly to the right. I turned and steered sharply to the right, into the skid, thereby halting the spin. As I felt the car catch its balance, I turned left to recover. And then I kept going round the track. The CLK55

AMG was so finely engineered I never had a moment of doubt about its brakes, its steering, its stability. I almost believed the car had corrected itself. "That was so great!" Mike said clapping his hands gleefully. "You have a real natural sense of left and right steering. Not many people do!" It all seemed elementary to me—the doughnut curves leftward, you turn in the opposite direction. But at the same time—and this is the real secret of skid pad success—you must look far ahead to exactly where you *want* to go, not off in the direction in which the car is pirouetting.

Mike pumped my hand, and as his next student took my place he called over his shoulder. "You're great for a beginner! I hope I get you again for open lapping."

The skid pad generated yet another rush—larger and louder than the lap track high. My heart was pumping fast, my blood volume felt it had tripled, my head seemed to rise in a spiral from my body. And when the buzz abated it was replaced, as before, by a sensation of clarity and peace. "It's much scarier to look at it than to do," I said to Attila and Joe.

The skid pad taught me to recognize driving, on or off track, as an exciting test of coordination, balance, and alertness, rather than a dangerous but necessary chore, best performed by someone else.

WE BROKE for lunch, sheltered beneath the same big white party tent where we had begun our day. I sat at a round table, bracketed by Attila and Joe. Midmeal, the AMG Challenge's forty participants stopped in freeze-frame, forks suspended before open mouths. A tow truck trundled down the road in front of the tent, hauling a black E55 AMG four-door sedan, the front end of which was creased like the bellows of an old view camera. The immobilized mouths started moving again: "*I* didn't do it! *I* didn't do it!" everyone around the table said. I whispered to Attila and Joe, "What a strange reaction! Do you know, Joe, is anybody hurt? How did it happen?"

"Nobody was hurt," said Joe, who had inside information. "You can see our ambulance is still idle. I can't say who did it," he said, lowering his voice to a whisper. "But I can tell you how it happened. The driver came to a curve, took his eyes off the track, failed to turn, and hit a tree, doing around fifty. The front end, by the way, crumpled just as it is designed to do—and the air bags deployed perfectly. The guy walked away without a scratch and he's going to continue racing during the afternoon session."

ADAM shepherded us back to the track (which now seemed even more fraught with dangerous possibilities) for open lapping. This was more or less like our first activity of the day, with the difference that this time there was no pace car. I was not paired with Mike, but I had the good fortune of having Bob restored to me. He graciously told me I had progressed since the morning, but he was much more interested in talking about Attila's driving prowess than my own. "Your friend's got the right stuff," he said proudly, his leathery smile large beneath his prescription sunglasses. "He's fearless. He's got more guts than I ever had. If he's got the money, he should get started. More track time, and he'll be able to join the SCCA—the Sports Car Club of America—and start in the amateur races. I'll get him all the information. I don't see this kind of talent every day."

The objective of our next activity, the autocross (staged in what was essentially a parking lot converted into a maze), was to drive the car as fast as possible through labyrinthine channels outlined by orange cones without knocking down any of these markers. We would be timed for this event, and whoever had the best time of the day would win a prize.

"You're going to win," I said to Attila. "Anyone want to place bets?"

"In the last three events I've done," Adam said encouragingly, "the winner has been someone in my group."

To relax me, Adam massaged my neck and shoulders. "I studied massage therapy," he explained as he loosened a knot. "I wanted to learn how to keep myself from getting tense behind the wheel." When Adam finished, Attila looked me over with a vague air of disapproval. "You're getting sunburned, Amy," he said. "Your arms, the back of your neck are bright red."

"My face too?"

"Yes, everything. You've got a farmer's tan."

"A farmer's daughter's tan! I can't believe it—I forgot my sunscreen. I'm ruining my skin! First on the Harley, and now here!"

"Eight hours in the sun will do it. What's going on with you, Amy?"

"You're going on with me."

He smiled.

Once again they announced, "Ladies first." The pro guiding me, Dan, advised me not to think about speed, but about precision. On the first try I knocked down a cone. On the second round I clocked in at a slow but more graceful 27 seconds.

When I rejoined the guys on the grass, Adam, Joe, and Attila each gave me a high five, which I didn't quite feel I deserved. I suppose their response to my autocross performance was a little like Samuel Johnson's to a woman's preaching, which, he said, resembled "a dog's walking on his hind legs. It is not done well, but you are surprised to find it done at all."

I gazed back at the autocross field, bristling with orange peaks.

"It looks harder than it is," I said.

"From this perspective it looks confusing, like a sea of cones," Adam agreed. "When you're in it, it makes sense. You just have to take care to respect the car."

The athletic woman from the other color group went next. She was impressively quick and sure. I congratulated her. After his turn, Joe walked up the hill to us jubilantly. He had copped the best score of the day so far—20.2. Attila gave him a hug.

He and Attila wandered to the edge of the autocross course, where they conferred about technique and monitored the times of the other competitors. "Look at those two," I said to Adam. "Joe's dropped to number three and now they're strategizing about Attila winning this competition."

"That's called testosterone," Adam noted.

Attila was kept waiting until the very end. And when his name was called, he strode toward the young pro on the auto-cross field like a cowboy on his way to a duel. Attila maneu-vered the CLK55 crisply and fluidly, a blade flexibly carving up ice. He brought it to a needle-sharp stop, perfectly centered within the terminal, a cone-outlined box. Attila got out and walked over to the timekeeper. He mounted the hill, his fea-tures set firmly.

"That was very pretty driving," I said.

"Beautiful," Joe said, shaking Attila's hand.

"Well done!" Adam said, clapping a hand on Attila's hefty shoulder.

"I may have driven well, but I drove too slowly. My time was 20.5," Attila replied stoically. "Not as good as Joe. The best score of the day was 19.65. Joe, it gave me great joy to see you do so well. And Amy, I am very proud of the way you drive today. What a long way you have come."

"Well, I guess we can head back now," I said, disappointed. "Attila's got to get back to his dog," I explained to Adam.

"If you guys cut out early, you'll miss the prize ceremony and the champagne!" Adam replied.

"We've got a long drive back to New York," Attila said. "As it is, we won't be home until twelve or one tonight."

"Well, then, I guess I'll have to give you the prize now."

"For what? To whom?" we asked.

"To you, Amy. You have won the award for 'most improved.' " And he went up to the big party tent, where waiters were popping open bottles of champagne. When he came back to us Adam was bearing a trophy—a five-and-a-half-inch high plastic orange cone, inscribed in black with the words AMG CHALLENGE MOST IMPROVED. I threw my arms around Adam and thanked him. Joe took a picture of us, and at the checkout table we received further souvenirs, including a metal participation trophy and a personalized diploma certifying that we had completed the Challenge at Summit Point.

Attila asked Joe, "Does this give us credentials for SCCA?"

"No," Joe said quickly.

"You can frame it and hang it on the wall when you open your driving school," I volunteered.

"It's not worth the paper it's printed on," Joe said.

But to Attila it was.

"HE WOULDN'T let me downshift," Attila said as we rode, exhausted, in Joe's CLK320 back to Georgetown. "Did you notice how much faster I was on the first run? That's because I figured out the key to the autocross was to start in first gear and stay there—that way you don't have to lose time braking too much. But for the timed run, the teacher told me *not* to downshift. I shouldn't have listened to him, but what else could I do? I would have clocked in at 19.0, and I would have won." He was bothered by the lack of resolution to a problem he knew he had solved.

We dined modestly at a sandwich shop across the street from the Four Seasons Hotel. "When we're back in New York," Joe said, "let's go out again for a real dinner, and maybe a movie."

"I'd love to. But it'll be tough to get Attila to come with us." I knew better than to expect Attila to commit to any plan, especially one so far in advance. "But maybe you'll have more influence on him than I do. What do you think, Attila?"

"That's a really good commercial," he said, taking a bite from his cheese steak (the first he'd ever tried), without lifting his eyes from the television above the deli case.

"Well, isn't that a double insult?" Joe said. "Not only is she ignored, but ignored for a TV commercial."

"She was talking about me to you when she could have been addressing me directly," Attila said blandly. "I'm sitting right here."

"Men tune out women with television as a matter of course," I explained to Joe while Attila stepped outside for a cigarette. "Don't men ever do that to each other?"

We retrieved the SL55 and our luggage from the Four Seasons, and underneath its porte cochere, first Attila, and then I, hugged Joe good-bye. "Attila is so comfortable with himself!" Joe said in an aside to me as I squeezed him.

"Would you like to go with Joe?" Attila asked.

"No, would you like me to?"

"Just thought I'd ask."

Both cars pulled out of the hotel and into the capital city, over which the summer sun was sinking. I stayed silent, because the quieter I was around Attila, the more expansive he became.

"It's a nice tired, isn't it?" he said, turning his face toward mine at a stop sign. He had done it again—reading my mind, lifting words from my brain as they formed. I nodded.

We hit the open highway, with Joe just behind us. Out of the windshield I was seeing the road with reconditioned eyes. The whole curving stretch of interstate ahead was a track, which I scanned, transfixed, for apexes and straightaways.

"It makes you look at driving in a whole new light, doesn't it?" Attila said, plucking more thoughts from my head.

"I didn't think it was possible," I said, "but your driving has actually improved."

"Yes. And so will my teaching. Do you know, now that I am acquainted with the electronic shifting of this car, I am really loving it. The difference between the SL55 and the Viper is that the Viper is a wild horse; this one comes to you already tamed. Do you see how I'm setting the speed for the other cars around us?"

"You're the pace car."

I dialed Joe, still directly behind us.

"Joe? Guess who's loving the SL55?"

"Isn't it great how it takes over the road, and moves the traffic whichever way you please?"

"That's what Attila just said."

"From out here you look like a UFO."

"It's like a spaceship inside too—this ambient light is supernatural."

A Japanese motorcycle, upsetting the pace we had established, caught Attila's eye. "Let's see how good he is," he said. With I-95 as a stage and the other motorists as the corps de ballet, he pursued the biker, and the biker pursued him, in one lane and out another, in an automotive pas de deux. When, after a few more minutes, Attila decided to release his prey, he realized he had missed our exit and lost Joe. He turned off at the next exit, somewhere in Maryland. Before circling back to the highway we stopped at a gas station.

"Water and cigarettes?" I asked. (He had given up on papers and Drum.)

"Yes, please, while I fill up the tank. Winston Lights if they don't have Dunhills."

When I was leaving the store, a familiar voice called out, husky with mock lust, "Hey, sexy!"

"Joe!" I cried, running over to the gas pumps to hug him. "How on earth did you follow us?"

"I DON'T know how he did it," Attila said, back on the interstate. "Joe is a really good driver."

"I've never heard you give that kind of praise before. I'm phoning Joe right now to tell him."

"Did he really say that?" Joe said, his voice cracking with happiness. "I'm so honored."

When we reached Manhattan our Mercedes caravan split up—Joe peeled off downtown, we headed up. It was almost one o'clock when we arrived at the garage. Before surrendering the SL55 to the attendant, we took snapshots of the car.

"I won't be missing this SL55 too much," Attila said. "Not when I've got the Hayabusa coming to me tomorrow."

"I hope you'll be able to come up to give me a ride on it," I said wistfully. I was taking the train back to the island.

"I don't like that place," he answered flatly. "I don't like the mood it puts you in. Islands are depressing. When I was in Jamaica, it depressed me."

221

"Jamaica is depressing because there are too many poor people. My island has too many rich people."

He laughed.

"Maybe I can take the ferry to the other side and you can pick me up there."

"That I could do. But let's wait two or three weeks. I need to put about five hundred miles on her, to break her in. Maybe sometimes around the twenty-third."

" 'Sometime,' " I corrected him. "The Hayabusa is a she? That bike looks one hundred percent male to me."

"Definitely a she."

"Why?"

"Because she's a woman—hard to tame." And then he looked a little embarrassed, as if he had revealed something not intended for my ears.

"So, I should pack my gear and take it back with me on the train?"

"Yes."

It was 2 A.M. before I turned out my Venetian blown-glass bedroom light. All night long I dreamt I was doing laps, finding the apexes, using up as much of the track as possible.

ON THE island, I settled back into the slow rhythms of summer by the sea—lazy lunches, swimming and tennis in the afternoons, sunset cocktails, houseguests arriving and departing. But every time I drove the Acura along the island's sinuous main artery, I was transported back to the track, looking high and far ahead, my rear end into the seat "so I could feel the chassis." My driving had improved dramatically, and when the car's battery died, I asked the man from the filling station to teach me how to jump-start it myself. One afternoon, when the rain was tumbling down in wide, wax-paper sheets, pools of water collected in ruts and potholes all over the ill-kept road. I drove through an enormous puddle, spewing plumes of water to either side of me. The slurping sound of this enormous double splash—like buckets being dashed against metal, then suctioned away—took me right back to the skid pad. I pulled over to a dry patch and phoned Attila. "It's a giant skid pad out there today," I said to his voice mail—he was in a lesson, no doubt—and plunged back in.

Every several days, I received a progress report from Attila on the breaking in of the Hayabusa. At 3 A.M. one night, with not a single motorist in sight, he flashed over the Queensboro Bridge so fast that "its pillars blurred into a solid wall."

Another night he informed me that thanks to the Hayabusa, one of his most troubled students, Hank, had finally passed his motorcycle road test. Hank was a Vietnam vet whose body was pitted with shrapnel scars. Attila had described him to me as "a haunted man, broken to bits." Hank had last been on a bike at eighteen, just before he was drafted. At the beginning of his first lesson, Hank had asked Attila, "Do you think I could ever learn to ride again?" and Attila answered, "You can count on it." After an hour and a half not only was he up on the school Nighthawk, he was able to perform figure eights. "When the lesson finished," Attila had said, "I saw a change in his eyes. I swear that he had recovered in himself the eighteen-year-old boy that he had been before he was sent off to war."

The day before his road test, Attila told me, Hank was vomiting. "He said it was from his medication, but I knew it was from fear of failing." For Hank's final lesson Attila showed up on the Hayabusa (normally he rode alongside or behind his motorcycle students in a car.) "Whatever he had to do on the Nighthawk, I demonstrated first on the Hayabusa. It calmed him down, and when he passed his road test, he cried from happiness." I could hear the ice chinking in the glass from which he was drinking. "I am so one with this bike, Amy. I can't wait for you to ride on it with me."

THE NEXT time I heard from Attila it was eleven o'clock on a Friday morning. I was in my bedroom in front of my vanity's magnifying mirror, applying makeup for a lunch party, where I was expected in an hour. It was unusual to hear from Attila in the middle of his workday.

"How are you?" I asked cheerily.

"Not so good right now."

"Why? What's wrong?" My heart started pounding.

"Amy, I'm calling you from the police station. The Hayabusa was stolen. Sometime last night or early this morning, from the garage."

"Oh God. How awful." The disaster had happened—but not at all the one I'd expected. Attila had been riding the Hayabusa for exactly six days.

"I have a policeman here, Officer Dan Levy, who'd like to talk to you."

Past-Future

After the initial wave of shock passed, my reaction to the theft of the Hayabusa was relief. There was nothing further to fear, no more cause for worry. It was gone. But I also felt an encroaching dread—of the sticky skeins of red tape waiting to entangle me, already unrolling from the police department, the insurance company, the Department of Motor Vehicles, the finance company. And I felt guilty. Attila was managing the mess—cleaning up yet another Augean stable—back in New York, while I stayed at a comfortable remove, on holiday out of town. Attila's response was more elementary. He was angry—so angry, in fact, that with each passing day he grew more sullen and silent. On the morning the crime was discovered, he had to cancel lessons in order to file the police report, losing a day's worth of income. But then the police told him he was not permitted to report the theft as the bike was not registered in his name. I had to overnight-express a notarized letter authorizing him to make the complaint, and so he missed most of the next day of work too. He also visited Stanley at Motorhead to cancel

225

the insurance policy—more wasted hours. Both Stanley and the police officer in charge proposed the same theory: that the theft was an inside job. Two metal gates at the garage had been hacked open, and—more incriminatingly—the car adjacent to the Hayabusa was moved. Stanley and the policeman also independently postulated that Attila's movements had been watched almost from the moment he rode out of the dealership on the new bike, a theory that made his skin crawl.

"The blue eye," Attila muttered. "I should have known better."

"What's the blue eye?"

"Nothing. Forget about it."

"Is that something to do with the evil eye?"

"Yeah. The eye of envy."

"That's what you ward off with the bracelets that Frank sells?" Frank, the Turkish cosmetician, had given several of these trinkets to my daughter and me. He kept them in a special case in his shop, among the eye shadows and lipsticks. The blue glass beads of the bracelets, strung on a silver chain or elastic thread, resembled watchful, disembodied eyeballs. If, Frank told us, a bracelet snapped and the beads popped off, then they had performed their evil-thwarting function. Attila's blue-eye bracelets, if he had any, apparently had not burst.

"Yes, that's what they're for," Attila said, his words floating in wisps from the telephone receiver. "Amy, I'm leaving this neighborhood. I can't stay."

"It could have happened anywhere."

"Maybe. Maybe not. The system in this country doesn't work. The police fill out their forms, and then make no effort to catch the criminals."

"The system is imperfect, but can you name a better one?"

"Whether or not I can, it still sucks."

I'd have to teach him a more eloquent way to convey this sentiment, I thought, but not at that moment.

"Officer Dan Levy said that the bike was probably already chopped into pieces and on its way out of the country," he continued. "It's the thieves who should be chopped up." He pronounced the word *teefs*.

"What would you like to do to them? Have their heads cut off?"

"No, maybe one finger. The head man, the organizer, he's the one who should have his head chopped off."

"Would you want to hire a private detective to do the work the police won't do?"

"Why waste the money? In this country, you're a victim of a crime, then you become a victim of the bureaucracy. Here, only money matters." His words got thinner, like razor blades pushed through his lips, and his voice more constricted. "It's time to get out of this country too."

"For where?"

"I don't care—anywhere. Canada, Australia. Does it matter?"

"You had said you were staying here. You had said you would stay because of a promise . . ."

"Maybe I made a promise yesterday, but now it's today."

"You are really angry."

"I don't like people taking things away from me. I feel raped. Can you understand?"

"Yes, but—"

"Good-bye, Amy," he said coldly.

I hung up the phone and burst into tears. "Mama, why are you crying?" asked my daughter, who had wandered out of her pink gingham bed into my room and onto my lap.

"Attila's motorcycle was stolen," I replied blankly.

"The one I saw?"

"Yes, that one."

"That is sad," she said. "But nobody should cry. A motorcycle is only a thing."

"Yes, dear, you're right. But I suppose it had a deeper meaning for him."

All the same, I decided I would not call him again, not for a while anyway. It was my turn to be angry. Why be so blistering with me? I had put my money, my name on the line, and here I was left with a hole in my pocket, and a pain in the neck. My financial involvement with him had exposed me to the same naked, violated feelings that a physical liaison surely would have, under these circumstances; thankfully, we had primly avoided those complications. But whatever had happened, whatever I had gotten myself into, whatever was upsetting me, I had done it to myself, eyes wide open—maybe too wide.

As Attila would say, "Each sheep hung by his own leg."

LATE THE next morning my daughter and I were bathing in my old-fashioned footed tub when the phone rang. I must have had a premonition about a call, because I had dragged our antiquated touch-tone into the bathroom with us before we submerged ourselves.

"Hello, Amy?" the voice came over the wire. "It's Attila. I'm sorry. I was very angry last night. I am too moody. You understand, right? I'm not angry at you."

This was the first time I had ever heard him apologize, for anything. He had never done anything before that required an apology, and on those few occasions when I told him I was sorry (for being late, for instance), he had stopped me, told me that such phrases were unnecessary between us.

He was right to be angry. How could he not be? "If you weren't furious," I answered, "you wouldn't be human—although sometimes I tell you that you *are* superhuman. All the same, I appreciate very, very much that you made this call. It's an important one. Thank you."

When I retrieved my voice mail from the city, the answering machine played back an ominous-sounding message from the insurance company's head theft investigator, Christopher. The starkness of his demand that I return his call made my blood run cold—it felt like a summons to the principal's office. Had I done something wrong? For what had I been caught? Another recurrent childhood nightmare seeped up from its musty hiding place. Once upon a time I had committed a murder, and though I had repressed the memory of it, my crime was about to be exposed by the police and discovered by my family.

But I was innocent of any wrongdoing, of course. I returned his call.

"Yep, it's always the crotch rockets that get taken first," Christopher was saying.

"The crotch rockets?" Here was a term to love. I grabbed a paper and a pen and, sitting on my bed, started taking notes.

"Yeah, the super sport bikes."

"That's a detail the salesman and the insurance guy neglected to mention."

"Which insurance guy?"

"Stanley, at the dealership."

"I never heard of a broker at a motorcycle shop," said Christopher, who was located upstate. "Well, I guess things are done differently in Manhattan."

Was Christopher implying that he suspected the dealer was mixed up in funny business of some sort—maybe that the whole theft had been set up in-house?

"Yeah, everything and everybody's pretty strange in the city," I answered.

"So you say you bought a motorcycle even though you only have a learner's permit?" The interrogation had begun.

"Well, yes. But my friend has his license, of course."

"I understand. I have a Harley, and I've been riding it with only a permit for almost two years. I've got to take the road test and get my license."

"It's too bad you're not in town. Attila could get you to pass the road test pretty quickly."

"You bought the bike for your boyfriend?"

I could see where this was going. It wasn't the dealer at all, it was Attila who was the prime suspect.

"He's not my boyfriend."

"You're telling me you bought a motorcycle for a man who isn't even your boyfriend?"

"I'm a writer," I explained. "This is research, for a book about him—*The God of Driving.*" I told Christopher some more about the project, and about the article coming out in *Travel + Leisure* that had inspired the Hayabusa purchase.

"That sounds like a book I'll want to read."

"Well, I'll be sure to send you an autographed copy. Incidentally, though it doesn't look like it on paper, this was a fifty-fifty arrangement. He was to make monthly payments to me. Do you usually resolve these cases quickly?"

Chris tossed off his good-cop hat. "Seventy-five percent of our claims for motorcycle thefts are fraudulent," he said stiffly —*Dragnet's* Jack Webb as Sergeant Friday.

"I guess some of us have to fall into the twenty-five percent."

"We catch a lot of these criminals."

"It seems like you do your job better than the police. You're more motivated because money's at stake."

"Yes, we do a better job than the police. But we also work with them. We not only catch a lot of these people, we send them to jail. Sometimes it takes as long as four years, but we usually get them."

"Well, I hope you get these guys." They wouldn't—it sounded like they saved their vendettas for the crooks who tried to cheat the insurance company, not the thugs who actually stole motorcycles. "I guess no one's going to make a movie out of this one."

"No. But we've had some pretty exciting cases. This one should be straightforward."

"Well, it's going to give me something to write about, that's for sure."

"You'll be hearing from one of my investigators. His name's Tom. He'll probably end up interviewing both of you. In the meantime, I'll be sending you an affidavit of vehicle theft. You and your friend will need to fill it out, sign it together, and get it notarized. You'll have to send it back with the title, a copy of your license, the registration, the police incident information slip, and the keys." I was taking more notes. "The cover letter will explain in more detail. The investigation process will take longer than the standard thirty days, because the bike was brand-new—we can't initiate anything until the title comes from Albany, and that could take three or four more weeks. Why don't I give you Tom's number?"

"Sure, and if Tom wants to talk to me in person, I'll be happy to come into the city to meet with him."

"He'll tell you what he needs."

If Christopher was suspecting us of scamming his insurance company, how would the con have worked? Attila wouldn't be grifting me—he wasn't the one who'd be collecting the insurance money.

Larry—who had a million plots stored in his head and the

231

capacity to generate that many more—proposed, "Maybe they think that Attila had it stolen so that the two of you could split the insurance money. Or that he faked a theft so he could sell the bike, and let you collect the insurance money."

Meanwhile, to make sure I did not behave like a guilty party, I called Tom, the investigator, promptly. He asked me for a few vital statistics about Attila—his date of birth, his social security and phone numbers, his address. I alerted Attila about Tom's intention to question him.

When I opened my mail, forwarded weekly to me from the city, bills from the insurance, finance, and credit card companies tumbled out of assorted windowed envelopes. Among this Hayabusa-generated correspondence was Christopher's affidavit of vehicle theft, a dense scroll of questions I couldn't begin to answer. I called Stanley, the insurance man at Motorhead, for help.

"Hey, Amy, stop mind-screwing yourself. Calm down. This is a big pain, but nobody's hurt. When you're back in town, come see me and I'll help you take care of everything. You can't hurry it, anyway. We need to wait for the title, and Attila's signature. The reason the insurance company's sending bills even though Attila and I reported the theft is because they want you to turn in a FS-6T form to them, proving that the stolen plates—not just the stolen vehicle—have been reported to the DMV. So everything's OK between the two of you?"

"Yeah, everything's fine."

Stanley took this reassurance as a cue to chat about his son, a documentary filmmaker. Stanley was a movie buff himself, with a penchant for Billy Wilder pictures. His favorite Wilder film was *Double Indemnity*.

"You must love the Edward G. Robinson character, Keyes. How often is an insurance guy the hero of a movie?" Rotund and pensive, Stanley even looked a little like Robinson, but with a head of white hair.

"Naw, it's the Fred MacMurray character I like best."

"Why?"

"Because he gets to have all of the fun with Barbara Stanwyck. Hey, you know, Attila is a really cool guy."

"You think so?"

"Not Jewish, though, but who am I to talk? I married a gentile."

"That's worked out?"

"Mmm, it's OK. You know, when Attila came in to see me the other day, he was looking at a Honda."

"Yes, I know, the VTX."

"Do me a favor, Amy. Don't think about buying another bike until you get your money back for this one."

"I guarantee you I won't."

"You sure everything's OK between you and him?"

"Everything's fine."

"Well, make certain he gets the MV-78B form from the police station. That's what you turn in to the DMV to get the FS-6T form. I don't want you getting any more insurance bills. This is something he can do for you while you're on vacation and we're waiting for the title. Hey, isn't that what he's there for? You shouldn't have to do that yourself."

"Thanks, Stanley, I'll see you in New York."

I DID not drive the Acura (whose muffler now emitted plangent groans, which reverberated noxiously all around the island) back to Manhattan, but left it behind as planned. I settled my daughter back into school, and visited Stanley, a bulging folder tucked under my arm.

"You won't believe what I see around here," Stanley said, as he scribbled in black ink onto the blanks of Christopher's affidavit of vehicle theft. (Body type of vehicle? *MCV.* Number of cylinders? 4.) "It can make you sick. I see the widows of young guys killed on their new bikes. ER doctors call these sports bikes 'organcycles.' "

"Thanks for not telling me that earlier."

"You're welcome, dear. Girls come in together, lesbians mostly. That doesn't bother me. But it turned my stomach one day when an old queer gentleman, late seventies, came in with his boyfriend, seventeen. He was buying him a bike. Most of our customers nowadays, though, are young black or Hispanic guys, heterosexual. And do you know how they buy their bikes?"

"No, how?"

"Their girlfriends buy them. The women are smarter. They're the ones with the jobs, money, better credit. They've usually got kids to support. And you know what happens after that?"

"No, what?"

"A few weeks later these girls come back to me, sobbing their hearts out. It's always the same story. 'I bought my boyfriend the motorcycle he wanted.' " For dramatic effect Stanley raised his voice several octaves. " 'As soon as he got it, he took off, and I never heard from him again. Now I'm stuck with the payments!' " Stanley looked up at me from the insurance paper he had been studying. "You're doing OK?"

"Yes."

"Here," he said, scooting the affidavit across his desk, back to me. "The details about the theft and the garage only Attila can provide. You shouldn't have signed this. The form has to be completed before you sign it. And the two of you have to sign it in front of the notary. Has he picked up the FS-6T form yet?"

"No." Although I had been back in town for a week, Attila had not yet agreed on a time to meet me. He had, at least, called the police station in Queens about the MV-78B form. The precinct house said that the records for our case had already been transferred to Manhattan headquarters at One Police Plaza, and so the MV-78B form would have to be picked up from there. At that point Attila passed the baton to me. I dutifully phoned One Police Plaza, and in contradiction to what Attila had just heard, I was told that the Queens station was still in possession of our file. Attila had also dropped off with my doorman the keys, the registration, receipts for owner-added options (a chain only—he had not yet purchased the gel seat, the grips, and the alarm on his shopping list), and a little folded piece of paper, signed by Officer Dan Levy from the precinct house, which appeared to be the police incident information slip mentioned in Christopher, the insurance man's, letter.

"Well, enjoy your relationship," Stanley said by way of a farewell. "One more thing, Amy."

I turned around. "Yes?"

"If I were you, I'd stay away from motorcycles. You've got too much to lose. You've got a little girl, don't you? I never allowed my daughter to ride."

"Stanley! You'll put yourself out of business! But thanks for your concern."

ATTILA asked me to e-mail him the remaining unanswered questions on the affidavit:

Specific location from which vehicle was taken: _____
Reason vehicle was left at this location: _____
Name and address of others who were present: _____

When his electronic reply came, I hand-copied his responses onto the affidavit.

Attila and I had reached a stalemate, it seemed, about which of us would make those two tedious trips—first to the Queens precinct house and then to the DMV. In the off chance that we could circumvent these city bureaucracies by speaking to the insurance company's billing department directly, I phoned the number printed on its latest dun. I was put through to Louis at Customer Service, who then funneled me to Jim at Total Loss, exactly where I felt I belonged. Jim, who listened sympathetically to my story, gave me the same information as Stanley—in order to activate the policy cancellation, I needed to submit an FS-6T form to Billing, which of course had to be picked up from the DMV. And in order to be issued an FS-6T, I needed an MV-78B form, from the precinct house.

"If the police incident information slip I have says that the vehicle was stolen, isn't that proof enough?"

"Not for us it isn't," Jim at Total Loss said. "We need hard evidence that not only the vehicle but also the plates were stolen. But maybe there's a possibility the DMV will issue an FS-6T to you with the document you already have. Why don't you call the DMV and inquire?"

Looking into the future, I could see nothing but an endless succession of voice menus, petty bureaucrats, forms, bills—on and on into infinity, mirrors reflecting mirrors reflecting nothing.

"Jim," I said woefully, "if I'm the victim, why am I being punished? The criminals have already sold the bike and collected their money, and I'm paying for their crime with my money and my time. Right now I should be working, or playing with my daughter, not making futile phone calls."

"Amy," Jim said, in honeyed tones one generation, at most, removed from the Deep South, "there's no need to look at this as a punishment. God is just giving you a little test. Can you think of it that way?"

"Yes, I can, thank you. That really helps." In fact, I *could* view this as a test—of Attila's and my friendship.

Acting on Jim's words, I called the DMV. Placed on hold, I listened to a recording that boasted repeatedly that the bustling agency serves 150,000 customers a month. I must have been the 150,001st in line for September, because I was kept waiting nearly twenty minutes. The woman in Theft who finally took my call confirmed that I would have to go to the precinct house to get the MV-78B verifying that the plates, not just the car, were stolen. And that valued document had to be brought, in person, to the DMV, in order for the Holy Grail—the FS-6T—to be granted to me. There were no shortcuts, no way out.

AT THREE on a Friday afternoon, between runway shows during Manhattan's Fashion Week (in which I participate seasonally and selectively), I took a car-service limousine from Bryant Park in midtown to the Queens precinct house. No more waiting around for Attila to get on his white charger for me. No more reliance on Stanley for help. What I had gotten myself into I could damn well get myself out of.

The woman who answered the phone at the precinct house advised me to arrive there by 3:45 in order not to miss Officer Dan Levy. I had to be back in Manhattan by five o'clock, so the visit to the outer borough was a tight fit in my schedule. Buoyed up by my newfound self-sufficiency, I entered the police station, a colorless, clunky building with the architectural distinction of a cinder block. Inside, however, it was an anthill of purposeful activity.

"Is Officer Dan Levy still here?" I asked the freckled rookie at the front desk.

"Dan Levy? There's no officer here by that name."

"There has to be," I said. What now? Had I stumbled onto the set of *The Twilight Zone*? "He handled my case." I foraged through the stuffed black leather portfolio that had lately become my Hayabusa file, and produced the folded slip of paper that Attila had dropped off with my doorman, in the packet that had also contained the key, the chain, and the registration.

"Oh," he said, looking me over curiously, puzzling over my black-and-white Geoffrey Beene jacket, tailored from a vintage Art Deco fabric, and my Manolo mules, fastened to my feet by means of silver chains. "I see," he said. "You mean Officer *Dunleavy*. He just left. But somebody else can help you."

But of course. An Irish cop, not a Jewish one. Attila's mistake made me smile.

"Have a seat. You won't be kept too long."

Smoothing my skirt, I sat down on a short, sooty vinyl bench, whose toast-colored foam rubber interior was poking through the cracks in its upholstery. I shifted around until I loosened the peeling strip of silver duct tape, meant to disguise these fissures, which had adhered to my dress. My seat mate was a stooped, bushy-haired man who hid his face behind his hands—and he was a cheerful companion compared to the other souls huddled in the antechamber. After a few minutes, a bosomy, bespectacled black woman, wedged behind a metal desk, signaled for me. I obediently positioned myself into the little folding chair set up beside her. Before she even had an opportunity to speak, or I even had a chance to consider what I wanted to say, I poured out my heart to her in one lumpy, wet eruption.

"I came in from Manhattan," I said, choking on my words. "I haven't seen my daughter all day. I got tired of waiting for him to come here—it's his neighborhood—to get this form, so I decided to take the bull by the horns, and do it myself. And I'm still stuck paying bills for a motorcycle I never got to ride."

"Oh honey, here—take a Kleenex. Now see here, I don't know who's been telling you that you've got the wrong form to report the plates stolen, because this one you got's the *right* one. This is *not* the incident slip you're showing me. It *is* the MV-78B and if you look close it indicates that both the vehicle *and* the plates were taken. See? You don't need no separate form. You give this right back to that biker man and tell him to go straight to the DMV with it, and report those plates stolen, so's you can cancel your insurance policy and stop throwing away your hard-earned money. If he don't have no kids and you work, he's got more time than you. Tell him I said so. And so you don't feel your trip is wasted, I'm giving you another extra form from us—the real police incident information slip this time."

I couldn't believe I had traveled out of my way for nothing. But if I had to journey this far to find a sob sister, then so be it.

That evening, exhausted after the last fashion event, I couldn't stand it anymore—I needed to be cured by the hair of the dog. I had to see Attila. We had not laid eyes on each other in over a month, since our day on the track in Summit Point, West Virginia. Just when I knew he would be concluding his six-hour class at the driving school, I called. "I'm stopping by," I said. He replied, "I'll wait for you by my car, on Sixty-second and Lex." It was a sultry evening, so I removed my black-and-white jacket, and, stripped down to a tiny sleeveless black crepe dress, I hailed a taxi.

Seven minutes later we were sitting together in his Camry and—just like that—the magic came back, tangible as a mist. There was no hurt, no friction, no recrimination—not even any words at first, just a familiar harmony.

"Amy, you are reliable," he said.

"Too reliable."

"And I'm unpredictable." He waved two ringed fingers, between which he held a lit cigarette, toward the darkening street. "Like the traffic."

"Even to yourself?"

"Especially to myself. Tomorrow I will cancel some students and bring this form to the DMV, in Queens, to report the license stolen, and get the FS-6T. After that we'll go to the notary together and sign the affidavit."

He threw the remains of his Dunhill out the car window, onto Sixty-second Street. Only then, as usual, did the rigid column of ashes shatter. (Yes, Attila was a litterbug; he didn't like a car to stink of tobacco.)

"Amy, you know, I never regret anything in my life."

"Yes, I know."

"But there is something now that I regret very much."

"What is that?"

"That I never was able to give you a ride on the Hayabusa."

WHATEVER it was that had been fractured—trust, affection, camaraderie—was fused back together again, whole. Maybe it had all just been a little drama of my own devising, a "mind-screw" as Stanley put it, enacted only inside my own doubting head.

Not long after, the title to the Hayabusa finally arrived in the mail, and Tom, Christopher's field investigator, interviewed Attila at his apartment in Queens.

"He had a huge file on me," Attila told me the next day, when he picked me up in the Camry for a quick visit between lessons. He drove us up to our old spot, near Grant's Tomb.

"Tom knew every single thing about me," he said incredulously, "starting from the minute I set foot in this country."

"All your financial information?"

"Everything."

Tom must have found out things about Attila's history that I'd never learn, or want to know. He and I existed in a perpetual present—or as he called it, the "past-future," because his sense of time was circular.

"I said to Tom, 'You've got everything on me. So you see I am clean.' He agreed, 'Yes, you're very clean.' "

"That's still disturbing," I said. "It used to be that only the FBI could collect data of that magnitude on a person. That's the sinister side of your computers and Internet—no privacy."

"You betcha. Anyway, I took Tom to the garage. The garage had told me that they had no insurance. That was a lie, of course. Tom says they'll go after the garage. I'm glad this is over."

It was time for Attila to go to his next student. "You know what I was thinking, Amy? I was thinking we should rent a motorcycle again, while the weather's still nice."

"Do you know, I was thinking the same thing?" It seemed like the reaffirmation we both needed. "Would you even go for the Fat Boy again?"

"Sure, why not the Fat Boy?" He pronounced it *Fet*, like an old-time Jewish grandmother.

"Well, if we're going back to the Harley dealership, let's see if this time we can rent the V-Rod."

He dialed Lighthouse Harley in Long Island, and asked for John. Not only was the V-Rod available, starting the following week for ten days, but John offered the bike to us at a discount.

"Amy," Attila said before he left, "your trust in me, your belief in me means more than I am able to say. Have I ever told you about my cave?"

"No, I don't believe you have."

"For a long time I stood in front of a huge cave, in the middle of nowhere, naked. I said to whoever wanted to visit my cave—and many people did—'Before you come into my cave you must first look me in the eye, shake my hand, and say hello. And you must enter my cave naked. Once you're inside, you can take whatever you want from the cave. But when you exit, you must shake my hand as you say good-bye.' Ninety-nine percent of the visitors to my cave went in and grabbed diamonds, they snatched gold. They stuffed it into their mouths, stashed it under their arms, stuck it up their asses. So, when they left my cave and had to shake my hand again, whatever they were hiding under their arms and holding in their right hands dropped out. When they opened their lips to say good-bye, more fell out of their mouths. I gave my trust to these people and they took advantage of it. If they had tried walking out with something in their left hand, and under their left armpit only, I wouldn't have minded. They could have helped themselves. They could have grabbed a little one day, and come back for a little more later. I would have welcomed that. So here and there, over the years I eliminated visitors, until almost nobody was ever invited into my cave anymore. This is my life story. My cave is still very huge and it is a warm place. But right now I'm down to three or four people who can go in and out, without even greeting me at the entrance. You're one of them. You've become someone I can trust blind."

ATTILA called that evening while he was out in the end-of-summer wind, walking his dog. During a pause in their rounds, Attila addressed his dog. "Ajan, forget about it!" He explained to me, "Ajan is in love with the neighbor's dog. She's a miniature Doberman, about the size of Ajan's head. She's looking down at him right now from a first-floor balcony. You should see the way he's gazing up at her. All he's missing is a guitar to serenade her. Ajan needs a girlfriend. But not this one. In Turkey, most dogs are not on leashes, and few of them are fixed, so it's not a problem if they want to mate. I've thought about getting Ajan neutered, but I haven't been able to bring myself to do it yet. Ajan," he said again to his dog, "forget about her!" They resumed their walk more briskly. "He looks so happy—he's smiling, with his ears flapping in the wind."

A second later, Attila was shouting, "Put the leash back on your dog!" The commotion that followed sounded like a *Hound of the Baskervilles* sound track—fierce growling, savage barking, screams, and snarls. "Amy," Attila said calmly into his cell phone, "I have to hang up."

Half an hour later he called and said, "I'm covered in blood. Ajan would have killed that dog to protect me."

"Are you hurt? What happened?"

Attila's fourteen-year-old neighbor, he explained, had been out walking his rottweiler, and had lost control of the dog's leash just as Attila and Ajan passed by. The rottweiler lunged toward them, and Ajan, fearing that the unrestrained dog was going to attack his master, jumped on the rottweiler and sank his teeth into the animal's throat. The two dogs were locked in a deadly battle when Attila intervened. Taking a 115-pound canine in each hand, he pulled them apart and hurled them both over a wall. The rottweiler went running off howling, while Ajan, his left ear split in half, was led home by Attila, whose shirt was soaked in the animals' blood, and whose hands and arms were harrowed by the teeth of his dog's adversary.

"Some people should not be allowed to own dogs," he said scornfully. "Just like some people should not be allowed to own cars. It's not the rottweiler's fault. The work it takes to train a dog properly—there are no short cuts, same as driving. I trained Ajan the way I have taught all my dogs—with hand signals, not words, with respect, not intimidation, and with barely any rewards. If my dog obeys me, it is out of love, not because he wants a treat. He knows by what I do with my fingers whether he should come or stay, lie down or stop. I taught Ajan 'Slow,' not 'Heel'—that's a demeaning command. He understands Turkish too, but I only speak it to him when he's done something wrong—not very often. I've got to repair this damaged ear, poor guy."

"Maybe he needs stitches. Can you sew?"

"Sure I can sew—I can knit too, by hand or with a loom. I had to learn when I studied textile engineering in Switzerland. Why are you laughing?"

"Because you can do anything."

"I do my best. A bandage is all Ajan needs. And some of the red stuff. What do you call it?"

"Mercurochrome. Actually, you'd be better off with Bacitracin—it's more effective against infection. Pediatricians don't recommend mercurochrome anymore."

"I'll go get some now at Duane Reade, and bandages too."

"Don't forget to change your shirt. You'll look like a murderer if you go out with blood on you."

"I've changed already, and put the shirt in the laundry." He pronounced it *loandry*. "I saved that rottweiler's life. Stupid kid. Next time, I won't bother."

"I can't believe you picked up those two beasts and threw them over a wall."

"I did what I had to do. What else could I do?"

The Red Convertible

I received many calls about my *Travel + Leisure* article about learning to ride a motorcycle. Most were from friends expressing astonishment that I had straddled a Harley and that I had been photographed in a wife-beater tank top and black leathers. The most interesting response, however, came from my father.

"First," he said, "be very careful on that motorcycle. Second, this article reminded me of something that I had nearly forgotten. Do you remember my red Corvair convertible?"

"Of course!" I said. "I loved that car, and I've been thinking about it a lot lately."

"It had an odd and unsafe design—the engine was in the back. Anyway, Amy, when you were seven, you and I went out for a ride in the red Corvair. Your mother was busy with your sister, so it was just the two of us. The top was down, and we were in the countryside around Bucks County. You begged me, 'Daddy, Daddy, please. I want to drive!' I said, 'Sure, honey.' And I pulled over. You climbed into my seat and sat in my lap—we didn't use seat belts then, of course. You turned on the ignition, took the steering wheel, and I showed you how to shift. You

247

complained bitterly, 'Daddy, my feet can't reach the pedals.' So I worked the clutch, accelerator, and brake for you while you drove. You kept saying, 'Daddy, more! Faster, please, faster!' You loved it. You were having so much fun. So was I. I said to you, 'Don't tell your mother.' "

"I have absolutely no memory of that incident—although maybe I was recalling it a little when I was in the Viper. Thanks for telling me. Do you have any idea why I liked it so much?"

"I suppose you loved the feeling of freedom and independence. You had a daredevil streak in you then."

"What happened to that little girl?"

"She grew up."

"But I mean, Daddy, where did she go? How did I end up becoming so scared of driving?"

"I don't know, Amy. You developed other interests—art, fashion, and so forth. Your female identity took over."

All these years that seven-year-old girl in me had been suppressed. And then along came Attila, reconstituting in me the child that I used to be—still was. On several occasions when I had thanked him for awakening in me a love of driving, he had said, "It was there already. I just helped you bring it out."

I had accepted this as a polite figure of speech. But at the same time I had known that he had to be right. I didn't understand why or how until my father told me his story.

I repeated my father's tale about the Corvair to Attila on the Long Island Expressway, while the two of us sat side by side in another red convertible—a 2003 SLK320 that Joe had sent for a four-day loan. Its color, Fire Mist, was a deep, mysterious pomegranate red (a close match to my favorite lip gloss)—not the obvious candy-red of Ferraris or Valentine's Day hearts. We had the top down, and we were on our way to collect the rented

V-Rod, which meant I would be driving the SLK320 alone on the return trip to Manhattan.

"Everyone has that child inside them somewhere," said Attila, who, as usual, occupied the driver's seat (he always did when we were together, unless it was a lesson, and then, of course, he was even more in control).

"And you recover that child for them."

"Yes, I do. But once that child is found, I don't automatically cut the cord and let my student become a driver—not right away. I have to show the child that he is responsible for the machine. When people first start enjoying driving, they usually still think that the machine's driving them. They say, 'Why didn't the car stay in the lane?' or, 'The car's slowing down.' Once they realize they are in control of the car—not the other way around—then I can let them go."

"Have I reached that point yet?"

"Yes."

"Still haven't kicked me out."

"No."

We brought John, our salesman at Lighthouse Harley, a copy of the October *Travel + Leisure*. He showed it to his customer, Jeff, and to Jeff's girlfriend, Jan, a willowy blonde with petite, Barbie-like features. She clearly had logged a lot of hours on Harleys because her bronzed, freckled skin was prematurely lined.

John asked me to autograph the magazine for him.

"John's been in a photo shoot too," Jeff told us, leaning against the dealership's rentals booth, flipping pages. "Last June a New York newspaper borrowed a bike to photograph, and they asked for a guy with it who looked good in leather. John was the man."

"But they didn't use any of the pictures they took of me," John lamented.

"I know someone else who looks good in leather, hey," said Jeff, nudging Jan with his hip bone while grinning with lecherous pride. She smiled back dreamily. I did not doubt Jeff's word for a minute.

John himself was wearing a leather vest over a Harley wifebeater tank top. His left arm was incised with a tattooed replica of a Jack Daniel's bottle. His right arm, evidently the work of the same artist, was illuminated with an equally elaborate homage to Budweiser.

"Like Jack Daniel's?" I asked John.

"Just a little," he answered. "I got drunk on it and then had the right arm done—you know, the chaser."

"Well, it's better than tattooing yourself with your girlfriend's name," I advised. "The tattoo usually outlasts the girl, unlikely to happen with your taste for beer and whiskey."

"That's the truth."

"The only woman's name you should ever get tattooed on you," I suggested, "is 'Mom,' because there'll only always be one of her."

The boys liked that.

Attila went downstairs to the clothing boutique and, without trying them on, bought a pair of Harley jeans. I purchased my first authentic pair of motorcycle boots, on sale for $112. Attila chose them over the full-price ones I modeled for him, a pair that laced up to the knee. I didn't know whether Attila rejected them because they looked too good, not good enough, or for practical reasons of economy and function.

"Want to buy something for your daughter?" he asked.

"I think nine is a bit young for motorcycle gear," I said.

"Why not start her early?"

Why not indeed?

ATTILA loaded up the passenger seat of the SLK320 with our purchases, and told me to raise the top of the convertible. "I don't want you to get distracted or disoriented," he said. He led the way out of Huntington on the V-Rod, more compatible with his physique and demeanor than the Fat Boy. A scintillating, six-hundred-pound silver bullet, the V-Rod had a more streamlined, Buck Rogers–esque silhouette than the traditional, heavyset Harley. Because of its anodized aluminum construction and its Porsche-designed, water-cooled engine, it was also lighter in weight, faster, and smoother to ride than its bulkier, hotter Harley brothers.

As long as I kept the broad back of Attila and the V-Rod directly in sight, I was content behind the wheel of my SLK320. But twice, invading the cushion of space that separated us (nature abhors a vacuum), cars changed lanes and leapt into the breach. Fortunately, the first intruder exited the expressway almost immediately, and the second trespasser made an equally hasty retreat back to the left lane, perhaps deflected by my scowl. Because I worried irrationally that if I closed the gap too tightly I would rear-end Attila, the interval between us kept widening. A third car jumped into the empty patch of road in front of me, obliterating my clear view of Attila and the V-Rod. What if Attila rode off at an exit? I would never see or know. I blinked my left indicator, looked into my left side mirror, and stepped on it. I landed in the left lane just half a length in front of the car behind me. I signaled right, accelerated again, and triumphantly reclaimed my territory behind Attila. No one, I vowed, was going to take that space away from me again, not for the rest of the trip. I followed him off an exit ramp. He stopped on its shoulder, and pointed for me to pull over ahead of him. In his heavy boots, he strolled over to the car and lifted the visor of his black helmet. (Attila's walk was part gunslinger, part gymnast; he had been his high school's top trampoliner.) I knew Attila was going to reprimand me for a driving faux pas. I looked up at him expectantly, waiting for the reproach.

"Amy," he said, "you've got to keep up with me. You're going too slow. It's not safe. We're the slowest vehicles on the highway."

"OK," I said.

"And I don't like the way you made that lane change. You've got to do a head check—not just a mirror check." I winced. How many times had he told me that before? "The car was coming much too fast and too close for you to change lanes. And you've got to be sure you see the bumper of the car you're passing in your rearview mirror before you switch back. It's OK. I won't lose you."

We stopped next when we were back in Manhattan, at the garage near me where we had parked the SL55 six weeks earlier, after our Washington trip. "It was a lot of fun watching you on the V-Rod," I said.

"What did I look like?"

"Like an athlete—or ballet dancer. Or maybe a mythological monster—a silver-and-black centaur, half man, half hundred-and-fifteen-horsepower beast."

"Thank you. It's a great bike. I already feel more one with it than I did with the Fat Boy. I got back that feeling of being the eight-year-old in Istanbul who used to sneak off to rent mopeds by the half hour."

"I guess both of us were kids out there today, seven and eight. How'd I do on the rest of the trip?"

"You kept up with me. The rest of your lane changes were excellent. I gave you some pretty tricky ones, but you followed me. You were observant, alert, and relaxed. You should buy that Mercedes."

"You think so? Maybe in a different color?"

Attila was not partial to red in cars or clothing, although he did tell me once over lunch at an East Side Turkish restaurant that the red wool jersey dress I was then wearing was becoming. "It gives you a glow," he had said.

"No, the Mercedes's the right color for you," he said. "You look really good in that car." And before I even had a chance to soak up that rare benediction, he laid on another, casually, in his Queens accent (which showed up from time to time in his speech in place of the stronger German-black-Turkish one). "Amy," he said, "you're a driver now." He pronounced it *drive-uh.*

The Best Cabbie in New York

If I was in fact a driver, as Attila said, I was not yet a good one, much less a great one. In any case, I was still an inveterate rider of taxis. While I had grown less tolerant of cabbies' ineptitude, I was at the same time no less dependent on them. Always running late, I seldom had time to go anywhere on foot.

So one September morning I found myself dashing to get to my daughter's school by eleven-fifteen in order to take her to an eleven-thirty orthodontist's appointment. She was scheduled to have her thumb-inhibitor appliance, inserted three months earlier, removed, and phase one of her braces installed.

In the pouring rain, I despaired of ever finding a cab, much less one traveling in the right direction. I pictured my daughter waiting anxiously inside the doorway of her school while I stalked transportation in vain. But then out of the drizzle emerged a shiny yellow cab, its TAXI light brightening the gloom like a beacon.

I hopped in and gave the address without looking up. When I laid down my umbrella I noticed the interior was twinkling with cleanliness.

"That's the girls' school, right?" the driver rasped.

I lifted my head. The voice issued from a buxom woman, whose hair was bleached and permed into curls the color, texture, and shape of uncooked fusilli. Her painted lips were the size and shade of pink party balloons. She had an unusual accent, possibly South American.

I was impressed with the fact that she not only had heard me (no distraction from radio or cell phone), but had also understood exactly where we were going. "I pick up a lot of girls in the morning and take them to that school," she explained. "I like the customers in this neighborhood. And I love the rain." She laughed, a merry gurgle. "Except on the weekends."

"Why do you like the rain?"

"More business. Weekends I'm off." She pulled up to the school.

"Could you possibly wait here?" I didn't want to lose time and get wet hunting for another taxi. "It won't be more than a second—my daughter is standing just inside the north door."

"I turned the meter off already."

"That's OK. You can turn it on again when we get back in— it's worth the extra two dollars. Here's a twenty, and then you can give me the change when we get to the next stop."

"OK."

I hurried in and fetched my daughter, who bounded out of the brick schoolhouse like a paroled prisoner. In the backseat, the two of us buckled up, and she absently reached over to hold my hand. I unpacked a peanut-butter-and-jelly sandwich and passed it to her; she would be missing her lunch period. While my daughter nibbled her sandwich, the cabbie and I continued talking.

"She's cute," the driver said, chuckling. "How old is she?" She looked over her right shoulder at us, exposing more of her blowsy, cheerful face, and spilling out further syllables of her mongrel accent.

"Nine," I said fondly. "In third grade."

"I've got three kids of my own, and five grandchildren."

"Grandchildren?" I said. "I expected you to say you had a child the same age as mine." I brushed bread crumbs off the pleats of my daughter's uniform, and then realized I had sullied the lady's pristine floor mats.

"Well, I got married at fourteen." She chuckled again. "I've been a grandma since I'm twenty-eight!"

My daughter (an aspiring novelist) and I glanced at each other sideways and exchanged smiles. The same thought bubbled up in our brains: *story!*

"Married at fourteen? It couldn't have been in this country."

"No, it was in Argentina, but I was living on Long Island. My mother gave permission. Thirty-four years later, I'm still married to the same man. My father's Argentine, my mother's French. My daughter got married at fourteen too! Fourteen plus fourteen, that's twenty-eight!" She chortled. "I speak six languages. Spanish, French, Italian, Portuguese, Greek, English."

"The Spanish came from your father, the French from your mother. But how'd you learn the rest?"

"You can only learn a foreign language if you're forced to speak it as a child. I lived in Rio, Rome, and Athens."

"Oh. My daughter has been learning French since she was an infant. At her school they don't teach any foreign language until fifth grade."

"Well, that makes no sense. You're doing the right thing. Look," she said as we rolled past a construction site—an inactive one that day, because of the rain. "Here's where the new Lycée's going up. They sold the old buildings for a lot of money, but not as much as they wanted."

"I didn't realize they had succeeded in selling them. Who bought them?"

"I don't know. I'm glad for the Lycée. That's where I went to school."

The elegance of her education surprised me, but I tried not to let it register in my voice. "You came in all the way from Long Island everyday to the Lycée? That's a big commute."

"My mother took me into the city every day. She worked at the French consulate. My mother was a diplomat."

"Your father too?"

"No, he did . . . other things," she said guardedly. "Anyway, it's really hard growing up all over the place—you don't have any real home or friends. The only good part is all the languages. But I like what I'm doing now. My job before this one was at a hairdresser's."

"Really?" Again, I studied her parched, fleecy tresses.

"Yes, I was a manicurist at Elizabeth Arden. I started there at fourteen. Of course, I didn't look fourteen, not the way I was built, not the way I put on my makeup!" This memory set off another series of cackles. "When I was nineteen I quit to start driving a taxi. I used to have my own cab, but since 1983 I'm with a company—my husband works for the same one. I still take care of the car like it was my own. I drive four days a week, he does five. I don't do July or August—that's when I visit my children and grandchildren in Florida. My daughter married a Chinese man. Those little half-Chinese grandkids are real cute. And I don't work at night—it's not safe for a woman."

"Have you ever had any problems?"

"Never! Because I know when to lock my doors and keep moving. I know who not to pick up. Mostly it's pretty safe. Although since Giuliani left, it's starting to change again."

I asked her who made better cabdrivers, men or women.

"Hey, what do you think?" She cracked a wide smile, threw up her hands, palms facing in, all ten fingers pointing to her chest—then let them fall lightly back down on the wheel. Her nail polish matched her lipstick.

"All right, you've answered my question. And who makes the worst cabdrivers?"

"The Indians, especially the ones in turbans. They smell. They don't know their way around the city. They don't know how to drive in the rain. Look at him!" She gesticulated to a cabbie riding too closely to us. He was indeed a Sikh. "They've always got their off-duty lights on. They're always talking on their phones." These two faults were also true of her careless colleague in the left lane. "And they don't learn the language— except they seem to have no trouble coming up with the curse-words. Have you noticed?"

I had.

"And they don't like women." That was the period at the end of her statement, the final condemnation.

"What do you think is the most common mistake of city drivers?"

"Not looking, not using the eyes."

"And what's the most important characteristic of a good city driver?"

"Being relaxed. If you're tense, you're already driving lousy. Look at me!" She grinned again, her big teeth gleaming beneath the thick pink lip gloss.

Her opinions echoed Attila's. As he would say, she knew what she was talking about.

"You see, I love driving," the lady babbled on. "I started driving at fourteen. I used to race cars."

"You did?" My daughter and I looked at each other again, savoring the arc of her tale.

"Yep. Corvettes. On the highway, on Long Island. Street racing. For money."

"Did you have your own 'Vette?"

"Nope, the cars belonged to my girlfriend."

We were approaching our stop. "What's your name?"

"Marie-Noelle. Born at Christmastime. Nearly—December 19th. Here you are, door to door. How much do you want back from your twenty?"

The fare was $7.50. "Nothing. Keep the change. You're the best taxi driver in New York. I hope we end up as your passengers again."

Marie-Noelle thanked me for telling her what she already knew—and drove off into the downpour, taxi light on, to seek her next fare.

Off- and On-Track

In tiny, leafy Lakeville, Connecticut, where Attila, his dog, and I stayed for three nights while we attended the Skip Barber Driving School (he was there to learn Formula Dodge racing, I was to study accident avoidance techniques), even the best restaurants stopped serving at nine. This posed a problem every night, and each evening we improvised a solution.

We learned about these early closings the hard way, when we pulled into town famished at 8:45 and found even the local pizza parlor dark. I phoned ahead to the hotel, the Interlaken, hoping at least to have a room service meal ready for our arrival. But its kitchen was already shut down. The sole exception to the nine o'clock closing rule was the Golden Wok in nearby Millerton. In its deserted parking lot Attila played carhop, first bringing the four-page Chinese menu to me in our borrowed black Mercedes E320 wagon, then going back to place our orders (dumplings, vegetable delight, chicken lo mein), and completing his job by carrying out four stapled, steaming, grease-streaked brown bags.

We spread out our feast from the Golden Wok on the dining room table of my two-story "town house" suite, while Attila's dog, Ajan, reposed sphinxlike at his master's feet. Attila stripped my idiot-proof corkscrew, which I had stowed in my luggage, down to its rudimentary component, an old-fashioned screw-pull, and popped open my bottle of Babcock 2001 pinot noir. "You know I like things simple," he explained. Even more basic was his technique for opening his Heineken bottle. He took a teaspoon out of the kitchen's silverware drawer, positioned it bowl-down beside the corrugated metal cap, and snapped off the lid. "The Turkish way," he said, pouring himself a glass.

After our Chinese takeout banquet, Attila cleared the table, took out the garbage, each bag neatly packed and tied, and moved to the living room, where he lit a cigarette and poured two Maker's Mark bourbons, neat. He motioned for me to sit on the sofa opposite his armchair. Maybe because our repast had about it the impromptu domesticity of a family dinner, Attila began to recount a few incidents from his childhood. Every afternoon when he was eight, he said, he and his friends would pass by a terrifying black dog on the way home from school in Istanbul. One day Attila decided to face their fear, literally. "I went up to the big dog, put my face up to his, and looked at him right in the eyes. He bared his fangs and, accidentally, we knocked teeth. I rejoined my friends, who thought I was crazy but brave. The next day, to our relief, the dog was no longer there. And then we found out he had been shot for rabies. I told my father what I had done and he said to me, 'Attila, you're never going to grow up.'"

"What did he mean—that you'd die soon from rabies," I asked, sliding an ashtray closer to him on the coffee table, "or that you'd remain a child forever?"

"Maybe both. As soon as my father said that, I froze myself right there, at age eight."

He stepped outside and walked Ajan around the Interlaken's grounds. When he returned, admitting with him a stray yellow leaf and a cool draft of autumn air, he sat in his armchair and said, "I was always a storyteller. Not a writer like you, but a storyteller."

"There is a difference."

"The stories were never about myself, though. In seventh grade I had a teacher who was bored with his job. He knew I told good stories, so he put me in a chair in the front of the classroom and asked me to start. My story turned into a serial—each day I added on another adventure, and it went on like that all year. The teacher would sit and listen with the rest of the class. It's weird—I can't remember the name of the story's hero."

"I know why."

"Why?"

"Because, though you might have given him another name, that hero was you."

"You're right. I hadn't thought about it that way before."

"I think you've always been your own hero, of your own life story. Now you're the hero of my book."

"That's quite a statement."

"Yes it is. And that's probably why for a long time I didn't know what kind of book to write. I already had a heroine. I needed a hero."

ATTILA had to awaken early for his first session of three-day racing school, but as my two-day program had not yet begun, I was able to sleep late. Andrew, Skip Barber's manager of con-

263

sumer marketing, drove me in his black VW Jetta from the hotel to the school in time for noon lunch—a grilled chicken sandwich, potato salad, Mountain Dew, and a brownie—track food in a tray that I would consume daily at twelve for the rest of Columbus Day weekend. Andrew had arranged for me to meet Divina, head of the racing series; Aaron, Skip Barber's CEO; and Bob, the school's traffic safety specialist. A pixieish Brit, Divina was one of just five women worldwide ever to have competed as a Formula One racer. Her present mission, she said, was to attract more women to racing school. I asked her why she thought females were such a hard sell.

"My theory is that women are too mean," she answered without apology. "They don't want to part with the money. They'll spend loads on clothes and jewelry—things to enhance their status—but not for an internal experience that doesn't 'show,' like racing."

Aaron noted that those women who do enroll typically make the best students because "they're good listeners and ask the best questions."

Why, then, I wondered, are accident rates going up for teenage girls?

"Girls have become more aggressive on the road as a result of their greater participation in school sports," Aaron answered.

"Racing should become a Title IX sport, then," I suggested. "That way we'd see both better teenage-girl drivers and more women on Divina's track."

Andrew and I next walked in on Bob, the traffic safety specialist, as he was concluding his lecture to Attila's group in a birdhouselike classroom overlooking the track. Bob, a sixty-year-old man with a schoolboy's brown bangs and rosy cheeks, preached the same doctrine as Attila, but at a more evangelical pitch. Ever since four of his friends were killed together in a car accident, Bob had been on a one-man crusade for automobile safety; he traveled to high schools around the country spreading the gospel with his program, "Survive the Drive." Like Attila, Bob believed that the automotive industry, insurance conglomerates, the medical establishment, oil companies, departments of motor vehicles, federal and state highway administrations, and some politicians had a vested interest in keeping accident and mortality rates high.

"It may not have started out as collusion," Bob said as his last students left the room, "but it sure has ended up that way." Consumer groups, Bob felt, misidentified the problem: "Drivers, not just cars, must be made safer. ABS brakes have not reduced crash or death rates. What they have changed are the *types* of crashes. In this country there are six million accidents a year. Two million people end up in hospital emergency rooms. Forty thousand a year die. In a decade that comes to sixty million, twenty million, four hundred thousand. The most common refrain in driving is, 'It wasn't my fault.' The most dangerous words in driving are 'All of a sudden.' There *are* no accidents—the iceberg didn't hit the *Titanic*! It all comes down to Isaac Newton's laws of physics, the driver's skill—and the condition of his vehicle. The most underdeveloped resource we have is driver ability. High school driver's ed courses and state licensing agencies churn out untrained, unprepared, misinformed pupils—potential killers or victims! In-depth education and training are accepted ways to improve ability and performance in every human endeavor, *except* driving a car."

Flushed, Bob halted his sermon only because Andrew dragged me outside to watch Attila do laps in the white Formula Dodge, number 99, which, after some Procrustean try-outs, had best accommodated his measurements (five eleven, 185 pounds).

"You have a racer's handshake," Attila's head teacher, Bruce, said when Andrew introduced us in the pits. A loquacious six-footer with a clean-shaven head, Bruce bored into me with his pale eyes.

"What's that?"

"A strong grip. Your boyfriend's doing great—he's perfect. Quiet. A Doberman pinscher with a hand grenade in his mouth."

"He's not my boyfriend. But you're a good judge of char-acter."

"I make my living by looking people in the eye."

A former Formula Ford national champion, Bruce, I learned, majored in pre-theology at Hobart and lived for a time in a VW bus. Among his thousands of ex-students were a serial killer from Australia and a man who hallucinated midlap that an air-plane was landing on the track.

THAT NIGHT Attila and I had dinner sitting on tall stools at Morgan's, the Interlaken's bar. We ordered beet salads and roast chicken from the barmaid, a twenty-two-year-old yellow-haired Hungarian. Attila flirted with her, but only enough to flatter her into looking prettier. She had difficulty filling our drink orders—Chivas on the rocks, red wine, and later on, co-gnac—and kept disappearing to consult with her supervisor, a man in a perky bow tie, who blushed with pride when Attila complimented his kitchen's food. The supervisor persuaded us to have a walnut tart with ice cream for dessert, and he complimented me on my dress, more formal than the occasion demanded.

Attila spooned the molten scoop of vanilla over the tart's round, warm, lumpy top, spreading it evenly all the way to its crispy rim. "It tastes better this way," he said. "Try it."

I took a bite. "Yes, it does taste better. You are such a baby!" I exclaimed, watching him trowel on more ice cream in uniform concentric circles with the back of his spoon, as if it were life's greatest pleasure.

And after we had devoured the tart, he told me how he had been on his high school's winning Ping-Pong team (he later challenged me to a game and lost), how he had extracted his lower left wisdom tooth with a pair of pliers, and how he had been shot in Turkey when he was twenty-three, with a .22-caliber bullet. "The man who pulled the trigger—I won't say who it was—wanted me dead. The bullet hit at the top of my right thigh, passed between an artery and a nerve, and exited through the other side. I couldn't walk for six months. The story ran in the newspapers, and the man went to jail." Distracted by the arrival of a new patron, he terminated his story there, without further elaboration.

The bar's new customer was a slender, dark-haired gentleman, perhaps sixty, with an intelligent Semitic face. He had walked into the room with an Asian woman and a boy of about thirteen, who wore a Hotchkiss sweatshirt. The boy and his mother played pool while the father nursed a vodka, straight up.

I surmised that the vodka-sipping man was a physician—judging by his long fingers, probably a surgeon—and that his wife had been his nurse. When I struck up a conversation, we learned that he was, in fact, a neurosurgeon from New Hampshire. He explained that he was not in town for Skip Barber but to tour boarding schools for his son. They had so far looked at Taft, Hotchkiss, and Lawrenceville, and he was eager to hear my opinions about these institutions. He hoped his son would attend a school close to home.

"Even though I'm not up here for Skip Barber, I am a car fanatic," the doctor said. "I collect classic cars—Lotuses, Ferraris, Cobras. I've got about twenty in all. I'm retired, so now I devote myself full-time to my hobby. Instead of the operating room I'm in my garage all day working on engines. I keep parts in a freezer."

"Do you wear a scrub suit when you work?" I asked.

"Yes I do."

"And gloves?" I could not imagine this fastidious man with motor oil under his fingernails.

"Yes," he said. "And a mask too. You see, car engines are more interesting than human brains. Each engine is different—every brain is the same."

He handed me his calling card. It showed a black-and-white drawing of a masked surgeon in a scrub suit spray-gunning the words "Barry's Motor Service Repairs and Restorations," in blood red paint.

MY TWO-DAY racing course was a more strenuous, Outward Bound–ish version of the AMG Challenge. Instead of sliding around in hundred-and-fifty-thousand-dollar high-tech German performance vehicles, my classmates—a cardiologist, a high school sophomore, an accountant, a real estate entrepreneur—and I were dropped into Dodge Dakota pickup trucks, economy manual-shift Dodge Neon ACRs, and on the last day, the Dodge Viper ACR, which, first time out, I threw into a 360-degree spin (a heart-stopping situation caused by accelerating and turning at the same time). In addition to trying out our luck on the skid pad and the autocross course, we practiced "panic" braking (without antilocks), emergency lane changing (the goal was to miss flattening "a child on a bicycle"), heel-and-toe downshifting (impossible in my tapered Manolo boots), and trail braking (the gentle release of the pedal while taking a corner). And there was classroom time devoted to line theory (taught by Spencer, a Porsche racer and mathematician), safety, and vehicle dynamics (presented by Dave, an art gallery habitué when not tearing up the track). The chalkboard diagrams of load transfers and turning ratios made sense—they were not the runes they had been just two and a half months before at Summit Point. My favorite activity (besides sweeping through orange-cone chicane in the Viper) was the "champagne slalom," a timed competitive event consisting of swerving around an obstacle course with a goblet fixed to the hood of our Neons. Inside the goblet was a ball, which, if spilled out of its container, cost us dearly in penalty points. Suited to my cautious temperament, the slalom required precision more than speed, care more than aggression.

Travis, the lanky blonde rally pro who took me for some hair-frizzling hot laps in the Viper, told me while we rocketed around in a thunderstorm at the tail end of my last day, "Right now I own thirteen cars. I like cars because I can control them. And the reason I'm single is because I don't want anyone controlling me."

ON OUR way home that evening from our three days at school, Attila sat at the helm of the black Mercedes E320 station wagon, which he had loaded down with our luggage, Skip souvenirs, and his dog, Ajan, who reclined languorously in the back. It had been raining hard all day long, and the dim, slick Taconic Parkway was littered with freshly fallen leaves, a brighter shade of yellow than the painted stripes on the road.

"Did you know we are driving in the most dangerous road conditions of all?" he asked. The E320's one long wiper was wobbling all over the window, unable to scrape away the sheets of rain fast enough.

"No, I didn't."

"Wet leaves can be as treacherous as ice. And dusk is more dangerous than nighttime." His dog, agitated by the gravity of his master's voice, began to stir nervously in the back.

"Ajan," Attila said, looking at his mutt in the rearview mirror. "Relax."

The dog calmed down immediately. "You speak to Ajan exactly like you do to your students!"

Attila nodded.

"And he obeys you just as they do."

He smiled. "All right, Ajan, go to sleep."

The dog lowered his long brown head and shut his eyes.

"Have you ever tried that command on your students?"

"No, not yet."

And then, as we were bending around one of the Taconic's notorious curves, a tree limb crashed onto the road, obscuring our view and impeding our path. It shuddered as it landed, scattering a whirlwind of yellow leaves and splintered twigs against the windshield.

Attila swerved, steering the E320 a neat fraction out of harm's way. No adjacent-lane cars interfered with his maneuver. Ajan barked once. Except for our exhalations of relief, we were both silent.

Attila spoke first. "You see, that is why, though I am an optimist in life, I have to be a pessimist on the road. You have to look ahead into the curve, anticipate, and expect the unexpected."

"What you just did," I had said, "is exactly what I was learning today in driving school—emergency lane changes." On an asphalt runway, we had accelerated one by one in our manual-shift red Dodge Neons, straight ahead toward three lanes, each marked at its dead end with a red traffic light. At the last instant an instructor would randomly switch any one of these semaphores to green, designating the lane that we had to enter suddenly and unprepared. I had not excelled at this exercise.

"Now you have a real-life example," Attila said.

The Mighty Maybach

Two weeks after attending Skip Barber Driving School, Attila and I flew to Hamburg to participate in the Maybach First Drive—a program organized by Mercedes to allow journalists to try out both the 62, the longer, chauffeur-driven model of the car I had first seen with Joe in June, and the 57, the shorter but equally sumptuous owner-driven sedan. Our Lufthansa flights, our routes, our meals, our rest periods, our excursions, and our hotel accommodations were all planned meticulously by our German hosts down to the quarter hour. I had, however, requested that Attila and I fly in one day early in order to acclimate ourselves to Germany. But when we arrived we found that the early-fall Hamburg weather was so gray and sodden, neither of us wanted to step outside the hotel, the Kempinski Atlantic. I napped, went to the spa for a massage and a swim, made phone calls, read, wrote, and showered. When I opened the door in search of Attila, he was already in the hall heading toward my room.

"Looking for someone?" he asked.

He came in to chat for a few minutes. I was in black lace

lounging pajamas, with pink ballet slippers and horn-rimmed eyeglasses. He was in a sweatshirt, jeans, and bedroom slippers embroidered with Old Glory.

"You're not going to convince anyone you're American in those," I said.

"I'm not trying to."

Attila was feeling even more dislocated than I, as he had lived in Germany for a number of years, but had not returned for thirteen years. He had been reluctant, then eager, to come back. Germany had been a door he had shut, but was now ready to prize open.

So far Attila had spent the day drinking beer in the bar and talking on the phone to Turkey, tantalizing friends and family with his sudden proximity to them. We agreed to have dinner in the hotel bar in fifteen minutes. I changed into a black wool jersey dress, applied some makeup, and was ready when he came to get me. Attila ordered more beer and a sandwich for himself and pasta and wine for me, in German; it was the first time I had heard him converse in the language, which to my ears sounded more fluent than his English. I knew German only as a dead, scholarly language, all that had been required by art history graduate school.

While we ate he told me about a laboratory supplies business, based in Frankfurt, that he had started after his move to Germany, when he was still in his twenties. Instigating a pattern that would be repeated at least twice more in the years ahead, Attila discovered one day that a trusted associate had drained the corporate bank account and left the company in debt. Not long after, Attila found a stranger sitting in his office waiting for him. The unanticipated visitor was Claude, a mergers and acquisitions man, who was there with an offer to buy what remained of the supplies company. From there the two men went on to start up several other businesses, including the one about which I had heard most—the firm that sold reusable, adjustable dress patterns. This was the era of the Rolls-Royce Silver Wraith and the hotel suites in Germany and Switzerland. After a while Claude, like his predecessor, absconded with the company's assets and patents, and Attila made America his home.

"It must have been a shock when you first landed in New York," I said.

"It was. I wanted to board the next plane and head back to Europe."

In New York he was president of a knitwear company in the garment district, putting to use his Swiss studies in textile engineering. After that enterprise foundered—his Turkish factories could not meet the American delivery dates—he briefly imported furniture from Turkey and exported shampoos and other toiletries. "While I was driving off my debts, numb to the world, I was thinking, this can't be my life. I knew that someday things would have to change. What goes up must come down, what goes down must also go up, right? And then I met you."

Noting the inquiring expression on my face, he said, "You're not going to be able to piece it into a whole. I'm only giving you fragments, bits and pieces, mostly out of sequence."

"It's all right," I said, grateful that he had acknowledged the sketchiness of his story. "It's probably better that way for both of us."

"Claude used to tell me I functioned at two thousand degrees Fahrenheit," he said. "I was so intense I burnt people up with my energy. But after Claude betrayed me, I closed my heart. I was lava and I cooled myself to stone. For me it's always extremes—never the middle."

"You've found the middle with me," I said.

"Yes, I have. It's been hard work. It still is."

"You say you're a stone, but you do have feelings."

"Yes, I do. But they are for me alone to know."

I looked at him. I had learned by constant observation to interpret the minute fluctuations of his face, but it was still a foreign text. At that particular moment I could read nothing. Attila had told me on the plane ride over that he had never once seen any emotion display itself on his father's face. It was an effect he was able to duplicate.

"What do you think it is that you've given me?" I asked, hoping my question would bring forth some legible expression.

"I've made you a driver, and taken away your fears."

"You have—but that's your job. You do that with all your students."

"But I do not sit with all my students in Germany at a hotel bar."

"That is what you're giving me?"

"If you're taking it, I am giving it to you."

For someone who could be so precise, Attila was a master of ambiguity. I doubt that he had an answer any more than I did to the question that, tired and tipsy, I suppose I was really asking: What were we doing together—and what would have happened to him if he had never met me?

ATTILA and I officially joined the Maybach First Drive program the next day. Our Mercedes sponsors transferred us to the Louis C. Jacob Hotel, a converted eighteenth-century summer villa on the banks of the Elbe. Framed by our rooms' floor-to-ceiling windows, the view of the river and its passing boats was filtered to monotints by the mist rising from the waves and the hail plummeting from the sky.

"It's typical Hamburg weather," said the driver of the green-on-green two-toned Maybach 62 to which we were assigned. "But," he added with the confidence of a true believer, "the sun always comes out for a Maybach event. It even did for us once when there was a blizzard." Attila took the back left chair, I took the right, and our hostess—a slender Nordic beauty in tight Burberry pants, a white blouse, and a black bra—sat in the front passenger seat. Our destination was Schleswig-Holstein, the land bridge near Denmark between the North Sea and the Baltic, two hours from Hamburg. And just as the chauffeur promised, thirty-five minutes into the trip the hail vanished, the clouds broke, and, incredibly, the sun came out, shining on peacefully grazing herds of eponymous Holstein cows. The bucolic scene could have been a poster for providence, pasted up for our benefit by the DaimlerChrysler corporation. "These are small, private farms that have been in the same family for generations," our fair-haired guide said. "The farmers let out their property for holidays so city children can breathe fresh air and milk cows. There are also lakes and beaches in this region which are popular vacation spots."

We played a Diana Krall CD on the twenty-one-speaker Bose Sound Surround system, opened and shut the gauzy rear window curtain, angled our seats' positions to a recumbent forty-seven degrees, and switched on our chairs' pulse buttons. The soft lumbar massage, which felt like babies' feet treading over our lower backs, "stimulated vertebral metabolism," we were told. Attila bantered with the guide in German, simultaneously showing off his linguistic skills and sharpening them. And then he dropped off into a sleep so deep he didn't stir—not even, it seemed, to breathe. I looked at his face with curiosity and envy—I wished I could nap so easily—and his eyelids fluttered open. His short nap had revived him so completely the circles under his eyes had disappeared, and his skin was a glowing pink.

"Look!" Attila said. *"Regenbogen."* Arcing over the marshy fields were two complete rainbows, visible from end to end—a meteorological phenomenon I had never before witnessed.

Even the driver was awed by this extraordinary fulfillment of his prophecy. "I knew we'd get some sun, but the rainbows are a first even for Maybach."

When we passed through the village of Bad Segeberg, two boys jumped and pointed. "Maybach! Maybach!"

"There has been a lot of publicity about Maybach on German television and in the newspapers," our hostess explained. "The Germans are very proud of this car."

We arrived at our "Relais station," the seventeenth-century Wensin Manor House, where we were served canapés, champagne, and coffee in a baronial carved-oak setting. And then we turned around and headed back to Hamburg and the Louis C. Jacob Hotel. The guide suggested we open the bottle of Veuve Clicquot that was chilling in the Maybach's refrigerator—there were Robbe & Berking silver goblets in the aboyna-wood cupboard waiting to be filled—but Attila declined. He later told me that he did not think the choice of champagne was worthy of the car.

THAT NIGHT we had dinner (first course: gnocchi in cream sauce) at a long banquet table with automotive journalists, Mercedes executives, and the Maybach's head engineer, at Hamburg's Elbe Lounge. A 1932 Maybach DS8 Zeppelin, the glossy brown-yellow of Hellmann's Dijonnaise mustard, was parked by the entrance of the lounge as a kind of welcoming talisman. Pelted by rain, the vintage V-12 passenger car, with its side-mounted tires, running boards, jump seats, and suicide doors, inspired gasps of admiration from arriving guests.

After dessert, the group repaired to a smoking room for Cuban Cohibas and cognac. I took a few puffs from the cigar of Dutch, the formidable editor of *AutoWeek*. Attila came to my side, indicating he was ready to go.

"It's a good thing we weren't seated together," Attila said on the way back to the hotel.

"Why? I sort of wished we hadn't been at opposite ends of the table."

"This way we each lit up an end. What were they talking about down there?"

"Dan—he's a freelancer based in the D.C. suburbs—was telling me how he spent six weeks stalking a robin who ruined three of his test cars by splattering them with its daily droppings. He finally hunted the bird down in the neighbor's yard and shot it with a BB gun. The guy beside him, Dave, was humming the Loony Tunes cartoon theme while Dan was speaking. What were they saying at your end?"

"They all kept asking, 'What do you do? Why are you here? Who are you?' "

"That's a bit rude. What did you tell them?"

"At first I told them I was with you, that we were working on a book. Then, when they pushed, I told them I was a teacher. When they asked, 'Of what?' I said, 'What do you want to learn?' I was playing with them a little. When they wouldn't give up asking, I finally said, 'You really want to know who I am? I am the God of Driving.' "

We both laughed. "Congratulations. You've grown into your title. You didn't used to think you were worthy of it."

"Yeah. I like it now."

ATTILA asked me to have a drink with him at the Louis C. Jacob Hotel's small ground-floor bar. We sat on stools beneath colorful spherical light fixtures suspended from the ceiling like inverted balloons. Attila ordered champagne for me, scotch for himself, and he returned to our conversation from the previous night.

"What exists between us cannot be more, or less, than it is. I cannot do with less. If it's more, it will be destroyed."

"Sounds like it's a pretty fine line we walk."

"It's so fine that it's invisible. But if we walk either above or below that line, that line will become visible, and then it will be too late."

"Have you thought about this a lot?" I asked.

"I think about it all the time. Am I a magician to be able to see everything so clearly?"

"You are a magician. You make fear disappear."

"You are a rare person, Amy. You're powerful—but you do not use your power to hurt people. Now I will tell you what happened to me in the back of the Maybach today. Remember when I fell asleep?"

"Of course I do. It was strange—so short and deep."

"I fell asleep for exactly three minutes. I saw the time on the clock on the rear instrument panel just before I closed my eyes, and just after I woke up."

"That is short."

"For those three minutes I stopped breathing. And I saw what's waiting for me afterward. What you would call a vision."

"What do you mean?" I asked.

"The vision was—very nice," he continued. "I liked it. He was showing me what's there, so I would not be afraid. And I'm not."

"What was it like? Did you see anybody?"

"There weren't people. No. It wasn't like that. It was . . . another dimension."

"The rainbow!"

"Yes, that is when the rainbow came up. You see, the moment I gain control of my life, then it will be time to leave."

"What do you mean?" I asked again. "I'm helping you to gain control—so I'm also helping you leave?" He was composed, I was agitated, and about to faint off the bar stool from fatigue.

"It could take forty more years. We don't know. I do know, though, that I'm not afraid." He looked so beatific, I was no longer alarmed. But I was still dizzy with exhaustion. "This happened to me once before, in Germany," he said serenely. "That time I was sitting in the back of a Rolls."

"Attila, I need your help. Would you mind taking me back to my room? I feel like I'm going to pass out—it's the jetlag."

He rose gallantly to the occasion. Attila was not only the hardiest man I had ever known, he was also the most fey. At my door he said, "I'm going back to the bar for one more drink." He looked radiant, and relaxed. "Good night, diva," he said.

"Good night, God of Driving."

The next thing I knew I was being awakened by an insistent, intrusive Teutonic knock, at 6:00 A.M. "I am here for your bags," a blonde bellhop said through the crack I opened in my hotel room door. "The rest of the group is already downstairs having coffee. You're late."

WE ALL had breakfast—pastries, kiwi juice, espressos—aboard the *Xenia,* a yacht that conveyed our band along the icy Elbe from the Teufelsbruck pier to the Hamburg airport. We were then loaded onto a sixty-eight-foot-long private Daimler-

Chrysler jet, equipped with six seats and a sofa. I threw my back pashmina over my face and tried without success to sleep during the one-hour flight to Stuttgart.

As I felt the plane make its descent, I lowered the cashmere shawl and looked around the cabin. Everybody was exactly where I had left them fifty minutes earlier—two of the journalists were still engaged in the card game they had started at takeoff. The man opposite me still had on his Bose headset. But there was no sign of Attila anywhere—only a vacant spot on the divan where he had been sitting when I closed my eyes.

We touched down smoothly, and the door to the cockpit opened. Out stepped Attila. "I was with the pilots for the landing," he explained. "In the jump seat. It was great. I'm going to have to get my license. You know, the copilot works harder than the pilot—just like the codriver works harder than the driver in rallies. Did I ever tell you I raced in rallies in Turkey?"

"No, you didn't—but I've got no doubt that it's your destiny to fly," I said. Attila's father, naturally, had wanted him to be an air force pilot like himself. But Attila's astigmatism (which inexplicably—maybe psychosomatically—corrected itself after he began to teach driving) had disqualified him. I told Attila that maybe cars and motorcycles were a stand-in for what he was really fated to do—fly planes.

AWAITING US on the tarmac was a royal flush of 57s, a prismatic formation of five Maybachs, sparkling in the sun. Ours was metallic gray and silver. Daunted by German road signs, limitless speeds, and jetlag, I did not even consider driving— the passenger chair was good enough for me.

Our fleet of Maybachs wove through apple orchards and gold-crested autumn trees, en route to the town of Sindelfingen, site of the Center of Excellence, "the epicenter of the Maybach brand world," we were informed. The head of the Center of Excellence and several of his deputies delivered brief presentations about the Maybach's styling and engineering. We learned, for example, that the grand napa leather upholstering of the Maybach's interiors came strictly from the hides of south German cows, and that the roof's thirty solar cells cool the dashboard, seats, and steering wheel when it's hot outside.

In the Maybach commissioning studio there were several cabinets, each like a giant mah-jongg set, stocked with magnetized color chips (which you could click together to see how they worked in combination), as well as with leather samples, rug swatches, and wood specimens. Ranged on shelves above the cupboards were made-to-order Maybach accessories: humidors, silverware, luggage, and golf bags. Stefan, the head of global product communication, switched on the configurator, a digital visualization device that simulated for the Maybach patron via computerized animation many of the 2 million existing design permutations. One option he showed us was a retractable flagpole for flying the family crest.

We ate lunch at the center (using Maybach flatware, of course)—beef consommé, followed by fish with lentils and apple tart. This time, at my end of the banquet table we talked about Bugsy Siegel, Barbara Stanwyck, and South Carolina's Clemson College, where students, one journalist said, could major in racing.

After lunch we returned to our Maybachs (one for every two guests) for a scenic, meandering drive to Frankfurt, about 250 miles away. Our hosts had programmed our route into the computerized navigation system, which Attila listened to in German (*"Links!"* it commanded him in a very imperative mood). We were also given a diagram-filled, step-by-step hardbound map booklet, unintelligible to me and too awkward for Attila to consult while he drove. Still, we lost our way several times.

The Maybach 57 performed equally well on the impeccable autobahn and the crooked streets of the quaint, tidy villages of our detours. At a rest stop near Würzburg, where we used the bathrooms, the car instantly attracted an exclamatory, photo-snapping busload of Japanese tourists. We stopped at a McDonald's too, for Diet Cokes and more directions. Inserting our *grosse*-size drink containers through the graceful, manaclelike Maybach cup holders seemed an act of desecration.

"Would you tell me what it was like—those three minutes yesterday in the back of the 62?" I asked Attila when we had reentered the autobahn. I had been longing to hear more, but until that moment had felt timid about probing.

"I don't go back, Amy. I lived it, and that's it. You know nothing's alien to me."

"If you're quoting Seneca, he said 'nothing *human* is alien to me,'" I replied.

"Notice what I omitted?"

With my new triband Vertu telephone I called the *Vanity Fair* offices to fact-check a story, and retrieved messages from my home answering machine. Attila took the car up to 140 miles per hour (even at that speed the car was silent), and then to 155 miles per hour, its maximum. Still the ride was smooth and quiet. The only way of gauging how fast we were going, besides watching the speedometer needle, was seeing how far and how quickly the other cars (even a BMW M3) fell behind us, as if we had put them on rapid-motion rewind. Then Attila braked the Maybach back down to 120. "Woo, whoa, woo," he said, as he felt the soft six-caliper electrohydraulic mechanism respond.

"Is this the best car you've ever driven?"

"You betcha. The best brakes. The best acceleration. I have a feeling this car senses which way the road is going—it's almost steering my hands."

"Does it feel alive?"

"No. It feels like great craftsmanship, with great intelligence behind it."

"It's nice to have intelligence behind a car's design, instead of greed. Are you in love with it?"

"You can't be in love with a machine."

The only blemishes on this otherwise perfect car were the specks of dirt accumulating on its windshield. To expunge them, Attila turned on the pressurized window cleaning system. Great foaming jets of water spewed across the thick, gray-tinted windshield, making a froth through which the wipers skimmed like straight razors through lather. Still, stubborn bits of grime remained.

"It didn't clean up very well," I said.

"Because it's greasy."

"Greasy dirt? From what? Other cars?"

"No, from insects."

"So, those are insects' carcasses splattered all over the windshield?"

"No, not even—only their internal organs stick to the glass. Their other body parts fly off on impact."

Soon after nightfall Attila found our designated way station, an inn called the Schafhof ("sheep farm") in Amorbach, built in the fifteenth century as a Benedictine monastery. As we pulled into this pastoral refuge, another Maybach—whose raking, spaceshiplike bi-xenon headlamps bleached the night air—was making its exit.

Dan, the robin stalker, was at the wheel. "Everyone else cheated and took the direct route to Frankfurt," he said, lowering the window, his face chalk-blue in the eerie light. "This poor innkeeper set out all these fancy pastries and nobody's touched them. You definitely should check it out, though. The place is beautiful."

We drank coffee beside the Schafhof's rustic sandstone hearth and promised the hotelier and his waitress that we would return at the first opportunity. And then we lit out for Frankfurt, which we reached around eight.

Our hotel—hovering vertiginously above the city on the upper floors of a glass bank tower—was as contemporary and cold as the Schafhof was ancient and picturesque. Attila and I changed quickly (I dressed down for him this time—pants and a cashmere twin set) and we caught up with our Maybach group, already seated for dinner, at Holbein's restaurant next to the Städel art museum.

AS OUR flight left late the next day, we asked for a car in which we could tour Frankfurt before departing for the airport. This was not to be a sightseer's circuit of the city, but a whirlwind time trip through Attila's Frankfurt past. Our hosts placed at our disposal not only a Mercedes but a driver and a guide. From the backseat Attila directed the two Germans to four of his former residences—a crescent-shaped apartment building; a hotel; a warehouse, the penthouse of which he had converted into a six-bedroom loft; and a house where he had roomed with his ill-fated friend, an athlete who died under mysterious circumstances. We also drove by the last house occupied by this same man, whose death had induced Attila to start smoking again, and the wooded park where Attila used to walk his rottweiler, Athos, named after Alexandre Dumas' musketeer. "This park is where my friend's body was found," Attila said. "He was the second close friend that I lost."

At the Frankfurt airport we left the comfort and privacy of the Lufthansa first class lounge for a self-service restaurant in the main terminal. Attila had not wanted to leave the country without reacquainting himself with the juicy, spicy-sweet flavors of *Bratwurst mit Curry*, which tasted to me like an exotically seasoned version of the cafeteria classic Beenie Weenie.

On the flight home on the upper deck of a 747, we drank a bottle of burgundy and polished off plates of cheese and chocolate. With his tray table heaped high with treats (and *Spider-Man* on the DVD), Attila reminded me of a contented baby in a high chair, and I told him so. I wanted to learn more about his life in Germany, and his two friends' deaths, but repressing my journalist's instinct to pry, I refrained from inquiring. Instead I asked him what his favorite moments of the trip had been.

"I liked coming to the Schafhof," he said. "And sitting in the cockpit for the landing in Stuttgart—and then seeing all the Maybachs lined up, waiting."

The plump, henlike male flight attendant, who had been fussing over us, asked Attila, "What was it like driving the Maybach?"

"It was like flying a 747, but on the ground," he answered. "It's that fast and that smooth."

When the limo service Lincoln Town Car we shared dropped Attila off at home in Queens, he said good-bye as casually as if we had just spent four minutes, not four days, together. Back in my apartment, when I played my answering machine, there was one message accidentally taped through my Vertu phone. It had recorded the otherworldly *whoosh* of the Maybach on the autobahn, reaching 155 miles per hour.

Ducati Dudes, Maserati Men

Angela, the president of a PR firm that represented Ducati, the Italian motorcycle company, saw my *Travel + Leisure* story and, not long after, read the *New York Times* Styles section article in which I publicly proclaimed my love for the Harley-Davidson V-Rod. Angela's colleague Seema phoned to say, "We were so upset about you and the Harley! We wished it had been a Ducati!" She asked if I would like to try out the ST4s, Ducati's sports-touring motorcycle (it had the performance capabilities of a race bike, but the relative comfort of a cruiser), as well as some Ducati gear.

As I had dug into my own shrinking pockets to pay for the V-Rod rental—which had brought us a week of two-wheel bliss—I readily accepted her offer. Besides, it always gave me a kick to present Attila with yet another slick new vehicle to drive. Ducati even promised to reimburse me for garage costs—a boon, because after the Hayabusa debacle, we decided never again to pinch pennies with cut-rate parking. "We're going to have fun with the ST4s," said Attila. "But the Ducati I'm really looking forward to trying is the 999."

The apparel Seema sent us, designed for cold-weather riding, could never be mistaken for Harley gear. Wholly synthetic rather than leather, it looked like the paraphernalia of an intergalactic athlete rather than the accoutrements of a heavy-metal outlaw. The knees of the thickly insulated pants were fortified with rigid plates, as were the vast shoulders of the jacket. The boots—shaped liked stiff, thick Christmas stockings—could have come from the shoe closet of the Caped Crusader. Encased in the total head-to-toe, boot-to-helmet getup, we no longer had any clear gender, nameable identity, or true scale.

I was in my street clothes (a Beene cardigan and black snakeskin pants) and Attila in his new black-and-red Ducati jacket when we drove his Camry to Cycle Connection, in Lodi, New Jersey, to pick up the ST4s. "You can't miss us," we were informed over the phone by the two men named Mark who helped us. "We're just behind Satin Dolls. It's the club you see on *The Sopranos.*"

The red Ducati ST4s that Mark number one (he spelled it with a *k*, wore his thinning hair in a ponytail, and owned Cycle Connection) presented to us, all tuned up and ready to go, might have been an abstract monument to speed conceived by the Futurist sculptor Umberto Boccioni. Its front narrowed like the nose cone of a missile, its middle was scooped out like a greyhound's, and its back flickered like a comet's tail.

I shadowed Attila back to Manhattan in the Toyota Camry, mimicking his lane changes, turns, and accelerations on a split-second delay. He sat aboard the Ducati as naturally as Pecos Bill on an Oklahoma tornado. Attila paid the tolls for two and we passed single-file into New York. In tandem we glided 212 feet above the Hudson River on the upper level of the George Washington Bridge—a task that a year before had filled me with a terror equal to my present exuberance. I was now a member of that club, a million strong, of motorists who passed annually over Othmar H. Ammann's steel masterpiece of engineering.

We arrived in the city with barely enough time to make my one o'clock lunch appointment with Larry at Michael's. Attila agreed to drive me there on the Ducati, in spite of the fact that it had begun to drizzle. He stowed my black LambertsonTruex purse in the left saddlebag, a picnic-hamper-like contraption fitted with a shallow, semicircular handle.

"So how do I ride on the back of a Ducati ST4s?" I asked.

"You have to crouch forward, not sit up like you did on the Harleys. And don't hold me. Hold the handle."

This sounded partly like technical advice, and partly like a biblical commandment: *Noli me tangere.*

"This handle?" I inquired uncertainly, sliding the pads of my fingertips under the semicircular grip of the saddlebag.

"Yeah, that one," he said absently from deep within his helmet. He was adjusting his gloves (always the last gear to go on), and his mind had already zoomed ahead to the ride. In Attila's cryptic code of chivalry, an elastic loophole opened up on the subject of how a man treats a lady when he's near his bike. As soon as he's shed his mufti for his gear, he is no longer obliged to help her on or off with her coat—especially if it's a motorcycle jacket. Nor is he required to pull out her chair from a restaurant table, or even open a car door for her (although I've seen Attila slip on this one).

The ride from the East Seventy-ninth Street garage to midtown was a clammy catastrophe. Though the rain was not much more than a fine mist, slowly but surely I was getting soaked—and all that moisture was chemically compounding with my Aveda Replenishing Body Cream to glue my snakeskin trousers to my own epidermis. (Later that day when I peeled the pants off inside out, my legs were mottled with a scaly black pattern left by the bleeding dye.) And every time Attila tried to turn west, we were blocked by blue police barriers, delaying me progressively later for lunch with Larry. These inconveniences, however, were tolerable compared with the persistent fact that whenever Attila downshifted (click, click, *click)* or braked the Ducati, I catapulted forward into him, helmet hitting helmet. And every time he upshifted or accelerated, I bounced backward. Bracing myself against a fall, I clung, knuckles whitening, to the saddlebags' left and right handles—which had become two blades cutting into my hooked, strained fingers. What on earth had Attila been thinking? Was he trying to boost my confidence with his misplaced, casual faith in my backseat abilities, or was he simply self-absorbed and indifferent?

He stopped the ST4s near Fifty-seventh Street on Sixth Avenue. "I'm going to have to leave you here," he said, finally lifting his visor so he could hear and speak. "I can't get any closer to Fifty-fifth Street." It was true. I wouldn't be able to alight in front of Michael's from the Ducati, as I had promised Larry— who for twenty minutes now had been awaiting my bike-borne arrival.

"That's all right!" I managed perkily. "I'll walk between the raindrops. Those handles are uncomfortable," I added nonchalantly. "I barely stayed on."

"You'll get used to it," he said sympathetically. As he spoke, I followed his sight line. It extended beyond the hateful saddlebags' handles to a sturdy metal red hoop rising at an angle from the backseat I had just vacated.

"*That's* the handle you meant?" I said incredulously. "I thought you had told me to hold on to *those.*" He shook his head, smiling. I wanted to give the ST4s another try, the right way—right away. "When do you think can we ride again?"

"Don't keep Larry waiting any longer, Amy. We'll speak a little later."

He always succeeded in detaching himself from me with those words.

The streets, I learned when I finally reached the restaurant, half an hour late for my appointment, were blocked for the Veterans' Day parade. Poor old soldiers—no one had been cheering or even watching them, just cursing them for clogging up lunchtime traffic.

OUR NEXT, more leisurely excursion with the Ducati, back to Bear Mountain, was not so much about seeing (as it had been on the V-Rod) as about pure riding. Somehow, once I was connected to the correct handle, I knew by instinct all the right moves to make. The faster we went (we made it up to 100), the lower and more forward I pitched my body. When the bike decelerated, I was able to lift my torso, but just a little. Mostly I hunkered down like a jockey on the homestretch and felt the wind and the speed. My arms, bent behind me like a pair of tailfins, become an aerodynamic appendage of the machine. I grew comfortable enough to grasp the handle with just one hand, sometimes with the fist facing in toward my body, sometimes with it turned out toward the receding road. When we reached our top velocity (which automatically brought the bike up into a low wheelie) I felt like a speed skater, so low was my body to the ground and so close together behind me were my hands. Curiously, it was at that moment that I felt most placid, and secure.

At a scenic point in the state park we took a break and, alone except for a pair of Asian tourists, snapped some photos with a disposable Kodak. "You won't believe how good you look on this bike!" I said, backing up against the sun to compose the picture.

"You've said that about every single bike you've seen me on."

"Well, it keeps getting better."

"Yes, it does. This is the best motorcycle I've driven," he said, puffing on his cigarette and squinting (right eye closed more than the left) into the sunshine at the slate-hued lake and the rusty foliage spread before him.

"I'm so happy to hear you say that—again." It was the most fun I'd had on a motorcycle so far. I felt as if I'd been riding the red Ducati all my life. "There's only one thing I miss, though, when we're on it."

"What's that?"

"The conversation."

"Well then, think of it as a silent movie—but a very fast one."

When the photos came back from the developer, Attila lingered over one that he had taken of me (normally he gave this kind of attention only to pictures of himself). "Amy, you look like you're about seven years old in this picture," he said.

I had noticed the same thing.

PARTING WITH the ST4s was not as difficult as I had supposed. Other exciting prospects awaited us—the 999, for example, which Ducati promised to have ready for us in January. In the mean time, Stéphane, a French publicist friend, invited me to a party to celebrate the U.S. launch of two new Maseratis—the Coupé and the Spyder—at the Four Seasons, in the Seagram Building, on East Fifty-second Street. Attila did not want to attend, so I recruited Joe from Maybach-Mercedes as my date. I wore a very short silver-and-black satin shift, thigh-high patent leather stiletto-heeled boots, and fishnet stockings. This was an outfit that modesty would have prevented me from wearing around Attila. As we crossed the forecourt of the Seagram Building, tented for the occasion, paparazzi bulbs flashed their applause. But the scene stealers on the Seagram's plaza were not Manolo Blahnik's tall, shiny boots, but the even glossier and more fetishistic Maseratis on display: the 2003 four-seat Coupé Cambiocorsa, in atomic red; the 2003 two-seat Spyder, in Mediterranean blue; and most alluring of all, a mouse-colored 1959 5000GT, formerly the property of the Shah of Iran.

Inside we bumped into Angela, the PR president, who suggested setting up a lunch meeting in a few weeks with some visiting Ducati colleagues from Bologna. The room became so crowded that Joe and I found ourselves pinned by the mob against a wall. A man elbowed by, spilling red wine down the front of my satin dress. That was our exit cue. Joe and I scuttled sideways out the door to the now-deserted tented outdoor space, where the two of us were able to inspect the Maseratis closely and at leisure. (At upscale Manhattan parties it was almost an unwritten law that guests ignore the object of the celebration: the paintings at an art opening, the bride at a wedding, the corpse at a funeral, or a two-hundred-thousand-dollar car at an automobile launch.) We seated ourselves inside the red Coupé, stroking its dark gray dashboard and its quilted ceiling. But we felt a little let down by the Coupé's exterior design. "The back looks like a Honda Prelude," Joe sniffed (he was a Mercedes man, after all). "But this Maserati is really all about the engine."

"Let's have a look," I suggested.

We climbed out of the Coupé and Joe slid his index finger into the seam of the hood, popping it open like a jack-in-the-box. We gasped at the red-and-gray V-8 engine suddenly revealed to us in all its virile glory. It rippled beneath our stunned gazes like the abdominal muscles of a Roman god.

A security officer, who had been keeping a tense eye on us, came over and admonished us for getting a little too familiar with the Coupé. Stéphane, the publicist, appeased the guard and escorted us diplomatically, his arm linked through mine, over to Jeff, Maserati's U.S. communications director. "Just wait until you hear the sound of that Maserati motor," Stéphane murmured in his runny French accent. "It eez the *sexiest* noise." Jeff promised to arrange a test drive of the Coupé for Attila and me in December.

So that is how Attila and I found ourselves back in New Jersey, this time at Maserati-Ferrari headquarters in Englewood Cliffs, on a cloudy early-winter day. Jeff welcomed the two of us at the reception desk and led us to a red Maserati Coupé Cambiocorsa—the same one I had examined at the party—and gave us his best insider's tips on driving it. Intimidated by the prospect of taking its wheel, I asked Jeff whether girls accounted for a significant percentage of his consumer demographic.

"No, not yet," he said knowledgeably. "But we're beginning to attract women buyers on the West Coast. They're catching on that pulling up in a Maserati is about the most emasculating thing a woman can do to a guy."

"Cambiocorsa," I learned, referred to the Maserati's paddle-shifting system, based on a Formula One race car's. The stick and clutch were replaced by a pair of ergonomic levers on the underside of the steering wheel—downshifting to the left at nine o'clock and upshifting to the right at three o'clock. Unlike the Tiptronic shift systems built into Mercedeses, BMWs, and Porsches, the Cambiocorsa's was mechanically identical to a manual-shift car's; it tended, for example, to roll downhill backward in first gear.

"The Maserati has a physical gearbox and clutch," Jeff elaborated. "Since you have no clutch *pedal*, it'll seem like there are gremlins inside operating the clutch for you. And you *will* feel the engine. You want that kind of feedback in a race car. The single most important thing to know about driving this car is that it's all in the throttle foot—the right leg. You'll get the most power out of the car if you understand that with the Cambiocorsa, the accelerator *is* the clutch."

I PHONED Joe as Attila gunned the Maserati onto the Palisades Parkway. "Joe, are you hearing that?" I asked. Joe was an excellent mimic, not just of people but of engine noises.

He was already making Maserati sounds into the phone.

"What's it feel like?" he begged to know.

"Right now—like a zipper sliding up a dress very fast."

"Tell him they did it," Attila weighed in. "The Italians know what they're doing. It feels like a race car. And Jeff is right—you get the best out of this car when you work the accelerator almost like a clutch, even when you downshift. But it still doesn't have the pickup of the Maybach or the Viper."

"Of those three cars, which would you choose?" I asked, clicking off with Joe. We were now heading into New York State on 87.

"The Maybach, of course—the Maybach's a sports car, and then some. The Maserati is beautiful, incredible, powerful, but for me it's a little *schiki-micki*."

"Where'd you get that term?"

"Germany. . I can see *you* in this, Amy."

"*Me?* In the Maserati?"

He nodded.

Clearly Attila was not the kind of man who'd feel emasculated by a woman in a Maserati Coupé.

"I guess I'll have to learn to drive it."

"Not in this weather." It had begun to rain. "But I still see you in the SLK 320. If not in Fire Mist, then maybe in all black."

"Why? In case you want to borrow it?" Attila's wardrobe consisted largely of black T-shirts, jackets, and boots, and his apartment (which I had never visited) had at some point been furnished exclusively with black leather sofas and chairs.

"Sure. Why not?"

Once again, Attila navigated us to Bear Mountain, which I had by now seen in all its seasonal variations. This time it was blotched with snow, a shiny white impasto smeared on metallic boulders and spidery trees. Without horizon or sunlight, the sylvan winterscape rose to either side of us like an Impressionist's painted stage flats.

"This Maserati can really corner," Attila noted as we wound up the mountainside. "Any other car would have tilted on that ninety-degree turn. This car's really fun when you know what you're doing. Learning to race the Formula Dodge at Skip really made me think different about my teaching and my driving.

"Differently."

"Think differently. The only problem is, I really miss this"—he stroked the air where a stick would have been. "I like using my right hand."

"It must be like dancing with a one-armed girl."

"I wouldn't know. They also could have made the brake a little higher than the gas pedal, like on the Viper, so it would be easier to do the 'blip' "—the heel-and-toe downshifting technique taught at Skip Barber to both the racing school and the driving school students. To execute the blip, you rolled your right foot laterally, inside to outside, from the brake to the throttle, as you passed through neutral. This kept the RPM high, smoothing the transition between gears. I never got the hang of it (my slender-toed boots were just part of the problem), but the best drivers did it instinctively.

"If I stepped on the accelerator in first gear I would spin the rear tires. I used to do that with my cars when I was a bad boy."

"When did you stop being a bad boy?"

"I don't know."

ATTILA hugged me good-bye at my corner and rode on to a Queens used-car dealership. He had his eye on a well-priced Volvo S80 for use as a teaching car. He hoped to return the Camry to Earl, owner of the driving school, to whom it actually belonged. Earl would then be obliged to pay Attila a higher hourly rate, and Attila would gain more freedom. The catch to having his own car was that the commercial insurance rates and repair costs, which Attila would then have to pay himself, would be so high they would, in combination with the monthly car payments, eat up the difference between his old pay rate and his new one.

The first time Attila had gone to the Queens dealership, he had taken me along, and Arnie, his salesman, told Attila he recognized me from magazine pictures. The second time Attila rode up to the lot on the Ducati ST4s. This third time, when Attila arrived in the Maserati, Arnie couldn't take it anymore. "Who *are* you?" he demanded to know. "You'll need thirty years to find out," Attila answered. He decided against the Volvo, realizing he'd be trading one yoke for another.

The whole driving-school business was exploitative. Not only did school proprietors take health insurance costs out of instructors' hourly earnings, they required that the men in their fleets pay for gas, parking, and towing. If a school car broke down, for example, or was towed away, an instructor was unlikely to be given another car to drive; he simply lost income until the auto was back on the road. And if it snowed or rained, instructors' earnings dropped to zero. Attila, I argued, should be taking in at least as much as a personal trainer or a licensed masseur (both former professions of his). He was the only instructor at the school willing to teach highway driving, stick shift, and motorcycle—the most labor-intensive and dangerous courses offered. For an hour of Attila's services, the school charged about $40 ($55 for stick-shift and motorcycle), of which he said he took home less than half, minus taxes. My masseur commanded $100 for an hour home-visit session, and my Pilates teacher netted $80 for a lesson in her studio. Attila's profession (which dealt with life and death) was grossly undervalued—as teaching of any kind generally is.

"At the very least," I had told Attila before he took off for the Queens used-car dealership, "Earl should be charging a higher fee for his top instructor, just as hair salons do with the best stylists, gyms do with the most desirable trainers, and bordellos do with their most beautiful girls."

"Who?"

"Brothels."

"I wouldn't know," he answered. "Earl's not a bad guy, Amy. He's got a problem with trust. He was cheated by his own family. That's why he started his own business." Attila could always see the other side of a story so clearly that he was usually able to short-circuit his own anger. And so particular were his powers of empathy, he told me one day that he knew what it felt like to give birth. "I had a dream once that I was having a baby," he had explained. "I experienced the labor pains."

"What did you have?" (He often gave me his dreams to interpret.)

"A dark-haired male infant."

"That," I had said, "would be you."

We both regarded his present situation as temporary, and knew that when the timing was right, and probably with my help, Attila would strike out on his own—somehow, be reborn.

FOR OUR second day with the Maserati, Attila decided we'd go back to Lakeville, Connecticut, home base of the Skip Barber Driving School. We would not be allowed on the track with the Maserati—it was closed for the season. But the Taconic Parkway, the route we were taking, posed its own set of challenges —hairpin turns, roller-coaster hills, speed-crazed lane changers. Before we took off I called our pal Andrew, Skip's manager of consumer marketing, to let him know we were heading his way.

En route, we stopped at a Mobil station for gas (we went 111 miles on a third of a tank) and a rest room, where I removed my snagged panty hose and threw them into the trash. Bare-legged and shivering, I warmed myself up in the Maserati, observing Attila as he smoked a cigarette in front of the station with a younger man. When they finished, Attila brought the dark stranger over to the car and introduced him to me. He was a Jordanian, the owner of a deli in Fishkill. He wrote down his number in my notebook for Attila, who promised to stop in for a sandwich. I knew the man fully expected to see us at his deli counter, and I felt just as sure that Attila would never show up. His knack for forging instant friendships was exceeded only by his ability to dissolve them quickly, without compunction. After his basic curiosity about a person was satisfied, he lost interest. After a point, for example, he tuned out his students' monologues, and once they had finished his course, they were out of his life forever.

"So what was that, a couple of Muslim guys standing around talking?"

"Yeah, something like that."

Attila piloted us from Route 44 to the Skip Barber corporate offices, a flat redbrick complex built in the style of a suburban elementary school. In the parking lot we took more pictures, and just across the building's threshold we ran into Bruce, Attila's head teacher from his three-day racing school, the ex-hippie who had tagged him "the Doberman pinscher with a hand grenade in his mouth." Bruce directed us through the warren of cubicles to Andrew's desk.

We lured Andrew (who did not exactly resist) away from his computer, ushered him out of the office, and installed him in the driver's seat of the Maserati.

"Amy, you'll have to squeeze into the back," Attila said. "You know I won't sit there."

Yes, of course. I had nearly forgotten the first of Attila's acknowledged phobias—the backseat of a two-door.

"In the city this car must feel like a caged animal," Andrew said. "I'll show you some of my favorite backroads where we can let this thing do what it wants." He drove the Maserati up to a bluff, and then, at the drop-off, opened it up, pushing the needle sky high, carving up both sides of the road. Naked knees jackknifed to cheekbones, I rattled around the back. The snowy landscape flickered by like old newsreel footage, then blurred to a smudge of gray. Andrew slowed down when we reached a larger road, with posted speed limits and stop signs.

"Thanks, Andrew!" I said, a little breathlessly. "That was exciting. You handled the car beautifully. I really enjoyed seeing you have so much fun." I stopped myself, realizing that I was repeating some of the phrases I had used before with Attila. Oh well—I remembered how it felt when I first heard him, on his cell phone, calling his other students "sweethaht" and "deah."

"Your place is near here? Why don't we drive over?" I suggested to Andrew.

"My wife and kids should be there now. Will they be surprised to see me drive up in a Maserati Coupé! This car's amazing. The brakes are unbelievable. It's got incredible grip. It just doesn't lift."

But nobody was home in his two-story colonial. Inside the open garage, the only vehicle to be seen was an FAO Schwarz toddler's yellow cab. "Any neighbors you want to show it off to?" I asked.

"No. Our neighbors don't speak to us. We're not rich enough."

We took more pictures in Andrew's driveway, and then, ceding his place to Attila, Andrew scrambled into the backseat. "I fit much better here than you," he said to me. "You guys want to go for a cup of coffee?"

We drove—within the speed limit—to a coffee shop, passing on the way a large house dominating a hill. "That's Skip's place," Andrew said, with the proud resentment of a serf toward the local lord. "The view from up there is fantastic."

"Should I get out and genuflect?" I asked.

"No, too cold today. There are a lot of other celebrities' houses around here, but we don't have time for a tour."

The girl behind the counter at the coffee shop said they could not serve us because they were closing early.

"Why?" Andrew asked.

"Because of the ice storm. It'll be hitting here in about a half hour."

"We'd better leave right now," Attila said.

303

"I wouldn't take the Taconic if I were you," Andrew cautioned. "It'll be safer on 684." We shuttled Andrew back to his office and his VW GTI.

Attila decided to take the Taconic anyway; with people and machines he liked a challenge. In any case, what began to fall from the sky was not ice but sleet, precipitation that afforded him an opportunity to practice finding the "rain line," a grip-seeking trick he had picked up at Skip Barber. "The line you normally follow on a track is scarred with tire marks, greasy with oil," Attila explained, "not a problem in dry weather. But when it rains, the 'dry line' of a track or road becomes too slippery." Even though our Maserati and the car directly behind us were both going 50 miles per hour, the distance between the two vehicles kept widening, Attila pointed out, because of his adherence to the rain line.

"Would you have liked to drive the Maserati the way Andrew did?" I asked as Attila plowed through the sleet.

"Yes, on a racetrack. I would never risk going speeds like that on a public road."

"You mean, risk getting a ticket? You went faster than that—a hundred fifty-five miles an hour, and more smoothly—on the autobahn in the Maybach with me."

"Yes, that's what I mean."

"I don't even think you'd drive the Maserati like Andrew did on a track."

"What do you mean?"

"Well, first of all, Andrew used the brakes a lot, like we did on the track. You've driven all this way without hitting the brake once that I've noticed—when you've needed to slow down, you've downshifted."

"True."

"Andrew drives more like the automotive journalists we met

in Germany on the Maybach trip than like you. Or like the race-car drivers at Skip and Summit Point—eager, excited by speed, a little aggressive with the machine. You like holding back, listening to the car, learning from it. Your approach is more . . . tender."

He was smiling, his dark eyes animated by pinpoints of light. Without saying a word, he had made me realize on my own what he had been thinking all along. This was the same way he had taught me to drive, and probably the only way anyone ever really learns anything.

"You are how you drive," he answered. "Something I've noticed about many American men," he added, switching topics, "is that they know one subject very well—motorcycles, football, banking, books."

"Or women," I proposed.

"But then, when it comes to the other areas of life, they're lost. Jeff, at Maserati, told me that some American automotive journalists had complained that the Maserati Coupé had no cup holder."

"*Cup holder?* As if any Italian would ever want to drink his espresso in his car out of a paper cup. Well, there's one feature the Maserati designers remembered that the Viper guys left out."

"What's that?"

"The vanity mirror," I said, flipping down the sun visor to show him the illuminated looking glass. "The Italians might have overlooked the cup holder, but they would never have forgotten about the girl."

"No. They would never forget about the girl."

ON THE last day of the Maserati loan, Seema and Angela, Ducati's PR girls, took us out to lunch with their colleagues from Italy at Michael's, while Larry observed us from the next table. Angela seated Attila beside Dan, Ducati's head of product development, who, like him, was a thirty-year veteran of motorcycling. I was on Dan's right and on my other side was David, the head of Ducati marketing worldwide, who tried to interest me in some of the events he was planning. His pet project, he explained, was "Fast Women," a program designed to promote motorcycling among females.

Later that afternoon, Larry, who had never before seen Attila in a jacket and tie, called me from his office. "Amy," he said into the phone, "Attila could pass as anything, fit in anywhere. He'd make a great spy." I reported this remark to Attila, whose nickname at school had been Ajan—"spy" in Turkish. He had named his dog after himself.

"Happy New Year"

Although I was spending most of my time on a new *Vanity Fair* assignment (on Kenneth, Jackie Kennedy's hairdresser), Attila and I saw each other several times in late December. Our most interesting meeting took place on New Year's Eve day. As on the preceding December 31, he took me to lunch at a Turkish restaurant in Sunnyside, Queens. I brought him a gift-wrapped holiday bottle of Johnny Walker Blue, as I had done the year before. He had been pleased with my choice; it turned out to be what his father drank. And he brought me a bouquet of roses—red, yellow, white, and pink—tied in a curling red grosgrain bow.

Attila was telling me over a meal of lentil soup, eggplant, and chicken kebabs that on January 1 he would be quitting smoking. He would begin working out again. He was going to clean out his apartment and renovate his bathroom. He was going to eat three meals a day and limit his work schedule to no more than sixty hours a week. He would put $15 in a jar daily, the amount he had been spending on cigarettes. And with the money he saved, he would finally "have some fun."

"Do you know how long it's been since I've been out on a date, gone to a movie?"

I left his question dangling rhetorically.

"Well, forget about the date part," he said, a little self-consciously.

"You took my daughter and me to see *Jimmy Neutron: Boy Genius* a year ago, and at that point you hadn't been to a movie in five years. And then this past summer you saw *Minority Report*."

"I forgot about that."

"What kind of fun do you have in mind?"

"I will buy a guitar again, and maybe an aquarium. Get a motorcycle if I can. Go snowboarding, go out to the movies sometime. Sometimes. Go out to a restaurant with you like this maybe every two weeks."

Every two weeks sounded like a reasonable schedule.

"Maybe I'll get you a guitar for your birthday," I answered expansively. Though he played saxophone, piano, flute, and even bagpipes, he preferred guitar because he needed no accompaniment. "I'd like to hear you play."

"I know you would." He rested his fork and knife on the edge of his plate, tines and blade inclined inward at identical angles in the "pause" position, and took a sip of his yogurt drink. "The last time we were here was for my birthday."

"But you were here once by yourself since, last summer."

"That's right, on the Hayabusa. I parked it right out there, where I could see it."

"Yes, and you told the restaurant's owner that you were 'bad to the bone,' in Turkish."

"Yeah, I did."

I don't know why Attila clung to this conviction that he was "bad." He had never, as far as I knew, even touched an illegal drug, and he was so peaceable, fur coats made him uneasy. The only "bad" thing he seemed ever to have done was defy his father, the general—by refusing to serve in the military, by dropping out of school and leaving Turkey, by growing his hair and piercing his ears. I had told him several times that there was no shame in evading compulsory military service, that in fact what he had done could be construed as honorable—that he was, to an American, a conscientious objector, and as such was in some pretty good company.

"Do you notice what's wrong with this place?" he asked.

I looked around the restaurant—at the fading travel poster of Istanbul and the gold-embroidered Turkish vest (Attila used to wear one like it in his folk-dancing troupe) displayed on the wall. I scrutinized the waiters, some dark, some blonde, a new crew since we were last there. I studied the faces of the other diners, solemnly bent over their food. And I took note of the refrigerator cases, cool cornucopias laden with meats, pastries, vegetables, and alien delicacies.

"No, what?"

"The floor's not level," he replied. "The restaurant's on a hill, but we shouldn't be noticing that. Nobody wanted to spend the money to even it out."

This flaw had upset his sense of order and quality.

"I like these faces," I said.

"Which faces?"

"Turkish faces." The physiognomies and the geography of the place—Fortieth Street in Queens—were as exotic to me as they were familiar to him. Attila himself both blended in with them and stood out; he could pass, as Larry had pointed out, as anything.

After lunch, while I waited in the Camry, Attila ran into a Turkish specialty store and bought a sackful of imported chocolate bars and a tub of chocolate-nut spread for my daughter, and a slab of cheese, a bag of pistachios, a spinach pie, and a jar of olive paste for me. I watched him through the car's and shop's windows as he made his purchases, with the remaining cash in his wallet. He came out and tossed two white plastic grocery bags (brightened with yellow smiley faces, and the slogan "Have a Nice Day") onto the backseat.

"Take a look at that," he said, indicating the city skyline toward which we were now heading via Northern Boulevard. In the hazy twilight, Manhattan was flattened to a ghostly two dimensions.

"It looks as if the city were cut out of a sheet of silver," I said.

He nodded, unimpressed.

I tried again. "It looks like a mirage."

"Yes. A mirage. I like that much better."

We parked the Camry on my block and sat for a few minutes. He thanked me for improving his English, and his life. "I know I've done things for you too," he proceeded. "Since you've known me, you've learned to enjoy machines. You are discovering that machines will never spit at you, or lie to you, or talk about you behind your back."

"But a machine is not a substitute for a human being," I objected, recoiling from the bitterness behind his words.

"Of course not. Amy, I know that I've helped you in other ways too. That first time I saw you, you were so . . . stiff."

"Like the suspension of the Maserati?" I was aiming to lighten the mood a little.

"I don't know if that's the right word."

"Severe?"

"You're not that way anymore." He had never before addressed the subject of his effect on me.

It was true. "I know I'm more relaxed, more patient, less fearful, more adventuresome than I used to be," I said. "And everybody tells me I look better, which doesn't make too much sense because I'm older. My friend Miriam says she's gotten back the Amy she knew at twenty."

"It's because what's inside of you is now showing through. And what's inside you is very nice."

This time he hugged me good-bye inside of the car, not outside, on the street, as was his custom. And he took my hand, just for a moment.

Right after midnight he phoned to wish me a happy new year. The friends who earlier in the day had invited themselves over to his apartment to celebrate never showed up, and so he spent the evening alone with a bottle of Moët & Chandon— "My idea of a perfect New Year's Eve," he said.

I told him that this year was certainly off to a good start if his first wish for it had already come true.

He told me that I was the only person to whom he had wanted to say "Happy New Year."

I NEXT spoke to Attila from the Palm Beach Four Seasons, where I had gone for the last few days of my daughter's winter break. He had been drinking Jack Daniel's, an activity that had put him in an unusually ebullient mood.

"I have some news for you, Amy. Are you sitting down?"

"No," I answered. "I'm leaning." Though it was a chilly night I was outdoors on a balcony, looking at the whitecaps and the stars, which in Manhattan are obliterated by city lights and smog.

"Keep leaning. The new government in Turkey is going to allow men who have avoided military service back into the country—if we pay a fee of eleven thousand dollars. Maybe I'll be able to return this year, or even in a few months!"

I'd never heard him sound so happy about anything that did not concern a machine.

"You are very much missed in New York," he said.

I noted his careful use of the passive voice.

"Thank you," I said, a little coolly, rather than let him know at that moment that he 'was missed' too. It was good to be the recipient instead of the giver of an homage for a change.

Back in New York, my daughter returned to school and I immersed myself in another *Vanity Fair* story. Everything with Attila settled into a normal routine too. He was working twelve-hour days, teaching the six-hour class, and taking on new students. His favorites of the new year were ex–Mayor Giuliani's seventeen-year-old son, Andrew, and Stephen Rubin, the president and publisher of the Doubleday-Broadway Publishing Group, who at sixty-one decided to earn his license. Attila bonded easily with both men. He had also succeeded in quitting smoking, and I noticed one afternoon when he came to get me in the Camry for a quick cup of coffee that the sclera of his eyeballs had cleared up to an almost spooky white.

"Spooky?" he said, examining them in his rearview mirror at a stoplight.

As he drove uptown he told me that once again he was on the brink of burnout. "I have to set three alarm clocks now to get out of bed in the morning. But then throughout the night I wake up every few hours thinking I'm hearing the first bell." A symptom of his fatigue was an increasing intolerance of careless drivers and pedestrians.

On the Upper West Side he denounced a mother for eating a yogurt while driving. "And she's got an infant in the backseat," he observed testily. "Eating is as much of a driver distraction as talking on cell phones. Driver distractions are responsible for twenty-five percent of all car crashes."

A block later he vilified a father, with a boy on his shoulders, who was running through an intersection as the Don't Walk sign blinked. Next, he fumed about a school-bus driver, his vehicle full of children, making an illegal U-turn.

"Look at that father teaching his daughter to play soccer," he said irritably at Riverside Park. "He has no clue how to play himself."

"Probably the same way she'll end up learning to drive."

"That's what I mean. To be a good teacher you need to have had a good teacher."

"For you it was your father?"

"Yes, my father—but also my uncle. I never talked to you about him. He was an engineer, and my physics tutor. This morning when I told Stephen, 'Think about what you're doing,' instead of, 'You're doing that wrong!'—while he was trying to parallel-park, he steered left instead of right—that was the influence of my uncle. Anyway, about fourteen years ago, my uncle was driving with his wife and son, and their car went off the road. Nobody was hurt except my cousin. He was eleven, their only child, and he didn't have a seat belt on. He died."

Before long we found ourselves at the foot of Grant's Tomb.

He parallel-parked in the tightest little spot alongside the monument, using just two economic maneuvers, and two fingers of his right hand.

"Why are you smiling?" he asked.

"That's how much I enjoyed watching you do what you just did. It's fun to see anything done that well."

313

Because it was cold, the swing sets in the park were empty, and as always, the tomb was unvisited.

"I hadn't planned on it," Attila said. "For some reason, I keep taking us here."

"I can think of at least three reasons why you're drawn to Grant's Tomb."

"Why? Because I am the general's son?"

"Well, yes. There's your father, and your attraction-revulsion toward the military."

"What else?"

"The second reason would be because we've spent some pretty pleasant moments up here in the past year. And the third reason is because the architecture of Grant's Tomb is a free interpretation of King Mausoleus's tomb from 350 B.C.—one of the seven wonders of the ancient world along with the Colossus of Rhodes, and the origin of the word, 'mausoleum.' It was built by his widow on Halicarnassus, in Turkey, near your family's beach house."

"Well, that explains it. I hadn't even made the connection." He looked up at the edifice, seeing it in a new light. "Of course, it doesn't exist anymore."

"But isn't that typical of the difference between you and me? I've got the book knowledge of Halicarnassus, and you've got the actual experience."

"We start out curious about things far away from us," he answered. "Later on, we end up interested in the places where we began."

"You must be very homesick."

"How can you be homesick if you don't know where your home is?" he said.

I rephrased my question. "You must miss your family and your friends."

314

"Yes, I do very much. And it's worse now that I know it's just eleven thousand dollars that separates me from them. But if I had the money, wouldn't it be better to buy a teaching car of my own? Is it more important to have my freedom in Turkey—or here, where I live and work?"

"That's a difficult question."

"New York is my home," he declared after a pause, as if he had just ended a long debate with himself. "I'll drive you back now, slowly."

He looped around Grant's Tomb, hitting the apex of the curve and accelerating on the straightaway.

He drove down to Eighty-sixth Street and turned east.

"I owe you something," I said as he cut through the park.

"You owe me something? No you don't."

"Yes, I do. I owe you a kiss. In Florida you said I did—for the news about Turkey."

He bowed his head about three degrees, his eyes still pinned high on the road. (Attila would never commit the racing-school sin of "low eyes"—a telltale sign of a poor, accident-prone driver.) "Let's wait until we get some more news—how the payments must be made, all at once or in installments, exactly how much, and when. The government will post the information soon. And then when it's time, we can also open the Johnnie Walker Blue."

He stopped at my corner, hugging me good-bye inside the car. After he let go, I spoke. "When I was out of town," I said, "I missed you." I felt I owed him that, too. Caught off guard, he was unable for once to regulate his feelings. His face registered first surprise, then delight. It lingered briefly at embarrassment, moved on to tenderness, and finally calcified into impassivity, its habitual expression. And when he collected himself he said, "New York is an empty place without you."

ATTILA and I returned to Cycle Connection, in Lodi, New Jersey, and the two Marks to collect our next plaything, the Ducati 999. I had already been treated to a sneak preview of the 999 when I attended the motorcycle show at the Jacob Javits Center with Joe the week before, as a guest of Ducati. To get us into the proper mood for this event—the most heavily attended trade show in recent memory, according to the man who issued us our laminated visitor passes—Joe bought each of us a shot of Jack Daniel's in a plastic cup, which had the immediate effect of an intravenous injection. I coaxed Joe onto the driver's seat of the 999 exhibited in Ducati's booth, and I swung my leg over the back. "I wouldn't ride on that backseat for anything in the world," the Ducati representative on duty advised. "But I'm old and fat, and not flexible in my legs." To me the high leather seat, which came equipped with a hang-on-to-your-life strap, felt cozy. And I did not need to be a contortionist to hoist my feet onto the posts.

Since our last visit to Cycle Connection, Marc with a *c* had bought out Mark with a *k*. Concerned about Attila driving the 999 back to Manhattan in the below-freezing weather (I would follow him as before in the Camry), Marc plied us with extra winter gear—one-size-fits-all thermal balaclavas, which made us look like weatherproofed bank robbers, as well as thermal glove liners (long underwear for the hands), in size medium for me and extra large for Attila. Marc also furnished Attila with thermal socks in XL; he had none in my size.

"Men will not buy gloves or socks marked size small," explained Rick, part of Marc's Cycle Connection sales team. "You're not gonna feel the cold," Rick reassured Attila. "The sex of the bike will keep you warm." I looked at Rick searchingly.

"You know," he said, slightly abashed, "the sexiness of it will warm him up." Then Rick did a little figure-eight dance with his hips to demonstrate how he rocked the bike between his legs to help get it started on a cold day.

I thought this was a good moment to ask Attila if the 999 were a she or a he.

"The 999 is an it," he replied.

"I don't know where Mark put the insurance card for the 999," Marc said. "While you're waiting around for me to find it, the mechanic can do a check on the bike and Mr. Klein can get you some coffee." Although Marc was half Italian, he was Greek Orthodox, the religion of his mother. He had about him an aura of calm—a trait shared, I had discovered, by the truly devout and the skillful motorcyclist (both understood well the uselessness of anxiety).

Mr. Klein was a slight, older gentleman with saucer eyes, a bulbous nose, and grizzled curls over which he wore a leather motorcycling cap, similar to Marlon Brando's in *The Wild One*. It was stamped with the word "Victory," in old-fashioned script, which in this case was not an abstract noun but a brand name, referring to a grassroots motorcycle company based in Minneapolis. Despite the hat, Mr. Klein looked nothing like Brando; he was, rather, a dead ringer for Burgess Meredith. "Hi," he said, offering his hand. "Joe Klein." When I mentioned his resemblance to the actor, he said, "Yeah, everyone's been telling me that for years. Nobody ever wanted to put *me* in the movies—though they did put me on the cover of a magazine." He pointed to a framed, four-year-old copy of *City Cycle Motorcycle Newsmagazine*, displayed on the wall. The headline read, "Who Is Joe Klein and Why Is He Smiling?"

Mr. Klein explained, "I was the first person ever to drive a

Victory, a V92C, cross-country from New York to California. They called my drive the 'Rock to Rock'—the rock of the Statue of Liberty to the rock of Alcatraz. I was sixty-eight at the time, and it took me just eight days, including a stopover in Minneapolis at Victory headquarters. I go for twenty-two hours at a time, you see, in a kind of hypnotic trance. I've ridden sometimes with a tank of gas strapped to the bike, so I don't have to go out of my way for fuel. I rode to Iowa and back on a V92C, twenty-six hundred miles, with one overnight stay each way. I took a long trip once with a broken leg, my crutches tied to the bike. I could drive just fine—only I couldn't walk. My license plate says, 'NY–CA.' Would you and your friend like your coffee with cream and sugar?"

It turned out that Mr. Klein was the father of Mark with a *k*, the former owner of Cycle Connection. He prepared one black for me and one with sugar for Attila, and then he pulled open a drawer beneath the coffeemaker, stuffed with press clippings about himself.

Attila, who had been quietly communing with the bikes in the showroom, came over to claim his cup. "I found a new buddy for you," I said.

"I did a ride as long as your 'Rock to Rock' once," Attila said, sipping from the foam vessel. "Berlin to Istanbul, twenty-three hundred kilometers, three days nonstop, in snow and rain. Nineteen eighty-one."

"Would you like to be a test driver for Victory?" Mr. Klein asked.

"Sure, why not?" Attila said. "Why not?" was one of Attila's verbal feints, a scrambling tactic effective for avoiding both the commitment of a yes and the disappointment of a no.

Marc found the insurance card at last, and walked us outside to where the 999, a virgin, zero-mileage bike, awaited its first driver. "Guess what?" Marc said. "The truck delivering the 999s arrived a minute ago. They're about to uncrate it. You want to have a look? The 999s is even faster than the 999, a superbike," he explained to me, "more torque, more horsepower."

Attila said, "It's *monoposto?*" This was Italian biker lingo for "one-seater."

"Yep," Marc said.

"Thank you, but we're only interested in *biposto.*"

Attila opened the door to the Camry for me. "That was very nice, what you just said. The old Attila would never have said that." I pulled the brown polyester tweed driver's seat about half an inch forward.

"No, he never would have."

Mr. Klein leaned over between us and kissed me good-bye.

On the way home, I was surprised to see how much of the 999's power Attila was holding in reserve. "It was because of the cold," he said when he removed his helmet at the Manhattan garage. "It was frustrating. Even with the winter gloves, my fingertips came close to frostbite." I had learned by reading the back of the balaclava box that if a bike is going 30 miles per hour, and the outside temperature is fifty degrees, then the motorcyclist experiences the air as twenty degrees. It was currently twenty-five degrees, and he had been going about 45 miles per hour.

He plugged in a device supplied by Marc called the Battery Tender, which performs more or less the same function for a motorcycle battery that a tea cozy does for a teapot.

"But you love it?"

"Yeah, I do," he said. "It's light, fast, and responsive. But we'll have to wait for the weather to warm up a little before we can take it out again."

"While we're waiting, maybe we can borrow something from Joe again."

"How about the SL55?" he asked.

I had been thinking precisely the same thought.

FOR THE first time since he had begun teaching four years earlier, Attila took two weeks off. He spent the first seven days alone, cleaning out his apartment—purging it of thirteen years' worth of old clothes, old computer equipment, and old papers, which he tore up in a shredder. "I've carried seven forty-gallon black garbage bags down to the basement," he said over the phone. "The super asked if I were moving out."

"He's right to ask—the old Attila *is* moving out."

"Yep," he said. "While I was clearing out my apartment these last few days, I was figuring out what kind of driving consultant I would like to be. I'd like to help people overcome phobias, anxieties, road rage. It couldn't be a coincidence, could it, that student after student tells me, 'If you taught me, you could teach anybody. You're better than a therapist. You've changed my life'? My new student from Ghana, the thirty-four-year-old political science professor, said, 'This is embarrassing to admit, but after three years of psychoanalysis, three times a week, I just left my shrink! I've been cured by my driving instructor.' Amy, I don't understand why this happened to the professor from Ghana, but it was after only ten hours with me!

"I could also teach emergency driving techniques and car control too, to kids and adults; advise clients on what kind of cars and insurance to purchase; instruct owners of Porsches, Mercedeses, BMWs how to get the maximum potential from their cars—how to have fun with them, but still be safe and responsible. Most consumers only know how to use twenty percent of their cars' abilities. I could bring my expertise—my six-hour class included—to high schools, police academies, corporations, insurance companies. I want driving and driving instruction to be taken seriously." He was talking fast, for him. "Too many people are dying on America's roads—we're ninth in safety in the world—I can help stop it. I've always wanted to leave a mark, and this is how I'll do it. Well, now you know more than anybody."

"It all sounds good to me," I said. "You've certainly been doing a lot of thinking."

"Too much, as usual," he said, easing his pace. "Have I told you about the three jars I keep in my apartment?"

I already knew he had one filled with Turkish blue beads and water, to ward off the evil eye. And I knew he had started another on January 1, where he placed the $15 a day he used to spend on cigarettes. "So what's the third?"

"A long time ago," Attila said, "a very wise man told me that the average male lives seventy-five years, which represents 3,900 Saturdays. If each Saturday is a penny, then we start life with a total of $39.00. By age seventy-five, a man has used up all of his pennies—after that he's living on borrowed time. Ever since I heard that, I have kept a jar of pennies. First I deducted the number of Saturdays I had already used up. Now, every Saturday I remove another penny. You'd be amazed at how quickly that jar empties out. I'm down to 1,664 pennies now—$16.64. In America they say that time is money. But time is not money. It's life."

"What do you do with the pennies you remove each week?"

"I throw them into a fourth jar."

"What's that one for?"

"That's where I dump my change."

"You really enjoy your own company, don't you?"

"Yes, I do."

"And I think, after your own company, you like mine."

"You're right. You're number two. Which really makes you number one. It's good to have you, Amy."

Two days later, on the way to a lunch appointment, I passed a driving-school car, a spanking-new one with a Hispanic man at the helm. The vehicle bore a white sign on its roof that read ANNIBAL—and below the boldface name was a local number. I reported this sighting via cell phone to the God of Driving.

"If Hannibal has his own school," I promised, "then so will Attila!"

Independence Day

Because I wrote down these stories about motor vehicles, Attila, and me as they were happening, I knew I'd have trouble coming up with an ending. The book is a diary taken from life, which I don't expect to be over anytime soon. For a while I was imagining a grand finale featuring a Grand Tour—a fulfillment of Attila's pipe dream of driving the Viper from Amsterdam all the way to Turkey. My idea was to substitute the Maybach for the muscle car and to reunite Attila with his country and kin. The war with Iraq complicated this ambitious plan, already problematic because of the $11,000 that we would have needed to cross Attila safely over Turkey's borders. I next tried scaling down the plan to a drive in the Maybach in this country, which Joe said he could arrange for us—but only after the final draft of my manuscript was due.

Searching for a conclusion, I was, so to speak, spinning my wheels, editing and re-editing what I'd already written, waiting for life serendipitously to deposit some new material at my feet. Attila, on the other hand, had made steady forward progress, in the direction of the signposts we had planted. He acquired a teaching car of his own, a bronze 2001 Nissan Maxima, which freed him from much of Earl's stifling control. With this new tool, Attila's pass rate climbed from 96 percent to 100 percent. In early spring Attila and I returned to Skip Barber—I repeated the crisis-driving course (I felt I could happily re-enlist for a dozen more sessions) and he enrolled in it for the first time, mostly "to learn new teaching techniques." We brought along Joe, who won a Michelin detailing kit for earning the best score in the relay race, and Andrew Giuliani, who displayed the kind of skid pad courage that only a seventeen-year-old male can muster. At the end of our two days Joe admitted, "I'm a convert. I love the Viper now." A natural amphitheater nestled beneath the Berkshire Hills, the Skip Barber Driving School began to feel a little like Alma Mater.

Attila, sensing she was ready, acted on his old promise to teach my daughter to ride a bicycle. In the same runwaylike cul-de-sac where I had nearly flattened myself under the school's motorcycle, the red Honda Nighthawk, he accomplished in three hours what no one else had been able to achieve in four years. "Teaching bicycle is harder work than teaching motorcycle," Attila said, cutting up a stuffed grape leaf for my daughter at the Turkish café where he took us to celebrate her success.

At their urging, I renewed my motorcycle learner's permit at the DMV, and in May Attila gave me a two-hundred-and-fifty-dollar driving school gift certificate for my birthday.

"Is this for motorcycle lessons?" I asked.

"For anything you want."

He said he had also intended to give me a silver cast of his sculpture, *One on One*. "But then I realized it was in Turkey."

Instead, he presented me with one half of a pair of new silver hoop earrings. He had lost his last one while removing his helmet after a ride on the Ducati 999—a vehicle that we had returned without regrets to Cycle Connection. Though Attila praised the bike, I had found the 999's backseat a little too much like riding the mechanical bull from *Urban Cowboy*. On the Staten Island Expressway one day, Attila—after doing a high-speed lateral four-lane change—reached behind him to feel my left leg. I thought he was trying to reposition my foot on the peg. But later he said, "I was checking to see if you were still there."

"I didn't exactly notice you crying," I had said.

"THE WAY you should end the book," Attila proposed when we drove up to Grant's Tomb in the bronze Nissan for another meeting, "is with me doing what I am meant to do—riding off on a motorcycle alone."

"That's very good," I answered. "But if you're riding off alone on a motorcycle at the end of the book, then I should be driving off alone too, in a car—the red SLK320."

I talked to Seema, the Ducati PR woman, about borrowing back the 999 for this purpose. Seema, said, "Do you and Attila really have to go off in separate directions at the end of the book? You're making me cry."

"It would be an open-ended ending," I reassured her. "Maybe our separate roads will meet up, and maybe there'll be a sequel."

But as the frigid spring days grew longer and then warmer, I found myself once again yearning for the V-Rod.

Although the previous summer, Tony, the motorcycle-leasing magnate, had told me that it would be impossible for him to procure a V-Rod for us, on a whim on the first sultry seventy-five-degree day, I called him.

"Amy, this is karma."

"Why?"

"Well, just this morning," Tony said, "I was looking at a photograph of you in a magazine, and then, an hour ago, I received an e-mail from a Harley dealer in Virginia, asking if I would consider a zero-mileage 2003 Anniversary Edition V-Rod for my inventory. Would you and Attila be interested in leasing it?"

"Definitely! But let me check with him first."

I caught Attila between students.

"Amy, you can't imagine how much you've brightened my day."

"Isn't that what I'm here for?"

I suppose we learned nothing from the Hayabusa heist— except maybe that we wanted a replacement bike and a safe place to park it. We agreed that Attila would pay for the lease and I would pay for the garage. He would strengthen his credit rating, and I, it appeared, would have a conclusion for the book.

"We'll drive down to Virginia in the SLK320 together," I suggested. (Bringing the bike to New York, Tony had said, was our responsibility.) "I'll come back in it by myself, and you'll ride off on the V-Rod. I'll get the road time and experience I've been missing, you'll break in the bike. Sounds like we have the ending I've been seeking."

But that's not the way it worked out. In order to miss as little teaching time as possible, and simply because he never did anything by halves, Attila decided that on a Monday night, after his six-hour class, he would go home, have dinner, walk his dog, sleep for an hour, and drive down to Virginia in a rented car at three in the morning. "I'll reach Shenandoah around eight A.M., drop off the car at the airport, take a taxi to the Harley-Davidson dealership, head back to New York around nine-thirty in the morning, and arrive home around six P.M. You don't want to put yourself through that, do you?"

That left me still flailing about for an ending. Larry reminded me, "Amy—don't forget, this whole adventure started out as your mission to learn to drive. By the end of the book, no matter what else has happened to you in between, you should have accomplished that mission."

Larry was right, of course. In the year and seven months since Attila entered my life, I had become a student, a scholar, an observer, and a critic of driving—but not, in my estimation, a driver. It was the habitual, academic way that I ended up approaching everything—art as an art historian, and as a journalist, life. I always contrived somehow for the printed page to mediate between myself and the exterior world. It was time to tear through that sheet of paper and see what was on the other side.

THREE DAYS before Attila was scheduled to make his marathon round trip, I was seized with an idea that should have taken hold long ago. Why not rent a car, any car, and just go, on my own, for a drive? A year earlier, Attila had said that after our lessons finished, he would devise a program of practice routes for me to take in order to encourage the habit of regular driving. "Otherwise you'll end up sitting on your license." He had never produced the list, but then, I had never asked him for it; nor had we ever "finished" with each other.

That Saturday I had exactly two and a half hours—the duration of my daughter's afternoon playdate—to make a drive. I reserved a medium-sized car at the neighborhood Avis and then called Attila to ask for directions to Bear Mountain. After all our trips there, I still didn't know the way.

"You won't make it there," said Attila, who sometimes appeared to have a MapQuest brain and (like the Tin Man) a pocket-watch heart. "You won't have enough time."

"Where should I go, then?"

"Just drive toward Bear Mountain for an hour and fifteen minutes, and then turn around and come back."

Then I realized that maybe I should consider another journey—up I-95 to Connecticut, the way to my beach house, a route I had driven only once, the summer before, and not by myself. Wasn't that one of my goals when I had first matriculated in driving school? But that itinerary was dull and featureless. The trip toward Bear Mountain would be scenic and romantic. Which path ought I take, and did it even matter? Marcel Proust certainly went to great pains to show how seemingly divergent routes (in his case Swann's Way and the Guermantes Way) met up in the long run.

Attila said, "Sweetheart, the point of your driving is not to learn your way to the beach or to Bear Mountain, but to have the freedom to go anywhere, at any time."

At the Avis rental agency, the chubby-cheeked girl behind the counter shook her braids. No, I was told, there were no reservations under my name. And there were no more cars left to rent either. After she punched around the computer for a few more minutes, she confirmed that no record of my booking existed—but wait, yes, there was in fact one car available, parked in space number one, a brown Chevy Impala. Would that do? Yes it would. And apprehensively I purchased every form of insurance that Avis corporation had for sale.

I took two little white cards from a Lucite display rack, one that gave directions "to I-95 and Connecticut" and another that read, "Upstate New York, Albany." After a moment's hesitation I replaced the second card and walked over to inspect my rented

328

wheels. The only attribute that the Chevy Impala had to recommend it was its color—the same pale, powdery, metallic brown as the '92 Acura Integra, left behind a year ago on the island.

As I rolled slowly out of the parking spot toward the garage door, I was thinking about how narrow and shallow the opening appeared and how wide and blubbery the Impala felt. But if its right side mirror was clearing the garage's doorjamb, then I had ample exit room, right?

Crunch, squeeeak, scrape—nails clawing on a blackboard. I leapt out and saw that I had grated fine, long strips of paint off the Chevy's back right door. The girl in the office and the attendant in the garage ignored my summons, so I coasted into the street, sweeping onto the FDR Drive, over the Triborough Bridge, and then beyond to the Bruckner Expressway, the New England Thruway, and finally Interstate 95. Because Avis's direction card had simply read, "Go from East 96th Street to the FDR Drive North and take the Triborough to I-95," omitting the intervening roads, I kept thinking I was traveling the wrong route. How could their instructions be so telegraphic? Betty Crocker wouldn't issue recipe cards that listed only ingredients, measurements, and baking times. Highway signage in general is perplexingly illogical, at least to a fledgling driver. Signs (like the ones for the Triborough Bridge and I-95) are thrown your way at the last moment, set up in ambiguous locations, or else missing entirely when you need them most. But if it was just the directions that were disturbing me, then maybe I was getting comfortable with driving itself.

I scanned radio stations until I found a soothing Connecticut oldies station ("Say a Little Prayer" was playing), adjusted myself to the whalish proportions of the Impala, and after chewing nervously through a pack of Big Red, finally relaxed. The Bad Thing had already happened to me in the most innocuous spot possible—the rental car garage, at point zero of my trip. With that ignominious incident safely out of the way, I felt there was nothing further to dread. All I had to do was drive for forty-five minutes more, find a rest station where I could stretch my legs, and turn around and go home.

An hour and fifteen minutes found me near Fairfield, Connecticut, with "Expressway to Your Heart" jingling on the radio. I left the interstate at a vividly marked exit for a welcome center; McDonald's certainly knew how to announce its proximity without ambiguity. When I stepped out of the Impala (parked rather well, I thought) I felt dizzy and tired. I used the ladies' room (it had more seating capacity than a hair salon), ordered a small fries and a Diet Coke, and returned to the car. Before I switched on the ignition I left a message for Attila: "I'm at a rest stop in Connecticut, the same one, I believe, where you once bought a map during a driving lesson—you had said at the time it was the first one you'd purchased in twenty years." Of course, I could be wrong; like 7-Elevens and Hollywood starlets, all roadside welcome centers looked alike.

I asked a compact, swarthy man at the Mobil filling station adjacent to the McDonald's food court how to get onto I-95 South, back to New York City.

"Take-a nex-exa, right traffic light left turny EYE southa."

Even so, I found I-95 South, more or less by following the herd. If the road had been unpopulated I would have made at least one false turn, at an incoherently labeled junction. The interstate system needs to market itself more like hamburger chains.

I passed by two accidents on the way back—one involved a rickety flatbed truck that had rear-ended a Ford Taurus, the other an SUV and a white sedan. Attila would have been able to reconstruct the circumstances of the collisions by observing the damage; to me the ruined vehicles were grim reminders of mortality, the human skull and guttering candle in the fruits-and-flowers still-life. As I went by both sites I muttered my father's old incantation, *"Nisht fur dich gedacht."*

At the homestretch, the Manhattan-Queens ramp for the FDR Drive, a police car nosed up to my rear bumper, sirens wailing. A yellow sign had warned automobiles to reduce their speed to 20 miles per hour, and I was dutifully decelerating. Oh no! Had I not slowed down enough? As I let the needle descend lower, the patrol car tailgated me even more insistently and stridently. Any moment now its loudspeaker would squawk at me to pull over. But because of a construction job on the ramp there was no shoulder, no safe place anywhere to pull over. Was I really going to be slapped with a speeding ticket on my first solo outing? Well, one Bad Thing had happened to me on the way out of the city, so maybe I was due for another Bad Thing to befall me on my return.

The police car was now fastened to the Impala's rump like a blinking blue-and-white caboose. *Waaa-naaay-aaa!*

And then the cop car darted into the right lane that had suddenly opened up, and sped on, its urgent caterwaul dying into the distance. They were chasing someone else, I surmised, and had only been trying impatiently to pass me on the right.

I laughed away the last of my anxiety and realized, as the radio station fizzled into static, I was two blocks from home. Overall, the drive had been fun, and—how about that?—it had ended too soon. I would do it again next Saturday, I decided—probably a longer repeat of the same route, and then a week after that, I'd tackle the twistier challenges of Bear Mountain.

Before returning the car to Avis I dialed Attila, but I couldn't get through—because at that very instant he was trying to reach me.

"How was it?" he asked, his voice deep with interest.

"Exactly like a lesson with you—a drive on a tight schedule to nowhere in particular, and back again. It felt like there was an invisible Attila beside me. It was fun. It's a great feeling to drive alone in a car."

"*No kidding!* Well, I've finally let you go, Amy—I mean, as a student."

"Yeah, the cord's finally been cut, and isn't it about time? But I'm sure there's still plenty more I could learn from you—and not only about driving."

"Probably there is. And I've got more to learn from you too, and not just about speaking correct*ly.*"

"Well done! Now that you've come this far I'm going to get tougher on you. You know, Attila, this drive today was more than fun. *I loved it.* You've turned fear into love—quite an achievement, my dear."

"Thank you. You don't know how good it is to hear you say that. Let's talk a little later."

TWO DAYS later, Attila flashed down to Virginia and back in fifteen and a half hours, including stops for gas and lunch. I asked him if the drive was pretty.

"I don't know, Amy. I didn't notice. To me it was just a task—go to one point, and then return. The Harley dealer thought I was crazy. He asked what hotel I was staying in, and I told him, 'The V-Rod.' I guess I *am* crazy. The rain and crosswinds were bad both ways. It was like doing the twenty-four-hour Le Mans —without a controlled environment. It was tougher than my trip in the snow from Berlin to Turkey, in 1981—but then, I'm twice as old."

I told Attila that while he was away, my daughter and I took our first horseback-riding lessons. "Use what you learned from driving," he advised. "Keep your eyes up, look to where you want to go, not down at the horse. If you're scared, not in control, or don't respect the animal, he'll sense it. I used to ride a lot in Turkey and Germany," he explained. "In Turkey on wild horses, bareback, and in Germany, in the snow, *galoppieren* . . . what's the English word?"

"It's the same. You galloped bareback in the snow?"

"Yeah. It's not as much fun as riding a motorcycle in the snow, though. You know I like horsepower better than horses."

"What are you made of?"

"I don't know, Amy. I'm a driving machine."

The following day he picked me up in the Nissan to have a peek at the V-Rod in the garage—an outing that felt like a hospital visit to a newborn. Attila explained that I could not ride the motorcycle comfortably or safely until he had changed the seat and added a backrest—"It's called a 'sissy bar,'" he noted. He did, however, let me sit on the parked bike. "No! Always mount it from the lower side, the left."

"It's a perfect bike," I said, admiring the cosmic symmetry of its gauges, the rakish slope of its double-barreled tailpipe, the faceted curves of its headlamp, the vigorous contrasts of its glossy chrome and matte aluminum bodywork.

"We made the right decision," he said. "But eventually, we'll have to get you a Sportster."

"What's that?"

"A little Harley that makes a lot of noise."

"Will two hundred and fifty dollars be enough to teach me how to ride it?"

"We'll see."

THE NEXT vehicle I drove, however, was not a motorcycle at all but an Aegean Blue Mercedes SL500 convertible (close kin to the SL55), another loan from Joe. I took the V-8 sports car, whose profile swooped like a folded bird's wing, to the island and back, driving through rain one way and through nightfall the other. The trip was not a chore—it was a pleasure, start to finish, and tooling around in the convertible by the beach with the top down was a far more alluring activity for both my daughter and me than swimming and tennis, our usual island pastimes. After that came a glamorous silver Bentley Azure Mulliner convertible, which the company had offered me for the long Fourth of July weekend, to help promote the model's final series. I tried to tempt Attila out of Queens and his Nissan with the 6.75-liter, turbocharged V-8 Bentley, but he said, "Amy, go ahead and enjoy that great car by yourself. But don't forget—though it may look civilized on the outside, inside it's a very powerful animal."

I drove the seductive four-seater all around Manhattan, over the Fifty-ninth Street Bridge to Queens and back, and to City Island, in the Bronx (where Attila and I had once gone on a lesson), for a seafood dinner. And, dressed to match the Mulliner in a silver suit, I conducted it onto the Taconic Parkway upstate to Stuyvesant, New York, to visit Larry at his country house on the Hudson River. Everywhere I went, girls gave me the thumbs-up sign, cops sidled up for a closer look, and men (black ones especially) asked to shake hands, trade places, or take my phone number (the California plates helped). "I could easily spend the rest of my life with this Bentley," I reported to Attila from the Hopewell Junction Mobil station.

But the most important voyage I made in the car was to Bucks

County, Pennsylvania, on Independence Day. With my daughter in the backseat, a baby blue kerchief like the ones I used to wear covering her head, I went in search of the country roads where my father had taken me decades before in his convertible. Widened now and better paved, they still existed. But the scenery through which they used to wind had vanished. Where there had once been woods, there was now a blight of housing—pseudomansions on postage-stamp patches of land, and "town home" developments with wishfully historic names. And where there had formerly been cornfields and barns there were now malls, parking lots, and fast food franchises. The colonial farmhouse that had served as my father's office had burnt down, and so had the Romanesque Revival schoolhouse where I had attended first through third grades. But the cemetery with my family's plots was still there—although the grassy, willow-shaded graveyard I recalled from childhood was now teeming with fresh headstones.

What I was really seeking, however—the real destination of this trip—was unaltered, running as it always had along the east flank of the cemetery. It was the steep hill from the recurrent nightmare—a two-thousand-foot stretch of inclined, two-way road. I paused at its summit, stepped on the gas pedal, and let the Bentley open up, top still down. With the heft of the 420-horsepower car augmenting the acceleration, we whipped through the wind, the sun stabbing the hood with its hot rays. We flew prow-down, a mesh-grilled cannonball shearing space. I brought the Bentley to a stop at the hill's base—the car's brakes were extremely dependable—and, the lone motorist at the crossroads, I exulted. Though the phobia had left its permanent mark—a breach in a wall where an intrusive vine had once grown—I knew it had been eradicated.

"Mama!" my daughter squealed from the backseat. "Can we do that again? Just one more time. Please, Mama? *Faster!*"

And then we drove the Bentley home in the dark—finishing one journey, headed for another—while fireworks crackled over a smoldering horizon.

BACK IN New York, Attila, unable to resist, took a brief turn in the Bentley, to his neighborhood and back. A few blocks away from my apartment, a sweating, mustachioed construction worker, shovel in hand, yelled out to Attila from his ditch, "Yo, man, have fun. Me, I need to work fifty years before I can buy that Bentley!"

"That's what I had to do!" Attila shouted back at him, bolting away at the green light.

"I rounded off the number," he said to me, with a smile.

And then, because he was in a good mood, I delivered the news I had been waiting all day (actually, for almost two years) to give him.

"I've found an entrepreneur who's interested in helping you start a driving school," I announced. "We've scheduled a dinner meeting for seven Tuesday night."

"Let's do it at a Turkish restaurant," he replied quietly. "I'll make the reservation. You'll be my partner in this?"

"You betcha."

"WHEN I met you," I said, studying his face as we completed the drive home, "you looked to me like a man with a secret that made him sad. Now you look like a man with a secret that makes him happy."

He smiled, and nodded once in agreement, a small movement. He double-parked the Bentley Azure Mulliner, opened the door for me, and out on the street, kissed me good-bye with feeling—on the cheek, of course. And on that particular day, that's how we left it.